M&A Titans

M&A Titans

The Pioneers Who Shaped Wall Street's Mergers and Acquisitions Industry

Brett Cole

WILEY

John Wiley & Sons, Inc.

For general information on our other products and services or for technical support, please contact our Customer Care Department within the United States at (800) 762-2974, outside the United States at (317) 572-3993, or fax (317) 572-4002.

Wiley also publishes its books in a variety of electronic formats. Some content that appears in print may not be available in electronic books. For more information about Wiley products, visit our web site at www.wiley.com.

Library of Congress Cataloging-in-Publication Data:

Cole, Brett, 1965–
  M&A titans : the pioneers who shaped Wall Street's mergers and acquisitions industry / Brett Cole.
       p.   cm.
  Includes bibliographical references and index.
  ISBN 978-0-470-12689-9 (cloth)
  1. Consolidation and merger of corporations—United States.   2. Investment banking—United States.   3. Corporations—United States.   I. Title.   II. Title: M & A titans.
  HG4028.M4C65   2008
  338.8'30973—dc22

                                                                    2008012005

Printed in the United States of America

10 9 8 7 6 5 4 3 2 1

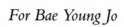

For Bae Young Jo

Contents

Acknowledgments

This book could not have been written without the patience and good humor of my wife, Bae Young Jo. Young Jo let me leave my paid job, supported and financed my research and writing, and spurred me to finish amidst a move from one continent to another. I am eternally grateful.

Dina Brunstein provided great friendship and support during my research. Dune Lawrence helped me crystallize some of my early ideas.

Debra Englander, executive editor of Wiley, agreed to publish my proposal. Debra was sensitive and supportive during my research and kindly gave me more time to finish the manuscript. I am grateful to a friend, David Riedel, for introducing me to Debra.

Susan Cooper painstakingly corrected the manuscript and improved the turgid prose. Kelly O'Conner, the development editor at Wiley; Stacey Fischkelta, Wiley's senior production editor; and Stacey Small, senior editorial assistant, all showed extraordinary patience with a neophyte author.

I owe John Canning a debt of gratitude for not only introducing me to many in his Chicago business circle but also for educating me on baseball and installing a fondness for the White Sox.

Sharon Smith arranged for me to talk with Bill Hambrecht in San Francisco. In Washington, Harvey Pitt spoke with me following an introduction from Arthur Fleischer. In New York, Tim Metz introduced me to Joe Perella. Steve Anreder did the same with Fred Joseph and John Sorte. John Ford at Blackstone facilitated my talks with Pete Peterson and Steve Schwarzman. J. P. Morgan's Adam Castellani arranged interviews with James B. Lee. Jay Roser set up my meeting with Boone Pickens. Tony Zimmer at William Blair arranged for Ned Jannotta to speak with me.

I was fortunate to meet Stephen Chan during my wife's MBA studies at the University of Virginia. Stephen kindly read my initial drafts, corrected errors, and was most supportive.

John Wells, an old friend from New York's International House, introduced me to John Whitehead and read parts of my initial draft. I am grateful for John's comments and friendship.

Marty Lipton kindly read an initial draft and corrected grammatical and factual errors with respect to his career and pointed out mistakes in reference to legal matters. I am most thankful.

John Whitehead graciously read an initial draft of the manuscript to check for errors, particularly with regard to the historical context of the merger business on Wall Street and the development of Goldman Sachs's investment banking efforts.

Any remaining errors are, of course, mine alone.

The Titans

At Skadden, Arps, Slate, Meagher & Flom
Joseph H. Flom

At Wachtell, Lipton, Rosen & Katz
Martin Lipton

At Salomon Brothers
J. Ira Harris

At Lazard Freres & Co.
Felix G. Rohatyn

At Goldman Sachs & Co.
Stephen Friedman
Geoffry T. Boisi

At Morgan Stanley
Robert F. Greenhill

At First Boston Corp.
Joseph R. Perella
Bruce Wasserstein

At Lehman Brothers
Eric J. Gleacher

At Drexel Burnham Lambert
Michael R. Milken

Remarks from Some
M&A Titans and Players

"Mergers and acquisitions; or as we used to say, murders and accusations."
                    —Scott Newquist, former Morgan Stanley managing director

"I don't think I would want to see a child of mine go into the M&A business. It's cruel."
                    —John Whitehead, former Goldman Sachs co-chairman

"It was very clear the career came first."
                    —Claire Flom, wife of Joe Flom

"We were the Oakland Raiders."
                    —John Sorte, former Drexel Burnham Lambert chief executive

"For an M&A guy, loyalty was not to the client. The loyalty was to the deal."
                    —Former Anderson Clayton executive

"M&A is a euphemism for fear and greed."
                    —Adam Chinn, merger banker and former Wachtell partner

Introduction

What most people think of as Wall Street's merger industry emerged in the 1970s. The Dow was swooning, the economy was in recession, and the Organization of Petroleum Exporting Countries (OPEC) had bludgeoned the world with its first precipitous hike in oil prices. It was then that a small group of men figured out a way to make money in trying circumstances. Those on Wall Street are people with practical intellects. They are people who can look at the reality of a situation and figure out a way to reconstruct the reality and make a lot of money out of it at the same time.

The leading investment banks at the beginning of the 1970s were tiny. Their capital was a sliver of the giant financial supermarkets of today. Advising on a merger risked none of a firm's precious capital. Moreover, advising an acquirer or the target of a takeover would result in a payday. How could an investment bank not get involved and push this business of merger making or merger defending?

Like many things under the financial sun, takeovers were not a new phenomenon. What was new was that bankers and lawyers were pushing it when previously it was the corporate chieftains who had arranged mergers without the help or the payment of a fee to Wall Street.

Marty Lipton, the merger industry's leading philosopher, has said there have been six merger waves that have consumed American industry since 1890. In a lecture delivered at Canada's York University Lipton identified the first merger wave as lasting from 1893 to 1904. It was characterized by the creation of basic manufacturing and mining industries. The second wave from 1919 to the Crash of 1929 was one of vertical integration. Ford had steel mills, railroads, ore boats, and assembly lines to build cars.[1]

The third merger wave was that of the conglomerates from 1955 to 1969. ITT, LTV, and Litton were built during this period. From 1974 to 1989 was the hostile takeover wave wherein bankers and lawyers took center stage and greenmail—payoffs to raiders who threatened to take control of companies—was popular. From 1993 to 2000 were friendly mergers to create companies of global scale and size. The sixth from 2002 to 2007 was characterized by the emergence of hedge funds and activist shareholders, the creation by some countries, such as Russia, of national champions, particularly in commodities and the power of private equity.

This book is about 11 men who dominated the fourth merger wave. They collectively created and shaped what people recognize as a merger industry on Wall Street. Like others who rise to the top of their trade or profession, they are quite singular. To use an adjective such as *driven* to describe them goes only part of the way to sum up their common character. They are obsessive and were nurtured and blossomed in the hothouse of New York, a singular place itself where the bottom line is indeed the bottom line.

One person interviewed for this book viewed New York as a city consisting of silos. Everyone who is part of a silo thinks their own silo is the whole world. There is a publishing industry silo, one for the music industry, the performing industry, and the finance–law industry. The finance–law industry is one in which less is known about the actual human life of people while they work. This book seeks to give such an insight.

The finance–law silo is democratic, many in the silo would argue. People can succeed in this area now regardless of whether they are Jews, White Anglo Saxon Protestants, black, Asian, Latino, or women, or whether they went to fancy prep schools or state universities.

It's performance that really counts. This was not always the case, of course.

These pioneers of mergers include the godfathers of the industry: Marty Lipton and Joe Flom. These two lawyers, often sparring on opposite sides of the boardroom table or courtroom, taught the bankers how to strategize and advise on takeovers. Lipton's friendships with Salomon Brothers' Ira Harris and Lazard Freres's Felix Rohatyn helped catapult them all into the spotlight, as did Joe Flom's relationship with Morgan Stanley's Bob Greenhill.

Steve Friedman and Geoff Boisi also tapped Lipton's expertise at Goldman Sachs as they led the charge of the firm into the upper ranks on Wall Street. Their blueprint of teamwork and cooperation helped make Goldman Sachs the world's preeminent investment bank.

Joe Perella, tutored by Flom, and Bruce Wasserstein, close to Lipton, took First Boston's moribund franchise and breathed new life into it with a series of daring and innovative takeover tactics. They made the firm's mergers and acquisitions department a magnet for some of the best financial talent from America's business schools.

Eric Gleacher, schooled by Lipton, established the merger department at Lehman Brothers which spurned its firm-wide talent in favor of Florentine intrigue. Michael Milken of Drexel Burnham Lambert is considered the most brilliant financier of his generation. Drexel's "highly confident letter" and Milken's proselytizing of the usefulness of high-yield bonds fueled the takeover boom of the 1980s and the ensuing popularity of leverage buyouts.

For a time, these 11 men bestrode Wall Street, the most identifiable personalities in American finance, promoted as rock stars by their firms and public relations executives.

After a while, the fickle public tired of them. Reports of their aggressive tactics and general cynicism following the financial scandals of the 1980s that landed Milken, among others, in jail and dented Wall Street's reputation. The new glamour boys of Wall Street became the managers of hedge and buyout funds, some of whom established their reputations as merger bankers, most notably Steve Schwarzman of the Blackstone Group.

Merger departments on Wall Street became less important to the overall bottom line of firms and with it the power of the men who led those departments waned. The revenue generated by Wall Street's traders after the 1980s dwarfed merger and acquisition fees. The cachet of a Wall Street firm may stem from its investment banking history, but many chief executives are from the trading side of the firm. Bankers who exert power in Wall Street firms today, such as J. P. Morgan's James Lee, are those who offer a vast array of lending services around the advice they give.

The 11 pioneers of mergers and acquisitions can be perhaps content that generations succeeding them will not have the impact they had when they first burst into prominence on Wall Street.

BRETT COLE
February 2008

Chapter 1

Genesis: Wall Street, Its Business and Culture

On Wall Street there were no merger departments or specialists in takeovers for much of the twentieth century. *Financier* was the term used to describe those few on Wall Street who had the ear of America's most powerful chief executives. If advice was sought on takeovers, it was given mostly free of charge as part of a service, which led to the main business of an investment bank—underwriting a sale of securities.[1]

There were no skyscrapers in lower Manhattan stuffed with thousands working for a brokerage or investment bank. There were no neon signs or ticker tapes running along the side of buildings giving the latest stock prices and proclaiming the site the home of a mighty global firm. The Great Crash of 1929 and the subsequent Great Depression made firms intuitionally conservative. They kept small payrolls. Most firms had no more than 100 employees and just one office up until the early 1960s. When Morgan Stanley began business in 1935, it was on the nineteenth

floor of a building at 2 Wall Street.[2] Goldman Sachs rented eight floors
of a building on Pine Street in 1947 and had hired virtually no one for
two decades.[3]

Wall Street was divided between brokers and investment banks. Brokers sold and traded bonds and stocks. Bear Stearns, Goldman Sachs,
and Salomon Brothers were brokers. Investment banks underwrote and
managed the sale of securities. Morgan Stanley, First Boston, Dillon
Read, Kuhn Loeb, Lazard Freres, and Lehman Brothers were investment
banks.

In the pecking order of the street, the investment banks in their manners, airs, education, and furnishings believed themselves to be superior
to the scrappy, blaspheming, uncouth, public school–educated brokers.

First Boston, Dillon Read, and Morgan Stanley were stuffy, white,
Christian males whose business largely centered on managing bond
offerings. The Jewish firms Kuhn Loeb, Lehman Brothers, and Lazard
managed the sale of securities but also invested in companies. The Jewish
and Christian firms all met when they formed syndicates to sell a bond
or a stock. "Banking was dominated by the Protestants, and the Jews
that were in the banking business acted like Protestants," recalled former
Salomon Brothers Chairman John Gutfreund who started working on
Wall Street in 1953.[4]

Investment banking was considered a gentleman's business. Firms
were suffused with a sense of probity because they were partnerships.
The capital of each firm was in the hands of those who were active in the
business. A partner had unlimited liability. Every year, Wall Street hired
very few new employees and promoted even fewer still to the coveted
partnership, where a select few shared in the profits of the firm. Few
graduates went to Wall Street. If you didn't have a personal connection
to a partner at a Wall Street firm and weren't marked by your professors
as brilliant, your chances of being hired were slim.

When John Whitehead graduated from Harvard Business School
in 1947, only one Wall Street firm came to campus to recruit. Along
with about 20 others, Whitehead signed up for an interview with the
firm. Much to Whitehead's surprise, he was the only one of the candi-
dates offered a job in the investment banking department of Goldman
Sachs.[5]

Most of Whitehead's contemporaries who finished the two-year master of business administration at elite universities such as Harvard went to work in industry or commercial banking. American industry boomed in the years after World War II. Companies generated cash for their expansion from their own operations. They rarely merged. It was a sign of failure.

Alan "Ace" Greenberg joined Bear Stearns in 1949 and worked on the arbitrage trading desk, betting on whether takeovers would succeed or not. "If a merger was announced once every two months, it was a lot. A lot," recalled Greenberg.[6]

If corporations asked for advice from Wall Street, it was how to sell bonds to fund a new production line. Most of America's 100 biggest companies went to one firm to fund their expansion: Morgan Stanley.

Morgan Stanley was the most prestigious firm on Wall Street by dint of its having sprung from the loins of America's most famous financier, J. Pierpont Morgan. By 1935 Congress had forced J. Pierpont Morgan's son Jack to split his father's firm, J. P. Morgan. Jack decided J. P. Morgan would now deal with Main Street, commercial banking. A new firm, Morgan Stanley, would do Wall Street business, investment banking. Henry Morgan, grandson of Pierpont, lent his name and unparalleled list of corporate contacts to Morgan Stanley together with Harold Stanley, whose father invented the Thermos bottle.[7]

Wall Street genuflected to the new firm. One firm, Dominick & Dominick, simply turned over its blue chip investment banking clients, Shell Oil and Coca-Cola among others, to Morgan Stanley after senior partner Gayer Dominick decided the firm would concentrate on broking.[8]

The bankers of Morgan Stanley were generalists. They, like others on Wall Street, prided themselves on their ability to advise chief executives on everything from loans to bond and stock sales and mergers and acquisitions. The firm headed and organized the syndicates of investment banks that underwrote and managed the sale of bonds. As head of an underwriting syndicate (it refused to co-manage offerings), Morgan Stanley took responsibility for the documentation that was a securities offering. The firm would take the lion's share of fees as manager of an offering and pay everyone else to sell it.[9]

Morgan Stanley established a protocol of how securities offerings were written. Its prospectuses were printed on cream-colored stock with lavender ink that people referred to as "Morgan Stanley blue." The agreements between the issuing company and Morgan Stanley, and the contracts between the firm and the sellers of the securities, were printed with the same typeface on the same cream-colored stock with ink that was "Morgan Stanley blue."[10]

As befits a firm that had its own color scheme, Morgan Stanley's culture was exacting. "Clients came first. Work had to be checked and rechecked. The worst thing was to go to a client with an error. No one was impressed if you had theater tickets that night. It was unpredictable when you would leave work," said Richard Fisher, recalling his days as a young Morgan Stanley statistician in the early 1960s.[11]

In the days before personal computers, work was done by hand on large spreadsheets. Down in the corner there was a string of initials, arranged according to a protocol, of people who had participated in preparing the original spreadsheet.

The first person who laid out the spreadsheet and did the initial set of numbers put his initials on it. Then there was a colon, and the next set of initials was the person who had checked it, every number. Then there was a slash, and the next set of initials was a person who had done any significant set of revisions to the spreadsheet. Then there was a colon, and the next set of initials was the person who had checked the revisions. Sometimes there would be 10 sets of initials in the lower lefthand corner of the spreadsheet.[12]

"First-class business in a first-class way" was Morgan Stanley's motto. Morgan Stanley was managed by committee. The partners met three times a week at 3 PM to discuss issues. Those partners who attended such meetings received $20, part of a tradition of the firm.[13]

Morgan Stanley prided itself on being part of the WASP establishment, and its partners carefully associated only with the pillars of New York society, serving on the boards of the Presbyterian Hospital and the Metropolitan Museum of Art. Morgan Stanley didn't court the press. It actively avoided it. "You led a very quiet, private lifestyle. You were always very careful who you talked to, how you handled yourself," recalled Harry Morgan's son, John Adams Morgan.[14]

To many, Morgan Stanley was the ultimate white-shoe Wall Street firm. Named after footwear that was popular on the campuses of Ivy League colleges in the 1950s, the term *white shoe* bore more than a smattering of anti-Semitism to some and reflected a stolid male patriarchy. Morgan Stanley didn't appoint a Jewish partner until 1973, when Lewis Bernard was named a partner.[15] In 1969, Morgan Stanley's usual outside counsel, Davis Polk & Wardwell, appointed its first Jewish partner, Joel Cohen, who remembered that when he joined Davis Polk in 1963 he was the only Jewish attorney in the firm.

"It was virtually impossible for a woman to get a job at a Wall Street firm unless they were going to be in trusts and estates," Cohen recalled.[16]

When Harvey Miller, who became America's leading bankruptcy and restructuring lawyer, graduated from Columbia Law School in 1959, he couldn't recall any women or blacks hired by Wall Street law firms. Miller's classmate was future Supreme Court Justice Ruth Bader Ginsburg, who graduated tied for first in her class. Ginsburg couldn't get a job. She had three strikes against her: she was a woman, she was Jewish, and she had a child. Someone, however, prevailed upon a tough, brusque federal judge, Edmund Palmieri, to offer her a job. Ginsburg became Palmieri's first female clerk.[17]

The hiring of Jews into Wall Street law firms was caused by a series of initial public stock offerings by companies in the garment district in the 1960s. As the garment district firms were run by Jews, Wall Street law firms hired Jews to help win business for them, Miller recalled.

"One of the great watersheds in American corporate life was that the law-finance silo that is Wall Street stopped being the domain of tweedy Ivy Leaguers," recalled a partner at a New York law firm. "That was probably around 1970. When I got out of Yale Law School in 1964, all of the non-Jewish big New York City law firms discriminated against Jews. Many of them were proud of it. For many, that was their lone distinction. Sorry, you're Jewish; you don't get a job here. We may be a third-rate firm, but what we don't do is hire Jews."[18]

■ ■ ■

Before the passage of the first federal law on takeovers, lawyers played a more central role than bankers in mergers. Acquisition agreements were

long and complicated, written by attorneys who directed the negotiations. Joel Cohen at Davis Polk helped buy and sell about 30 companies
for R. J. Reynolds.[19] Prior to the 1960s there was little discussion on
the legal rules that should apply to a company that was the target of a
takeover. The conglomerate building of the late 1950s and 1960s would
change that.

What brought mergers to the fore and set some on Wall Street
thinking that advising on takeovers could be a viable, long-term business
were men such as Jimmy Ling of LTV, Harold Geneen of ITT, and Tex
Thornton of Litton Industries. From 1955 to 1969, LTV, ITT, and Litton
bought hundreds of companies as accounting rules favored acquisitions.
Pooling accounting meant that goodwill wasn't charged against earnings.
This meant you didn't have to write anything off in the context of
a deal.[20]

Ling, Geneen, and Thornton believed professionally trained management could run any type of business and many different types of
businesses allowed a corporation to prosper through changing economic
conditions. There was also a belief that businesses had to be big to
succeed.[21]

A partner at Lehman Brothers, Warren Hellman, remembers taking
a telephone call from Jimmy Ling. Ling wanted to merge his Braniff
Airways with Continental Airlines, whose banker was Hellman. Hellman
recalled asking: "'Mr. Ling, how are you going to do it?' He said, 'We're
going to borrow money to buy Continental Airlines.' I said, 'Okay, but
I've looked at it and I think it will be too highly leveraged. This is
a business with a ton of operating leverage and you heap a bunch of
borrowing on top of it, it won't work.' He said, 'You don't understand
leverage.' I said, 'I don't?' He asked, 'How do you define leverage?' I
used my best Harvard Business School speak: 'the appropriate amount
of debt for the continued operations of a business.' He said, 'No, no, no.'
I said, 'Mr. Ling, how do you define leverage?' And he said, 'Leverage
is the last dollar some sucker will lend you.'"[22]

Wall Street investment banks had an almost exclusive relationship
with their clients. Bankers at rival firms generally didn't try to lure away
a company from its long-established bankers. If a banker had an idea for
a company that wasn't his client, he was expected to go to the company's
traditional bankers first to pitch the idea.[23] In the case where a Wall Street

firm went directly to a company and bypassed its traditional advisers, a chief executive could be counted on to call his usual adviser.

Lehman Brothers were the bankers for Philip Morris. Lehman rival White Weld approached Philip Morris, suggesting it buy fellow cigarette maker Lorillard. Warren Hellman was called on the morning of White Weld's proposal and asked if he could be in the office of the Philip Morris chief executive at 2 PM to discuss White Weld's idea.[24]

Bankers were keen to keep mergers friendly. There weren't any federal laws governing takeovers. Control of a corporation could pass to someone who bought the majority of the company's stock on the stock exchange. It could be done overnight if lawyers didn't take out an injunction. Some who sought control of a company after buying a large percentage of a target's stock got into proxy fights. They submitted proposals to shareholders to replace management and the board with their own allies. Proxy contests were considered so déclassé that the major Wall Street investment banks and law firms stayed away from them.[25]

It wasn't until 1968 when Congress passed the Williams Act that America had a federal takeover law. In the wake of the Williams Act, two men went around the country giving seminars on mergers. One was Arthur Fleischer, a tall, self-effacing attorney with a preference for three-piece suits and a deep resonant voice that reminded many of a stage actor. The other was an unassuming lawyer whose diminutive stature and pithy homespun wisecracks belied his intellect. His name was Joe Flom. Flom had a head start over others in mergers and acquisitions. He was familiar with the tactics and methods of how to gain control of companies by dint of being America's foremost proxy fighter.[26]

Chapter 2

Godfathers—Flom and Lipton

J oseph Harold Flom was a child of the Depression. His parents were Jewish immigrants from a small town in the Ukraine that was later wiped out in the Holocaust. His father and mother came to America separately—his father around the time of World War I, and his mother in the 1920s. They had married in Russia and had a son who died there as an infant. Joe was born on December 31, 1923, in Baltimore, and the Floms quickly moved to New York in search of work.[1]

Joe's father worked in the garment trade and was a union organizer. His mother did what was called "home work," cutting a pattern from cloth and getting paid by the garment makers for doing it. She kept a kosher home.

The Floms lived in Borough Park, Brooklyn, which was fast becoming a Jewish neighborhood in the 1930s. New York City landlords during the Great Depression would offer three-month rent-free apartments in the hope that the people who moved in would be able to find some work and afford to pay rent after the third month. The Floms moved frequently. When he began going to school, Joe got a dime for breakfast from his mother. He would go to a diner and buy two doughnuts, orange juice, and coffee for breakfast. If he saved a doughnut, Joe had lunch.

Flom always felt his calling was the law. In high school, his senior book review was *Evans Cases on Constitutional Law.* One of his boyhood heroes was the famed trial lawyer Clarence Darrow. Flom passed an exam that got him into Townsend Harris High School in Manhattan, a school for academically gifted pupils. The teaching staff was comprised of university professors at City College. Mayor Fiorello LaGuardia closed it down after Flom graduated because he thought it too elitist.

Every day after his high school classes finished, Flom tried to work. "Anything," he said, "to make a buck." He was a delivery boy in Manhattan's garment district, pushing hangers with dresses down streets. During summers, he ran a drill press on 8th Street and Broadway, which stamped out letters on uniforms. After graduating from high school, Flom worked as an office boy in a law firm during the day. At night he attended City College, taking prelaw and liberal arts classes. His studies were cut short by America's entry into World War II in 1941.

Drafted into the Army, Flom never saw any fighting, partly through circumstance but mostly because of his intelligence. The Army tested its recruits. Flom was part of a group of 60 men chosen from 300,000 soldiers. These 60 men were sent to Rutgers University in New Jersey. At Rutgers, Flom studied civil and then electrical engineering. At the end of Flom's studies, 20 of his classmates went to help build the first atomic bomb in New Mexico, 20 went to Alaska to monitor enemy radio signals, and 20 went to radar repair school, including Flom.

After the end of World War II, some universities waived minimum degree requirements for graduate schools such as law. While playing the dummy hand in a bridge game, Flom wrote to Harvard Law School seeking to enter its first post–World War II class. He was asked to an interview but was placed on the reserve list. One weekend when his parents were out of New York, a telegram arrived. It said that if he wanted to be in the law school, Flom should be in Cambridge the next day. He packed, left a note for his parents, and took a night train to Boston. He was at Harvard Law School the next morning.

Flom reveled in the law school's Socratic teaching method, a method of learning where legal trends were outlined and debated. He loved the arguments that raged back and forth in the law school classroom and thought about becoming a litigator. Flom took no notes. He had a superlative retentive memory. When that was discovered by a classmate, he was asked regularly to correct his fellow student's notes. Sometimes Flom skipped class such as corporate law if he was bored with the subject. He went to the movies. Charlie Munger, who would later team with Warren Buffett, was a classmate and gin rummy partner. Flom graduated 18th in a class of more than 300.

After graduation, Flom found it difficult to find a job. He felt awkward talking to the large New York law firms. They were not for him. He was, in his own words, "very fat and socially inept." Several months passed. Flom got a call from the law school's placement office. He was asked whether he would like to talk to some young lawyers who were starting a firm. At lunch, Les Arps, Marshall Skadden, and John Slate explained the risks involved in going with a start-up. They had only one client. But the more they talked, the more Flom liked them. He was hired in 1948 at the then going rate for law school graduates, $3,600 a year. For the first two years of the life of Skadden, his annual salary was more than the three founders made collectively.

Skadden started life at 1 William Street which at the time was the Lehman Brothers building in lower Manhattan's financial district. Its whole office was half a floor in a tiny building. Then Lehman Brothers said they needed Skadden's space and paid them to move to Fifth Avenue and 45th Street. There, Flom did a little of everything—tax, aviation, and corporate work. He made partner after six years, during which time Bill Timbers joined the firm. Timbers had been the general counsel of the Securities and Exchange Commission, the regulatory agency that administers Wall Street. Timbers asked Flom to handle a proxy contest. Proxy contests intrigued Flom because they involved litigation, public relations, and accounting. After Flom did his first proxy fight, he was hooked.

Proxy contests brought out Flom's ruthless side. When asked by a chief executive what he should say to a shareholder demanding a board seat during a proxy fight, Flom replied, "Give him an evasive answer. Tell him to go fuck himself."[2]

Proxy contests were completely absorbing. Flom's wife, Claire, said of them, "You just went under and you didn't come up for air for months." One year, Flom had taken on a whole bunch of them. Claire said if he took one more, she would leave. The Floms went on vacation. On the day Flom returned to the office, someone wanted him in a proxy contest. Flom told them he would get back to them the next day. At home that night, Flom told his wife that somebody showed up with a proxy contest. She asked what it was about. Flom said he didn't know, but Roy Cohn, who helped fuel the anticommunist hysteria of the 1950s, was on the other side. His wife, who as a high school student got on a soapbox to make a speech in support of the Spanish Republicans, said, "I don't care if you kill yourself, go kill him."

Flom met his future wife at a party in New Jersey while he was on crutches because of a broken hip. He had been at Harvard Law School trying to recruit associates. It was very tough, Flom recalled. Most at Harvard Law School in the late 1950s had never heard of Skadden. Flom was leaving Harvard in a taxi that was involved in a head-on collision. The cab driver was killed. Flom went to the hospital and was strung up for two months in bed "like a Christmas tree."

The lawsuit resulting from the accident paid Flom $15,000—enough to buy a New York apartment. He was invited to a New Jersey party by one of his former law school classmates, where he met Claire, an interior designer. Flom started to talk about decorating. Claire told him she didn't talk business outside work. "Give me your card," she said. "You can talk as much as you like Monday." Flom's card read Skadden, Arps, Slate & Timbers. Claire looked at it and said, "You said you were a lawyer, but this is a building materials firm." After touring the apartment Flom planned to buy, Claire talked him out of getting a king-sized bed. "How many girls can you sleep with at once?" she asked him. A year and a half later they were married. Claire was soon pregnant, sleeping with her husband in a bed she quickly discovered was too small.

Flom worked incessantly. On weekends, his pace barely slackened. Claire decided to give up her interior design business and stay at home to care for their children. Her first son was born two months prematurely. By the age of three, it was obvious he had learning difficulties. Peter Flom couldn't draw a straight line. In 1965 there were no schools in New York to teach children with these problems. So Claire started one: the Gateway

School. It is now world famous. Claire did all the noneducational work for the school. She did the fund-raising and administrative work, often typing through the night in the dining room, away from the bedrooms, so as to not disturb the rest of the family. Peter later got a PhD.

Throughout their marriage, Claire didn't want to move out of New York City because she was afraid her husband would never see his children. She had one rule for her husband, telling him that if it were remotely possible, he must come home for dinner at night. If he wanted to go back to the office, that was fine, but she wanted him to be home for dinner. Flom's youngest son, Jason, who has done stand-up comedy, said he grew up in a single-parent home.

When Joe Flom did stay home, there was a bulge in the back of his pocket. They were phone messages written on little square slips of paper. He would start at the beginning and go right through to the end. At Skadden, the rule was to return calls within 24 hours without fail. As part of a service business, you have to give service, Flom told his Skadden colleagues. One night ITT's Harold Geneen called the Flom home. Claire answered. Geneen, a very hard taskmaster, wanted to talk to Joe. "I'm sorry, Mr. Geneen, but he can't come to the phone because he's upstairs reading to the kids," Claire said. A guest who heard Claire's words to Geneen dropped the drink he was holding, shocked Claire would tell America's most famous businessman her husband wasn't available. One client called the Floms' home on a Sunday morning and, when Claire picked up the phone, asked her immediately, "Is Joe there?" Claire told him no, and continued to do so as he called throughout the morning. Finally, Claire told the caller that it was a Sunday morning and the Floms' home was a private residence, not an office. The next morning a basket of flowers arrived at the house with a short note that said, "Never on Sunday."

Flom's growing reputation as America's foremost proxy lawyer attracted a group of lawyers in the 1960s. They would become among the most influential takeover attorneys in America. Jim Freund, Fin Fogg, and Morris Kramer joined from other firms. Peter Atkins and Roger Aaron were hired out of law school. Morris Kramer said, "One of Joe's aphorisms was the 80-20 rule. His rule was as long as you spent no more than 80 percent of your time fighting with your own client, you could do an excellent job with the remaining 20 percent of your time. If you spent more than 80 percent of your time fighting your client, then they would not have gotten the best out of you."[3]

Skadden, Arps was still a tiny firm, with fewer than 20 lawyers, when in 1966 Congress tabled legislation to inhibit takeovers. Alarmed by the slew of acquisitions made by men such as Geneen and Jimmy Ling, Congress thought it put the era of mass mergers and acquisitions behind it when it passed the Williams Act in 1968. Instead of stopping takeovers, it put the imprimatur of acceptability on them. There was now a road map courtesy of Congress on how takeovers should be done.

Flom and Arthur Fleischer toured the country, giving lectures on the Williams Act. Fleischer remembers lecturing all day and then gambling until 3 AM in Las Vegas. That didn't seem to satisfy the hotel management, who later vowed never to have a group of lawyers again because they would actually sit in the meetings from 10 AM to 5 PM instead of being out on the gambling tables.[4]

In 1973, a Manhattan lawyer wrote a piece in the *Michigan Law Review* that said the first question asked by an arbitrageur, a trader who bets on takeovers succeeding or failing, is which side Joe Flom is on. Soon the other side would want the article's author. His name was Marty Lipton.

■　■　■

It is an irony that the two men who were perhaps the most influential in shaping Wall Street's contemporary merger business struggled to get hired. Martin Lipton, born in Jersey City, New Jersey, on June 22, 1931, wanted to be an investment banker. He had received an undergraduate degree in business in 1952 from the prestigious Wharton School at the University of Pennsylvania. Lipton wrote to various Wall Street firms. No one offered him a job.

On the spur of the moment, he decided to go to law school at New York University School of Law. It turned out that law school was Lipton's thing. He became the editor in chief of the *New York University Law Review.* When he graduated, Lipton wanted to teach. He did further study under Adolph Berle at Columbia University.

Berle was one of the seminal thinkers on corporate law. He wrote a famous series of articles and books in the 1930s and had been a key member of Franklin Roosevelt's administration as a lawyer and economist. In 1955, Berle recognized and wrote on the impact institutional investors would have on corporation law, corporate governance, and the stock markets. Berle called attention to the so-called agency theory, which states that with diverse public ownership of companies, it would be difficult to control management of these companies. Not one shareholder could police management so that they were true to their fiduciary obligation to shareholders. Berle picked up something from Adam Smith's 1776 treatise *An Inquiry into the Nature and Causes of the Wealth of Nations*. In *Wealth of Nations*, Smith said people who operated joint stock companies with a diverse group of stockholders would not be as careful in the operation of the company as would be partners who run their own business. Agency theory now runs rife through corporate law. Lipton has inherited Berle's mantle as its foremost expert, advising boards of directors and chief executives who are faced with hostile takeovers or unhappy shareholders.

Before Lipton could return to NYU School of Law in a full-time teaching position, he was told by its dean that he should have some practical experience of the law. Lipton went to clerk for Edward Weinfeld, a federal judge. Lipton's predecessor as Judge Weinfeld's clerk was Barry Garfinkel. Garfinkel had joined Joe Flom at the Skadden law firm. He tried to interest Lipton in the firm and introduced him to Flom in 1957. It wasn't appropriate for a law firm to try and recruit a judge's clerk, so Flom made no formal offer to Lipton.

After clerking for Weinfeld, Lipton was told that if he wished to teach corporate law, he should practice corporate law for a few years. In 1958, he began work for Seligson, Morris & Neuburger. Although a tiny firm of 10 lawyers, Seligson, Morris had important clients. They included John Kluge's Metromedia, Schenley Industries, Pepsi Cola, and several Pepsi Cola bottlers.

The firm's lawyers included J. Lincoln Morris, was a board member and general counsel of Pepsi-Cola. Leonard Rosen worked with Charles Seligson representing financial institutions such as Walter Heller. Harvey Miller did creditor and debtor work with Seligson and merger work with Lipton.[5]

Lipton worked most closely with Lincoln Morris, who possessed a photographic memory. Morris was able to look at a piece of paper with complex financial figures and memorize it. Morris and Lipton's relationship was akin to father and son.[6] Lipton quickly exhibited a talent for drafting documents and negotiating.

Asked to sell a whisky dealership, Harvey Miller and Lipton were told the sales contract couldn't be more than one page or the firm wouldn't be hired. Miller worked until 11 PM and couldn't get the contract to less than six pages. He called Lipton, who said to drop his draft off at his apartment. The next morning Lipton came into the office with a $2\frac{1}{2}$-page contract.[7] Seligson, Morris won the contract to sell the whisky business. Lipton gave up on the idea of a full-time career as a law school professor, though he would teach securities law at his beloved NYU School of Law for more than two decades.

Richard Nixon was indirectly responsible for the break up of Seligson, Morris. Pepsi chairman Donald Kendall was fascinated with Nixon after the Soviet leader Nikita Khrushchev had a debate with the then vice president in front of a Pepsi booth in Moscow in 1959. Kendall enticed Nixon to New York after the former vice president lost California's 1964 gubernatorial election and helped Nixon start his law firm. Nixon's firm was appointed Pepsi's counsel, replacing Seligson, Morris.

Lincoln Morris, who had spent much of his time at Pepsi's headquarters outside New York, resigned from the Pepsi board. He was not happy in the firm he had started and built and quarreled with Lipton. Lipton decided to resign. Not only did Lipton leave Seligson, Morris, but he took the Metro Media account with him. Leonard Rosen, a schoolmate of Lipton's at NYU, resigned and joined Lipton, as did George Katz, a litigator and real estate lawyer who was also an NYU graduate.[8]

Lipton, Rosen, and Katz moved in with Herb Wachtell, a litigator who specialized in white-collar crime. Wachtell had started a firm with Jerry Kern, Wachtell & Kern at 50 Broad Street. In January 1965, the two sets of lawyers formed Wachtell, Lipton, Rosen, Katz & Kern.[9]

Seligson, Morris was liquidated. Throughout 1965, Lipton, Rosen, and Katz were paid a total of $110,000—enough, they thought, to stay in business for at least a year.

It turned out that it was a fortuitous year to start a Wall Street law firm. Many brokers and investment bankers who were working for established firms left to start their own small companies. The white-shoe

New York law firms such as Sullivan & Cromwell; Davis, Polk, Cravath, Swaine & Moore; and Simpson, Thacher & Bartlett weren't interested in representing them. A number of these start-ups gave their business to Wachtell. Soon Wachtell was part of the deal network as work on one small transaction led to more.

In 1969, Lipton met Ira Harris, who worked at Salomon Brothers in Chicago. Lipton's relationship with Harris and Salomon Brothers would help transform Wachtell into the trusted counselors for chief executives and investment bankers.

Chapter 3

Seducers—Harris and Rohatyn

Ira Harris was born Ira Horowitz on April 13, 1938, in New York City. From an early age, Ira had a love for the number 13. When he later became an investment banker, he once charged a client a fee of $1,313,313.13. In Chicago, while working at Salomon Brothers, Harris's home address, personal and office telephone numbers, and his car's license plate all contained the number 13.[1]

Ira's father was a salesman who sold lace trimmings for lampshades, tablecloths, and handkerchiefs. His mother was a housewife. Ira would often travel with his father to the cities in the Northeast. Together, they observed the Jewish holidays. Ira's mother brought him up as a Christian Scientist. The family rented a three-bedroom apartment in the Bronx near 196th Street and Grand Concourse. It was a predominantly Italian neighborhood. Ira got his first job, delivering groceries, when he was $8\frac{1}{2}$ years old. Later, he won a newspaper sales contest for the *Bronx Home News*. A proud Ira took his mother, father, and sister to the circus.

In the streets, he played touch football and stickball with sticks stolen from the custodian closets of the apartment buildings.

To his mother's great disappointment Ira refused to go to the prestigious Bronx High School of Science after passing the entrance exam. The school didn't have a football program, Ira told his mother. Ira went to Dewitt Clinton High School also in the Bronx. In 1955, he graduated fourth out of 900 and embarked on a tour of colleges. After a visit to the University of Pennsylvania in Philadelphia, Ira told his parents he wouldn't go there. The campus reminded him too much of the Bronx. Ira decided to attend the University of Michigan partly because he was a fan of the university's legendary football player Tommy Harmon. His mother, ill with breast cancer, died during his first semester.

At Michigan, Ira wrote sports stories for the *New York Post,* joined a Jewish fraternity, studied history, and changed his name from Horowitz to Harris. In his third year, Harris transferred into the business school where he barely graduated due, he said, to holding down two or more jobs while attending classes. Having grown up watching his salesman father earn his own living, Harris wanted to be his own boss. In 1959, he came back to New York and applied to 32 stockbrokers for a job. He was rejected by every firm.

A friend introduced Harris to her father who worked at a brokerage, Jacques Coe and Company. Harris was hired at a salary of $60 a week and sold mutual funds by going door to door at apartment buildings often after 5 PM when people had just returned from work. Harris left the brokerage and took a job with Granbery Marache, the predecessor firm of broker Blair & Company. In 1964, Blair sent Harris back to the Midwest as manager of Blair's Chicago office. His research reports on food and beverage companies began to generate a following among fund managers.

Harris became a banker by accident. In 1968, he was on a plane heading to a mutual fund conference in Palm Springs with Dick Samuels, the executive vice president at CNA Insurance. Harris got up, drink in hand, to converse with Samuels in the aisle. Samuels told Harris that CNA was looking to acquire a mutual fund company and mentioned a name. Harris told Samuels the company mentioned wouldn't do and suggested that CNA merge with a famous brand. Fidelity and Putnam were too big, Harris said; what about Tsai Management? Samuels said it was an idea. But Jerry Tsai, one of the hot stock pickers of the 1960s, would never do it. Harris said he knew Tsai. Perhaps Tsai would talk about it. At 7 o'clock the next morning, Samuels grabbed Harris at breakfast and asked if he could arrange a meeting between CNA Chairman Howard Reeder and Jerry Tsai. Two weeks later, CNA acquired Tsai Management.

Harris's role in the merger caught the eye of Salomon Brothers. Harry Brown was the partner in charge of Salomon Brothers' Chicago office and was close to retirement age. Brown recommended Harris to Salomon Brothers' managing partner Billy Salomon.[2] Harris started work for Salomon Brothers in April 1969, the first outsider hired as a partner.

He felt right at home in the blunt, blaspheming Salomon Brothers culture. Many at the firm were products of New York public schools. Billy Salomon, a founder's son, and 12 other general partners never went to college.[3]

■   ■   ■

When the future president of the World Bank, James Wolfensohn, arrived to work as an investment banker at Salomon Brothers in 1977, he was in for a culture shock. Wolfensohn had spent most of his career working in the U.K. The Australian-born Wolfensohn went from being served coffee on a silver tray by a steward in striped trousers and a black jacket at J. Henry Schroder's London headquarters to bagels at Salomon Brothers' New York cafeteria. "You would go in at 8 in the morning and eat breakfast. Cigars would be smoked, people would be swearing at each other, criticizing each other, and then the team coalesced," recalled Wolfensohn nostalgically.[4]

Salomon Brothers had no formal investment banking department when Harris joined. Its business from the time it was formed in 1910 was managing the sale and trading of bonds for governments and corporations. "We didn't decide to have an M&A [mergers and acquisitions] department according to Harvard Business School principles," recalled Billy Salomon dismissively. "We hired individuals and backed them. We saw an opportunity and looked for someone to exploit that opportunity."[5] Harris sought to exploit Salomon Brothers' role as a financier for many companies by also offering corporations advice on corporate strategy, especially mergers. Harris thought he fit in better in Chicago than in New York. To a chief executive in Chicago, it didn't matter that his banker hadn't gone to Princeton or Yale with him. Harris plunged into Chicago society, attending charity dinners throughout the week. Chicago's business leaders were regulars at charity events, and Harris would mingle with them over cocktails and play golf with them over the weekend. He lived with his wife, Nicki, and their children in an apartment by Lake Michigan in Chicago's tony "Gold Coast." The area was known for its nineteenth-century brownstone buildings that gave it a whiff of Europe.

Harris "wasn't puffed up," said Ned Jannotta, a rival investment banker who would rise to be chairman of Chicago-based investment bank William Blair. This endeared Harris to many in the Midwest, who were usually treated with a degree of condescension by New York bankers. "You poor fellows in the Midwest, you don't know when to come out of the rain," was the attitude of many, recalled Jannotta.[6]

Many New York firms insisted on their name appearing on the top left of any deal announcement, as it signaled to Wall Street that their firm led the transaction. But Harris didn't. He preferred to give firms such as William Blair their due if they had a longer-standing relationship with a company than did Salomon Brothers.[7] This, along with his natural gregariousness and wit, won him friends and allies in the Midwest business community.

Often struggling with obesity, despite a series of diets and prescribed exercise, the 6-foot-1-inch, 300-pound Harris one day leaned against the boardroom table of lawyer Tommy Reynolds and split it lengthwise. Reynolds was horrified. Harris, who never lost his Bronx accent, simply said, "I'm just antiquing it for ya, Tommy."[8]

Harris called his first deal for Salomon Brothers the "crapper deal." Chicago's Illinois Central Industries was a client of Salomon as it helped finance the company's purchase of railroad cars. Illinois Central wanted to expand outside the railroads and had formed a holding company. Chicago's Pepsi-Cola General Bottlers were in talks to be acquired by Westinghouse. But the bottlers' executives were reluctant to be acquired by Pittsburgh-based Westinghouse, letting it be known privately they favored a merger with a Chicago company, partly because they liked where they were living.

One day while reading annual reports sitting on the toilet, Harris noticed that Illinois Central had a map showing where their railroads were, and Pepsi-Cola Bottlers had a map showing where their bottling plants were. The railroads passed by the bottling plants. The maps gave Harris the impetus to fly to New York for a meeting with Pepsi-Cola Bottlers' banker Mel Sieden. Harris suggested to Sieden over lunch that Pepsi-Cola Bottlers should merge with Illinois Central, which wanted to diversify its business beyond railroads. Marty Lipton, who was counsel to Pepsi-Cola Bottlers, was at the lunch. "The maps, the maps," an excited Harris told Lipton. "It's an overlay." Lipton looked at Harris in disbelief after Harris explained. Bottles of Pepsi weren't shipped by railroad. But Seeden, Lipton, and Harris knew Pepsi-Cola Bottlers' reluctance to a merger with Westinghouse. After the two chief executives met, Westinghouse was cast aside. Pepsi-Cola Bottlers agreed to a takeover by Illinois Central.

Lipton and Harris became friends. Both were pessimistic and conservative. Harris said Lipton taught him to be even more conservative, particularly when it came to Wall Street. Harris's office looked like a lawyer's, with stacks of papers and documents on desks and on the floor. He wrote down ideas for deals on three-by-five cards and kept paper by his bed in case he awoke with an inspiration. In the days before mobile phones, people speculated, only half jokingly, that Harris's secretary knew the telephone number of every pay phone in every airport in America. Harris had a propensity to call as soon as he got off a plane.[9]

Harris got one of the first mobile phones in America. Chicago was one of the test areas of the cell phone in the 1970s. Harris had a test phone in the car. He called it the brick phone and wrote memos on how the phone worked to the Federal Communications Commission.

Salomon Brothers' freewheeling culture enabled many such as Harris to feel empowered. One other firm operated in a similar fashion, affording its partners considerable autonomy. That was Lazard Freres. By 1970, Lazard partner Felix Rohatyn was ready to take the role of senior deal maker away from an aging and ailing Andre Meyer.

■   ■   ■

Felix George Rohatyn was born in Vienna, Austria, on May 29, 1928, to a prosperous Polish Jewish family. The family left Austria to escape the rising anti-Semitism of the 1930s. They went to Orleans,

France, where his father was a director of a brewing company. In 1937, Rohatyn came to Paris with his mother after she divorced his father. When the Germans invaded France in 1940, Rohatyn and his mother left Paris, their wealth in gold coins stuffed into toothpaste tubes.[10]

The Rohatyns' flight to freedom took them to Marseilles, Algeria, Morocco, and Rio de Janeiro. Brazil's wartime ambassador to France, Luiz Martinas de Souza Dantas, provided some 800 Jews trapped in France, including the Rohatyns, with visas to Brazil, saving them from the Holocaust.[11] Felix and his family didn't stay in Brazil long. They got U.S. visas and took a ship to New York, where they set up house on Park Avenue.

Felix initially struggled to learn English, He went to Middlebury College, where he studied physics. Rohatyn joined Lazard's foreign exchange department in 1949.[12] It was dreary work, and he longed for a change. The impetus came in a meeting with whisky magnate Samuel Bronfman, who advised him to work under the mercurial French-born Andre Meyer. Rohatyn approached Meyer and, after much grumbling, allowed the younger man to work under him crunching numbers.[13]

Despite its French name and cachet, Lazard had been founded in New Orleans in 1848 as a dry goods business. By 1876, Lazard's business was finance because of the firm's experience in managing the risk of shipping goods back and forth between continents. By the early twentieth century, Lazard had offices in New York, London, and Paris.[14] When the Germans invaded France in 1940, Andre Meyer fled Paris and, with Pierre David-Weill, took control of Lazard's New York office. When David-Weill returned to Paris after the war, Meyer stayed in New York and ran the firm with an iron fist. Lazard's New York office under Meyer is best described, according to one who worked there at the time, as a wagon wheel where Meyer sat in the middle.[15]

Andre Meyer said a good banker needed just three things: paper, a very sharp pencil, and what's up top. Meyer was also quick to remind those he worked with at Lazard that finance isn't about money, it's about people. The people who matter in mergers are chief executives. Chief executives are important people. Meyer said the job of a banker was to know important people. If you know important people, important people will want to know you, he said.[16]

Meyer was the quintessential banker to important people. He coun-
seled David Rockefeller, Katharine Graham, Jackie Onassis, and Gianni
Angelli. He would talk with Lyndon Johnson at the White House and
at his Texas ranch.[17] Meyer was also tough, controlling, and nasty. "Brilliant but also a quintessential son of a bitch," according to one who
worked with him.[18]

One New York lawyer remembers a meeting with Meyer. Discussion
on a deal had moved from grand theorizing to workmanlike discussions,
removing Meyer to the sidelines. A call had to be made to another party.
Meyer offered to make it. Meyer couldn't manage to dial the number,
and it was obvious he was doing so deliberately. Another senior Lazard
banker got up and dialed the number for Meyer. "He took back control
of the meeting by everybody's focusing on him. Playing with the phone,
not placing the call because that was beneath him, he was going to get
one of the princes to do it because he was the king. The king isn't going
to ask," recalled the lawyer.[19]

When Meyer held court in meetings, Rohatyn sat quietly soaking
up the experience. To be a great man, one learned by watching other
great men. "Felix might not be prepared to admit it now, but Felix
hated him with a passion," said a colleague who worked with Meyer
and Rohatyn at Lazard.[20] Many years later, Rohatyn said Meyer was a
"volcanic genius" and added that he had a "complicated relationship"
with the older man.[21]

Rohatyn, like Meyer, possessed the exotic, cosmopolitan manner
that beguiled many American chief executives. His European gracious-
ness and manners combined with a calm, self-assured manner gave Rohatyn a romantic exoticism, according to Arthur Fleischer.[22] He also
had a first-rate mind. Michel David-Weill said of Rohatyn that he could
thumb through an annual report and in 10 or 15 minutes estimate the
company's worth within 10 percent of its true value.[23]

Like his mentor Meyer, Rohatyn also worked extremely hard. He
would be in the office 16 to 18 hours a day. "Very literally in one year I
had two years' experience, and in five years I had 10 years' experience,"
Rohatyn once told a colleague.[24] In the 1950s and 1960s, Rohatyn
began to emerge out of Meyer's shadow by advising Harold Geneen of
ITT. Years later, Rohatyn said Geneen "taught me more about business,

about finance, about what the numbers meant and how to interpret them" than anyone else.[25]

Rohatyn became the first deal investment banker whose relationships with chief executives transcended the firm he worked for. For bankers who began to specialize in mergers and acquisitions in the 1970s, Rohatyn provoked an Oedipus complex. Rohatyn was the father they wanted to kill, said J. Tomilson Hill III, who started work as a merger banker at First Boston in 1977.[26]

Another firm realized that by the 1970s its success depended not on hiring the next Rohatyn, but on training and getting the firm to cooperate so that it thought like a many-headed Rohatyn. That firm was Goldman Sachs. One of the men responsible for the growth of its mythical culture of teamwork was Steve Friedman.

Chapter 4

Systematizer—Goldman Sachs

O n his first day at Goldman Sachs in 1966, Steve Friedman thought he wasn't dealing well with the pressure. He was sweating, and there was a buzzing in his ears as he sat there trying to do financial analysis. Friedman felt progressively more ill during the day and wondered that evening if he would have to call in sick for his second day of work. The ex-wrestler with the broken nose dismissed the idea and came in the next morning running a fever. After all, he reasoned, he couldn't leave all the work in Goldman Sachs's merger department to Corbin Day.[1]

Day had joined the firm three years earlier and was the head of the merger department. He was trained for a life as an investment banker, having graduated with an MBA from Wharton. Friedman was a lawyer who had gravitated to Wall Street because he found he liked dealing with people more than contracts. When John Whitehead, Goldman Sachs' courtly head of investment banking, interviewed Friedman for a job, he said that lawyers were often people who said you couldn't do something. "We don't want people who are always negative," Friedman recalled Whitehead telling him. "I told him good lawyers were people who recognized the problems and tried to figure out a legitimate way to accomplish things. I told him I hoped I was that sort of lawyer."

Friedman offered to take a pay cut to join Goldman Sachs, as his salary as an attorney was higher than the firm's investment banking associates. Whitehead said the offer wasn't necessary. Friedman's annual salary was set at $18,000. He was assigned to an investment banking department that was considered a backwater—mergers. Whitehead had just started it.

John Cunningham Whitehead was Goldman Sachs's answer to the WASPs at Morgan Stanley. The son of a porch furniture salesman from Montclair, New Jersey, Whitehead was every inch a Wall Street chief—polished, urbane, articulate, gray-haired, and given to wearing elegant Paul Stuart suits. Whitehead was perhaps the first person who brought modern management techniques into Wall Street. He sought to organize and execute business goals through a firmwide effort. Many of Goldman Sachs's competitors were partnerships that were haphazard in their planning.

Whitehead worried that Goldman Sachs's investment banking efforts was Sidney Weinberg, the senior partner, whose first job at the firm was as an assistant porter in the basement. Weinberg, despite never having finished high school, got the first merger fee for Goldman Sachs. The firm was paid $1 million after Weinberg helped arrange the merger that created the drug company Warner Lambert. Weinberg's personal and business relationship with the Ford family enabled Goldman Sachs to manage Ford Motors' initial public share sale. He sat on about 30 boards.

Goldman Sachs's traditional business since it was founded in 1869 was commercial paper—short-term, unsecured loans to companies. The firm didn't have the extensive blue-chip relationships of Morgan Stanley. Among America's biggest companies, Goldman Sachs could only count on Sears, Ford, and Procter & Gamble as loyal clients. Morgan Stanley, in contrast, had the most extensive blue-chip client list of any Wall Street firm, including the seven major oil companies and two-thirds of the 200 biggest U.S. corporations.

After he was made partner in 1956, Whitehead set up a new business department with Sidney Weinberg's tacit approval. Whitehead divided the United States into four regions and initially recruited 10 men to cover the 1,000 largest companies in the country. These new businessmen would call on chief executives and chief financial officers to see if they would sign up on Goldman Sachs's commercial paper program. The hope was that once a company borrowed money from Goldman Sachs, they would be enticed to sell their stocks or bonds through the firm or ask its advice if it wanted to do a merger.

"It was considered very degrading for someone to go out and say, 'Mr. Smith, my name is John Jones, and I'm here to solicit your investment banking business,'" recalled Whitehead. "The poor guy who ran the company didn't know what to say to that. He had never heard of an investment banker coming to call on him. Sometimes he was a little impressed. 'Isn't that nice? I've never been called on by an investment banker. Who are investment bankers and what do they do?'"

Whitehead's methodical and well-organized approach to win new business for Goldman Sachs included seminars for his new businessman, such as "How to get an appointment with the CEO" and "How to treat the CEO's secretary." Whitehead was careful to make sure that his new businessmen stuck to making calls. When a company needed investment banking help, Whitehead's new businessmen turned it over to the specialists in the firm.

Every Goldman Sachs new businessman who made a call on a company had to write a call report for the files. Whitehead would get a copy of all these reports as they went into the file. He assigned fellow Harvard Business School graduate Bill Stutz to get a copy if the reports pertained to mergers. Stutz accumulated two big spreadsheets, one of companies for sale, and one of companies that were potential acquirers. Goldman Sachs got some merger and acquisition business from matching the buyers and sellers of businesses in the 1950s and 1960s.

Whitehead got the merger department to take an assignment only if Goldman Sachs was hired on an exclusive basis and paid whether it brought in the buyer or someone else did. The firm's efforts were hardly remunerative in the beginning. In 1966, the year Steve Friedman joined the merger and acquisition group, Goldman Sachs generated $600,000 in revenue advising on mergers.

■ ■ ■

Born in Brooklyn on December 21, 1937, Friedman was raised on Long Island in a town called Rockville Centre, 45 minutes by train from Manhattan. His father had his own insurance business, and his mother was a housewife. Growing up in the Eisenhower years of the 1950s, Friedman remembers his generation as non-descript. His life at Oceanside High School revolved around athletics and the opposite sex.

"We were the Eisenhower generation. We were bland," said Friedman.

One day his father drove him to Yale College in New Haven, Connecticut. Yale's director of admissions told Friedman that he was in the bottom half of his class in a not particularly distinguished public high school. Friedman had no chance of admission into Yale. But the admissions director did offer Friedman a reprieve. If Friedman managed to get a 90 average for all his classes during the first half of his senior year, Yale would accept him. This challenge set the pattern of Friedman's life—goals set and then achieved. Friedman got the required grades, and at the end of high school, Yale, Cornell, and Harvard accepted him.

On the athletic field, he had similar success after a rough start. After ditching basketball in favor of wrestling, Friedman was, in his own words, "pinned, crushed, and decimated" in his first six matches. In his seventh match, the 106-pound Friedman had his father in the audience, curious as to what sport caused his son to arrive home black and blue. Friedman considered the seventh match of his wrestling career a moral victory; he was beaten but not pinned.

Friedman eventually became the Long Island champion among 50 high schools in Suffolk and Nassau counties. More importantly, it instilled in him self-confidence. "The thing about wrestling is that you're alone on the mat with somebody. It's difficult to make excuses," Friedman recalled. "There is a certain necessity to push yourself in difficult and painful situations. I think I learned some valuable lessons from that sport in terms of the necessity to pay the price for what you want to achieve."

Despite being the captain of the wrestling team and the quarterback of the football team, Friedman couldn't join his high school's athletic fraternity because he was Jewish. He shrugged it off. Friedman can't remember anyone protesting about anything in Rockville Centre during the 1950s.

Friedman chose to go to Cornell University because its wrestling program offered a chance to become a national champion. He had ambitions to make the U.S. Olympic team. Plus, Cornell had women undergraduate students, unlike Harvard, Yale, and some other Ivy League universities at the time. In his first week of classes, he met Barbara, his future wife. At Cornell, where he majored in sociology, Friedman learned another valuable lesson that would serve him well in his future business life, how to cram. Friedman married after graduation. In the fall of 1959, he entered Columbia University's law school.

In law school, he thought he had found his calling. Coming home after his first classes, Friedman told his wife an odd thing was happening: The professors were forcing him to think. Friedman's wife would often join him at the law library, falling asleep beside him as he worked into the night. The two "were happy as clams" in their small apartment. They went for long walks around the Upper West Side or went to the movies. Friedman continued wrestling through his first two years of law school, trained at the New York Athletic Club, and won a national championship.

Columbia's law school students had to hone their written and oral arguments before a panel of distinguished alumni in a law school exercise known as moot court. Friedman's wife cooked a meal for her husband and his moot court partner before their presentation. Friedman tried to calm his nervous partner with a few shots of scotch. His classmate proceeded to empty the bottle and pass out drunk. Friedman had to shake him awake so they could make their arguments in front of the moot court. Seemingly unaffected by alcohol, Friedman's partner impressed the judges and won the moot court prize. The experience persuaded Friedman he should not become a litigator.

After he graduated 10th in his class, Friedman clerked for a judge and then worked for a New York law firm for two and a half years. But Friedman found himself casting around for something more to do than drafting legal documents. His wife's brother had gone to Harvard

Business School, and Friedman found he loved reading the business school's casebooks. He started to read the *Wall Street Journal* to acculturate himself to finance and wrote to several investment banks asking for a job.

No one replied. In frustration at Wall Street's "blithe indifference" to his ambition, Friedman mentioned his rejection to a friend. The friend knew L. Jay Tenenbaum, a Goldman Sachs partner who ran the firm's arbitrage department. He suggested that Friedman have lunch with Tenenbaum. Friedman was initially reluctant. He viewed Goldman Sachs as an old-line, stuffy kind of place. The lunch with Tenenbaum led to a series of interviews, culminating with John Whitehead's job offer. Lehman Brothers, which had also met with Friedman, offered him a job as well. He stuck with Goldman Sachs.

Friedman and Corbin Day worked well together. Both men initially concentrated on giving private companies merger advice. As both men sought to expand the business, they began pitching their services to public companies. Two others, Bob Blank and Dave Remington, were hired to help Day and Friedman. Despite Whitehead's efforts, Goldman Sachs was not considered a first-tier investment bank at the beginning of the 1970s. It was considered a second-tier firm on par with Kidder Peabody.

In the summer of 1970, Whitehead was walking the floor of Goldman Sachs' investment banking department with his aide. Whitehead greeted the department's first summer intern, a six-foot-two-inch-tall Wharton MBA student named Geoff Boisi. As they exchanged pleasantries, Boisi pointed to the department's cathode ray tube (CRT) monitor, forerunner of the computer. He told Whitehead that soon every desk on the floor would have a CRT monitor on it to do the financial calculations that he was doing using a slide rule. Whitehead nodded and moved on. His aide said to Boisi as his boss moved out of earshot, "If you ever want to work here, you have to stop saying stupid things like that."

■   ■   ■

Geoffrey Thomas Boisi was born at New York's St. Vincent's Hospital on May 8, 1947. His father, James Boisi, and his mother, Edith Mullen Boisi, had six children. Geoff was the second-oldest. His maternal grandfather came to America from Ireland virtually penniless as a teenager and became a taxi driver. He had four daughters, who all graduated from college.

Geoff's paternal grandfather was French. He fought in the U.S. Army during World War I and met his wife in America. Boisi's father and grandfather never laid eyes on each other. Geoff's paternal grandfather died from the mustard gas poisoning he received in the trenches during World War I a few months after his wife became pregnant.

To support her family, Boisi's paternal grandmother worked as a cook and cleaner for various Catholic rectories in New York. Boisi's father was brought up in Hell's Kitchen and the Lower East Side. He passed an exam to enter New York's prestigious Stuyvesant High School and graduated from Brooklyn College and Fordham Law School, where he was top of his class.

Boisi's father worked as first vice president of real estate for New York Central Railroad. He helped develop much of the property on Park Avenue and created the notion of air rights. He later became the head of J. P. Morgan's first real estate group and rose to become the only non–Ivy League–educated member of the firm's corporate office.

James Boisi taught at Pace University for 50 years, partly because as a teacher at Pace his six children would be able to go to the college cheaply. When Geoff Boisi worked at Goldman Sachs, he would meet chief executives and taxi drivers who told him they had taken his father's courses at Pace University.

Geoff Boisi recalls his father as a demanding disciplinarian who ran conversations around the dinner table like the chair of a university debating society. Geoff's and his father's views on religion and politics sometimes clashed. The two engaged in fierce arguments at meal times.

Geoff went to Catholic elementary and high schools on Long Island, where he played sports and was elected president of his school. He became an altar boy in second grade and got tips helping to serve mass at funerals and weddings on weekends.

In eighth grade, Geoff gave his first public speech on service and Catholic activism, a theme that would be dominant throughout his life. "For the greater glory of God" was a phrase James Boisi would write at the end of letters to his son at the university to remind him of life's purpose.

As a teenager, Geoff shared a room with his maternal grandfather, who told taught him baseball, golf, and how to drive a car. They watched the Friday night fights together. His grandfather's death from cancer when Geoff was 15 deeply affected him.

As he neared the end of high school, Boisi sought to study international relations. He considered himself a patriot and wanted to become a diplomat, a cold war warrior, to protect America from the threat of communism. The U.S. military involvement in the Vietnam War was building, and when Boisi began attending Boston College, he wanted to go to the battlefields in Southeast Asia and fight.

Initially, Boisi wasn't identified as someone with establishment sympathies. Within 72 hours of arriving on campus, he got a note from the dean of students. "PYB Boisi, see me." He went to see the dean, who told him to get rid of his beard. "PYB" stood for "pack your bags." Shave or go home. Boisi shaved.

At Boston College he met his future wife, Rene; continued voicing his opinions in the classroom, much like he did to his father at the dinner table; and sought to evict Students for a Democratic Society, who had taken over buildings protesting the war. Boisi argued that they were interfering with the rights of students who had paid and wanted an education.

He sought admittance into Officer Candidate School. An illness and a subsequent high lottery number in the draft caused him not to go to Vietnam.

Boisi married after he graduated from college in Pittsburgh on August 16, 1969, one of the days of the Woodstock festival. Seeking entry to Wharton after admission to its MBA program had closed, Boisi was accepted on the strength of the entrepreneurial spirit he showed while still a teenager.

As a 19-year-old one summer in the mid-1960s, selling real estate door to door in New York, Boisi had noticed there were few skyscrapers in lower Manhattan. He wanted to build a high-rise building in an area on Broad Street where Fraunces Tavern, a historic landmark owned by the Daughters of the American Revolution, is located. Boisi got an architectural student to do a rendering of a 40-story building, He then found a developer from England to back the idea. Boisi went around to the 28 buildings on the block that surrounded Fraunces Tavern and got all to agree to sell their businesses to him in return for stakes in the proposed office block. He visited the Daughters of the American Revolution. They said they would never sell. It is now one of the few blocks in lower Manhattan that does not have a skyscraper.

Boisi and his wife lived in an apartment in Beverly, New Jersey, next to an X-rated drive-in movie house while Boisi attended Wharton. His wife taught school, and her $5,500 a year salary supported them both.

During his summer at Goldman Sachs in 1970, Boisi would take the 5 AM bus into Manhattan. As he would arrive just a few minutes before the bus pulled up, those ahead of him in line at the bus stop got a seat. Boisi stood all the way during the hour-and-a-half journey into Manhattan. On the same bus was a thin, sallow-faced man who read in the dark with the aid of a miner's cap affixed with a light. He was Michael Milken. Asked if he ever talked to Milken, Boisi said years later, "Why would anyone talk to someone who's got a miner's cap on?"

Boisi worked on real estate transactions during his summer internship at Goldman Sachs. But Boisi didn't want a career as a real estate banker. He wanted to carve out a business career separate from his father's field. After observing Goldman Sachs's merger group from his desk, he asked Bob Blank, one of its associates, out to lunch. He asked Blank to explain what he did. Listening to him, Boisi thought he could do the job.

At the end of the summer, John Whitehead called Boisi into his office and offered him a job in the commercial paper department. Boisi declined the offer. He told Whitehead he wanted to work in mergers. Whitehead said the firm had never hired someone straight out of business school to do mergers. Chief executives, Whitehead said, don't typically seek advice from 22-year-olds.

Four months after his internship finished, Boisi called Corbin Day. He had spent days thinking about how to convince Goldman Sachs to hire him. "Give me half an hour of your time," Boisi pleaded with Day and trekked again into Manhattan to pitch for a full-time job.

In Day's office, Boisi went down all the reasons the firm might say no and then his counterarguments and the reasons why he wanted the job. Boisi told Day that he had always related well to older people, was able to gain people's trust, possessed an analytical mind, and was numerate.

Two days later, Boisi got a call. Day invited him to join the merger department as its first associate.

■   ■   ■

Gus Levy was the senior partner when Boisi joined Goldman Sachs in 1971. Levy was one of the inventors of modern risk arbitrage and block trading on Wall Street. According to popular myth at the firm, Levy never gave his colleagues more than three minutes to make their point. He also had a deep southern drawl, which made it hard for others to understand him. Sometimes bankers would emerge after meetings with Levy, scratch their heads, and ask one another, "What did he say?"

Robert Rubin who worked under Levy called him "very difficult, very demanding." Levy managed people, said Rubin, "by yelling—all day long."

Corbin Day invented what were termed "Gus-O-Grams" by the merger department. Whatever the issue was, Day would write it out on a piece of paper with "yes" and "no" boxes for Levy to tick or a line on it for Levy to scribble what they should do. He brought along the 23-year-old Boisi when he met Levy with bad news, hoping Goldman Sachs's senior partner wouldn't yell in front of the young guy.

Boisi had great respect for Levy. Ben Heinemann, chairman of Northwest Industries, once called Levy up to complain about "this kid Boisi, who's making my life miserable." Goldman Sachs had been defending a company called Microdot from a hostile bidder and approached Northwest Industries to ask if they would be a friendly acquirer. Heinemann didn't like the price Boisi suggested he should pay for Microdot. Boisi was asked by Levy to come and see him. "Ben Heinemann is all upset. What's going on?" Levy asked Boisi. Boisi gave Levy his story. Levy told him to sit in a chair and got Ben Heinemann on the phone. Word for word, he repeated Boisi's story to Heinemann, with the price Boisi suggested. Then Levy said: "Boisi, is that all right with you? Ben, is that all right with you? Fine. Done."

Levy, who got to the office around 7 AM, the same time as Boisi, once called the younger man soon after he got in and asked to see him. He explained he had a friend who owned horses in Florida. "Go down to see him and help him," Levy told Boisi. "But I really know nothing about horses, Mr. Levy," a baffled Boisi said. Goldman Sachs's senior partner replied: "You'll learn, you'll learn."

Boisi searched around Goldman Sachs for somebody who knew about horses. He found someone working with computers named Richard Santulli. Santulli had worked his way through college and two graduate degrees by betting on horse races. Boisi took Santulli to Florida, and there they met Levy's friend, William McKnight, the former chairman of 3M. Then in his 80s, McKnight owned Calder racetrack. In McKnight's den was a huge picture of the famed racehorse Man O'War. As soon as Santulli saw the picture, he began talking horse racing with McKnight. The two men spoke for hours while Boisi quietly sat and listened. Goldman Sachs was hired to do McKnight's work.

Some years later, Boisi told Santulli that Goldman Sachs was thinking of putting him up for a partnership. "Geoff, please don't do that," Santulli told Boisi. "What are you talking about? People would give their right arm to be a partner at Goldman Sachs," Boisi said. "I understand that as a partner you can't have any individual leverage, and I believe in leverage. I have interests outside my activities at Goldman Sachs; my brother and I do entrepreneurial things. Please don't put me up for partnership," Santulli told Boisi. Within a year, he had left. He would later be a founder of NetJets and sell the company to Warren Buffett for $725 million.

Chapter 5

Originators—Morgan Stanley

A t Morgan Stanley in the late 1960s, a group of young associates wanted the firm to move beyond just raising money for companies and nations. They felt there was a risk that Morgan Stanley could be left behind if it didn't move into other businesses. The firm had to exploit its unparalleled relationships with corporate America, Bob Greenhill and Richard Fisher told their older partners.[1] The young associates found a sympathetic audience among the firm's two senior partners, Frank Petitio and Bob Baldwin.

Baldwin, the firm's chairman, who had worked under U.S. Defense Secretary Robert McNamara in the Pentagon, recognized that Morgan Stanley needed to plan its future and diversify its business model.[2]

In 1971, a year after Fisher and Greenhill were appointed partners, Morgan Stanley added brokerage and research functions. The firm cautiously expanded its trading of equities and debt. Its capital, like others on Wall Street, was tiny, then only about $10 million.[3] As partners left, they could withdraw their money from the capital account. As Morgan Stanley and its rivals expanded throughout the 1970s and 1980s, their low levels of capital that supported their burgeoning trading operations forced many to transform themselves into publicly owned companies through share sales.

Frank Petito, who was in charge of Morgan Stanley's buying department—later renamed corporate finance—had observed Lazard's Felix Rohatyn winning millions of dollars in fees advising ITT. Petito thought Morgan Stanley could do the same with even more success because of its raft of blue-chip clients.

In the late 1960s and into the early 1970s, Wall Street firms were hardly making any money because of a stagnating economy and a sliding stock market. Petito thought a merger department could at least generate some transaction fees for Morgan Stanley while risking none of the firm's precious capital. He enticed Bill Sword, an experienced corporate finance partner of the firm, to head the fledgling effort. In 1972, Sword, Greenhill, and two young associates, Joe Fogg and Brad Evans, made up the founding members of Morgan Stanley's new merger department.[4] Petito, who had mentored Greenhill, thought the young Morgan Stanley partner possessed the necessary drive to generate transactions for the firm. After all, Greenhill did everything at top speed. His energy level was volcanic.

Robert Foster Greenhill was born in Minneapolis on June 20, 1936. He was the son of a department store executive who kept his job throughout the Depression. Greenhill's father imbued in his son a love of the outdoors by taking him canoeing on Minnesota's Lake Minnetonka, where the family lived. Later, Bob would own a canoeing magazine and take his children paddling as far north as the Arctic Ocean.[5]

From a young age, Bob Greenhill stood out. At the two-teacher schoolhouse where one teacher taught two classes that sat beside each other, Bob's father, Raymond, recalled getting notes from his teachers telling them what a joy he was to teach. In 1950, Raymond Greenhill was transferred to Baltimore. Bob went to Gilman, a prep school in the area. There, he cultivated an ambition to be a great physicist or painter, ran track, and played lacrosse, a game almost wholly the domain of American prep schools. Greenhill shunned the University of Virginia and Princeton, the traditional colleges of Gilman graduates, for Yale in 1954. After a year at Yale, he found he had the top marks in the sciences and the bottom marks in the arts. Greenhill dropped physics and mathematics in favor of a major in philosophy. One night his roommate brought back a girl from Vassar College. She had been brought to a dance at Yale, only to see her date pass out drunk. Greenhill married the girl, Gayle Gussett, in Des Moines, Iowa, after they had both graduated in 1958.

Greenhill enrolled in the Naval Reserve during his Yale days. In the summer of 1957, while on a destroyer cruising between Virginia and Canada, he met Jack McAtee, a fellow Naval Reserve officer who was a student at Princeton.[6] It was the beginning of a lifelong friendship. During their military service after college, both men found themselves on the same group of ships going to the western Pacific. Greenhill sent air tickets to his wife, Gayle, and she flew to Japan and Hong Kong to see her husband. The Greenhills took language classes in Japan and celebrated Christmas with the aide of plastic tree on the balcony of their room at the YMCA in Hong Kong next to the city's famed Peninsula Hotel.

In the second year of their military service, Greenhill and Jack McAtee were on a shore base in California with their wives and had little to do. They played tennis or golf almost every day and applied to graduate schools. Greenhill got into Harvard Business School, and McAtee into Yale Law School.[7]

At Harvard, Greenhill had 650 classmates including two women who were not degree but certificate students. He was assigned Section F, along with Richard Fisher.[8] From almost the beginning of their days in each other's orbits, they were bitter rivals. No one could pinpoint their antipathy toward each other except that both men were ambitious and talented men, driven to get to the top. At times it was almost petty, like any feud.

Greenhill said he had a hazy memory of Fisher at Harvard. This statement left Fisher speechless when it was repeated to him. They were, after all, section mates at business school.[9] Fisher claimed he was a resource for those at Harvard Business School who sought work at Morgan Stanley.[10] Greenhill denies having asked Fisher for help to gain an introduction to the firm and said he got a job offer by dint of his own efforts. When Fisher died in 2004, Greenhill didn't attend his memorial service.[11]

Outwardly, Fisher was a more circumspect, gentler figure. He had contracted polio as a child. Despite having to walk with crutches, he won a spot on the wrestling team at his Philadelphia high school, the William Penn Charter School. Fisher graduated from Princeton at the age of 20 and in the university's history department made a lifelong friend, William Hambrecht.

"I was one of his left-brain friends," Hambrecht recalled. "He was attracted to people who did things differently. Mary Meeker, a Morgan Stanley analyst, once told me that the basis of your relationship was that you were a jock who wanted to be an intellectual and Dick was an intellectual who wanted to be a jock."[12] Hambrecht played football for Princeton and later co-founded San Francisco investment bank Hambrecht & Quist.

At Harvard Business School's Section F classroom, Fisher took a backseat, literally, to the more outspoken Greenhill. In the tiered seating arrangements during classes, "you didn't have any question where Bob would be sitting," recalled classmate Jerry Pearlman. "In the center of the front row. He was going to be prepared, and he was going to have his hand up and a case solution laid out. It was often not the kind of solution everybody thought of. It would be different. Well thought out."[13]

During the summer between his first and second year, Fisher went off to work at Morgan Stanley.[14] Greenhill worked at the Baltimore investment bank Alex Brown. Offered a job at the firm after graduation, Greenhill shunned Baltimore for New York. He tells of going to Wall Street on his own outside recruiting season and seeking interviews with firms such as Lehman Brothers, Morgan Stanley, White Weld, and Smith Barney.

Greenhill remembers being nonplussed by Wall Street until he met Frank Petito. The men took a liking to each other. Greenhill started work for Morgan Stanley in 1962, along with Fisher. They joined a 110-person firm still at its original headquarters at 2 Wall Street. The firm's revenue that year was $8 million.[15]

Fisher and Greenhill were almost immediately put to work doing financial analysis for the Rothschild family on the feasibility of Canada's massive hydroelectric power project at Churchill Falls. Morgan Stanley was the first Wall Street firm to utilize computers to build cash flow models in 1963.[16] The firm made both men learn Fortran and Cobol programming languages. Greenhill would go on Saturday mornings with his daughter Sarah to IBM's Manhattan headquarters to use the mainframe computer, which spat out Morgan Stanley's analysis. Placing four-year-old Sarah on a printer as he went to talk to the white-coated IBM personnel, Greenhill would notice pedestrians staring in amazement at Sarah, thinking, he thought, that she was a child genius.

The Greenhills lived across from lower Manhattan in Brooklyn Heights, as did his friend McAtee, who was working at Morgan Stanley's usual outside counsel, Davis Polk. They continued their tennis rivalry at the Heights Casino courts and developed a close business relationship. Davis Polk and Morgan Stanley were almost one firm at the time, recalled McAtee.[17]

■　■　■

The late 1960s and early 1970s was a subdued era on Wall Street. The stock market was in a swoon, credit was being rationed, and the antitrust climate was bad. Regulators were looking at the conglomerate mergers of the 1950s and 1960s for antitrust violations. Bankruptcies of major entities such as Penn Central Railroad in 1970 further depressed Wall Street.[18]

In 1972, little of this mattered to the four bankers in Morgan Stanley's new merger and acquisition department. They realized they had to do deals or their short-lived careers as merger bankers would end. Much of the distinct character of Morgan Stanley's new department emanated from Greenhill. Almost from the beginning, Greenhill thought of the merger and acquisition group at Morgan Stanley as an elite force within the firm.

At five foot nine inches tall, Greenhill was built like a Sherman tank clad in suspenders. He sat at a rolltop desk used by Morgan Stanley partners in the 1930s, and behind him was a cartoon of a man whose body was a series of gaping holes as a result of gunshots. The caption read, "Merely flesh wounds." He relished charging ahead. His maxims seemed forged in battle. They included: "Damn the torpedoes." "Ready, fire, aim."

Greenhill hated to lose. At tennis, he swung his racket like he was trying to kill someone, recalled Barton Biggs.[19] Getting to bed was

competitive for Greenhill. If he wasn't negotiating a deal, Greenhill
set himself a self-imposed deadline of lights out by 9:30 PM. He would
abruptly leave dinners and parties, including his own birthdays, to meet
it. Greenhill spoke as though he were back on the bridge of a destroyer
as a midshipman. His sentences were short, sharp, and rarely contained
a verb or adjective. Few could interpret them. Joe Flom was one.

Greenhill and Bill Sword sought out Flom in 1972 after hearing of
the lawyer's success in winning proxy fights. There was an almost instant rapport. They made an odd couple. Greenhill in his bespoke Savile
Row suits, cuff links, and forthright manner, compared with Flom, who
was content to sit unobtrusively in meetings, head down, rarely speaking, sketching doodle after doodle. After a stream of lawyers each gave
long-winded speeches on tactics to repel Saul Steinberg's 1969 effort
to acquire Chemical Bank, Flom stopped doodling for a moment and
asked those in the room, "Has anyone thought to check for bugs?"[20]
Flom had a way of speaking with self-assurance that bankers, especially Greenhill, appreciated. When Greenhill discovered Flom, Davis
Polk's stranglehold over Morgan Stanley as its outside counsel was
broken.[21]

Peter Atkins, a colleague of Flom's, remembers Greenhill at one end
of a conference room table and Flom at the other. A conversation ensued
between the two men in which neither used more than three words.
Flom started and then Greenhill interjected and said, "No, you mean."
Flom immediately said, "Yup, that's right." After this kind of exchange
went on for some time, both men ceased talking. Apparently, they had
reached a decision. No one else in the room knew what it was.[22]

Flom seemed to be able to shrug off Greenhill's impatience and
incessant demands. Greenhill viewed time as a "competitive weapon,"
always seeking to move the "ball forward," according to a colleague.
Another oft repeated Greenhill command was, "Do it NOW."[23]

Flom realized that a successful business relationship with Morgan
Stanley would prove integral to developing Skadden's reputation and attract new business to the tiny law firm. Flom's commitment to providing
the best service to Morgan Stanley was soon tested.

In the summer of 1973, Joe and Claire Flom rented a house in
Malaga, Spain. Claire Flom recalled picking her husband up at the
airport and driving 50 minutes to their vacation home. When they

arrived, the phone was ringing. It was Greenhill. "Get on the next plane and come back to New York," Greenhill demanded of his lawyer, who still had his sweat-stained coat on. Flom dutifully returned to the airport without changing. This was repeated seven times in all, Claire Flom remembered.[24]

The transaction that tore Joe Flom away from his family never turned hostile, as both companies agreed to a friendly merger. By 1974, sentiment toward hostile bids had changed. The depressed stock market encouraged foreign companies such as Dutch electronics giant Philips to try and snap up American companies cheaply. Foreign corporations weren't subject to Federal Reserve restrictions on borrowing money. Philips took advantage and purchased Magnavox's consumer electronics unit. Swiss chemical and agricultural concern Ciba-Geigy bought Funk Seeds International the same year.

Morgan Stanley partners noted these foreign acquisitions. They had a potential one of their own they could advise on. Blue-chip Canadian miner International Nickel wanted to acquire another blue-chip American corporation, Electric Storage Battery, after its efforts for a negotiated merger were rebuffed.[25]

Many Morgan Stanley partners were against the firm advising International Nickel on a hostile bid. They thought it would signal the firm was a hired gun and alienate Morgan Stanley's traditional clients, driving them into the arms of competitors. For others at Morgan Stanley, advising on hostile takeovers was simply not how business was done. Morgan Stanley's partners prided themselves on its gentlemanly image. The whitest of the white-shoe firms on Wall Street was Morgan Stanley. White-shoe firms, let alone Morgan Stanley, weren't associated with hostile takeovers, even if it were for blue-chip clients such as International Nickel.[26]

Those within Morgan Stanley who argued against advising on hostile transactions lost the internal debate within the firm because they had no other ideas on how the firm was going to make money amid an economic recession. The Dow fell 28 percent in 1974, its worst year since 1937.[27]

The firm's partners agreed initially it would do hostile takeovers only for long-established clients the firm had advised on business for many years. Moreover, the older partners stipulated that if Morgan Stanley were to advise on a hostile transaction, the acquisition must be crucial to the future of the company.[28]

International Nickel's chief executive, Edward Grubb, was trying to overcome a slump in nickel prices. Grubb thought that the nickel powder used in rechargeable batteries made Philadelphia's Electric Storage Battery (ESB) a perfect acquisition. Charles Baird, International Nickel's chief financial officer, had worked with Morgan Stanley's Bob Baldwin at the Pentagon. The business and personal ties between the two companies were as close as any between a Wall Street firm and a corporation. For Grubb and Baird to embark on such a controversial strategy as a hostile takeover, they needed the best firm on Wall Street. That was Morgan Stanley.[29]

Bill Sword and Bob Greenhill insisted that Joe Flom be retained.[30] Talks between International Nickel and ESB on a friendly merger, mostly at Skadden's offices on Third Avenue, through the summer of 1974 floundered. "Those days, Wall Street wasn't air conditioned. One meeting at our office in our biggest conference room, there were about 25 people. Temperature was 100 degrees plus. Everybody sweating and dying," recalled Skadden partner Morris Kramer.[31]

■   ■   ■

In July 1974, International Nickel launched its hostile bid for ESB. A shell-shocked Frederick Port, ESB's chief executive, had not hired any investment bankers to advise him, confident that a strong personal rebuff to International Nickel's efforts would suffice.

Port called Bob Hurst, an investment banker from Goldman Sachs who had visited ESB just weeks before. Hurst was one of Whitehead's new businessmen. In his meeting with Port, Hurst had discussed Goldman Sachs's merger advisory business. He had asked if ESB would like to be a friendly acquirer of cigarette lighter manufacturer Ronson, which had been the target of a hostile raid. Hurst after receiving Port's call called Steve Friedman. The two men agreed to meet at Penn Station and take the first Metroliner to Philadelphia the next morning.[32]

Hurst and Steve Friedman spent two weeks in Philadelphia trying to fend off International Nickel. They tried to get the offer enjoined by the courts. A hostile takeover wasn't in the best interest of the company,

Goldman Sachs and ESB's lawyers, Sherman & Sterling, argued.[33] However, Flom and his Skadden colleagues Morris Kramer and Alf Lawler,
working for Morgan Stanley, successfully argued International Nickel
was living within the law with a hostile bid. They cited the Williams
Act.[34]

When it was clear that legal maneuverings had failed to stop International Nickel, Friedman brought in United Aircraft as a friendly acquirer
or "white knight" for ESB.[35] A bidding war ensured. Bids for a company
at the time were open for seven days. Joe Flom decided International
Nickel should offer to pay ESB shareholders, who accepted their bid
before the seventh day. Flom also gave a guarantee to ESB shareholders
that if by the seventh day they wanted their shares back, they could have
them if they returned the money.

Flom effectively made International Nickel's final bid of $41 a share
worth more because it was willing to pay shareholders earlier for their
shares than United Aircraft. It was a tactic that would later be copied,
most notably by Joe Perella and Bruce Wasserstein at First Boston. Flom
had shown an ability to take the rules and stay within them but manip-
ulate them in such a way that it advanced his client's interests.[36]

Morgan Stanley's merger bankers were euphoric. Their gamble of
backing a hostile raid paid off. They were paid millions of dollars by
charging a fee based on the size of the acquisition, broke internal and ex-
ternal taboos, and cemented an alliance with a critical legal ally, Skadden.
Petito's confidence in mergers being a money spinner was justified. Advising on takeovers would prove to be one of the few lucrative practices
on Wall Street amid the economic recession of the 1970s.

Chapter 6

Attack or Defend

Morgan Stanley was the impetus in a subtle change on Wall Street. Investment banks went from reacting to a client's wish for a takeover to recognizing that advising on mergers was such good business that firms should go and talk to clients to suggest this is what they should do. More motivation for Wall Street to be more proactive came the year after International Nickel's successful hostile takeover of Electric Storage Battery (ESB). On May 1, 1975, the Securities and Exchange Commission decided that commissions paid on stock transactions were no longer to be based on fixed rates. They were to be negotiable, subject to a free market.[1]

Wall Street began scrambling to replace the fat fees it earned from brokerage commissions. It turned to advising on takeovers to replace part of the revenue it lost on the trading floor. After International Nickel's hostile takeover of ESB, some within Goldman Sachs argued the firm should work both for those who wanted to do hostile takeovers and for companies seeking to defend themselves against them. John Whitehead, the firm's head of investment banking, refused to let Goldman Sachs advise on hostile acquisitions.[2]

Whitehead pointed to analysis done by the firm, which showed that most of the unfriendly mergers that had taken place were unsuccessful. Management of the acquired company was angry at the acquirers, whom they had been fighting for control of the company. When a hostile takeover succeeded, most of the key people in the acquired company who knew how to run the business left for other jobs. The acquiring company was left with a shell of what they had acquired without the management. If a hostile bidder succeeded, he was left with nothing but trouble, Whitehead said.[3]

Whitehead decreed that Goldman Sachs would give advice to companies on how to keep their acquisitions friendly, but if their approaches were regarded as hostile, the firm didn't want to be involved. This would enable Goldman Sachs to become the preferred firm to defend a corporation. Chief executives knew Goldman Sachs wouldn't be around representing someone else who wanted to acquire them.[4]

"I must say, instituting that got a lot of opposition from my partners," Whitehead recalled. "They asked questions such as, if a General Electric, who had been one of our best clients, came to us for help to acquire a company that did not want to be acquired, would we turn down our client and force them to go to another investment bank to do the transaction? I said yes. If we are going to have a policy, we can't make exceptions because the policy is a principled policy."[5]

Whitehead's policy proved to be prescient. Morgan Stanley's aggressive backing of hostile takeovers would drive many clients, America's biggest corporations, into the arms of Goldman Sachs. But before Goldman Sachs could cash in on its self-promotion as Wall Street's chief defender and adviser to company chief executives under attack, it had to educate potential clients about exactly what it had to offer as a firm.

Goldman Sachs's merger department recognized that it needed much more sophisticated selling skills. Their pitches for business would be in front of boards of directors and chief executives. They got Xerox salesmen to teach them how to sell themselves. Xerox would later develop a sales course for all of Goldman Sachs's investment banking division.[6]

Steve Friedman stressed to a company that if it wanted to remain independent, it had to get its business in order well before a hostile bid was launched. He advised that a corporation's excess cash, if not used productively, could hold down the stock price and attract a hostile bidder. The acquirer would sell the unit, churning out the excess cash to finance its raid. Companies had to run their business efficiently, unit by unit, department by department. That would help bolster their stock price and perhaps make an acquisition too expensive.[7]

In the 1970s, companies that were the subject of a hostile takeover didn't think they needed investment banking help until it was too late, as in the case of ESB. Some thought their stockholders were loyal. A ringing letter denouncing the hostile offer was all that was needed. Goldman Sachs sought to disabuse corporations of that notion.[8]

Goldman Sachs was not oblivious to the fact that a lot of the restructuring they were advising companies to do required investment banking help. The firm was duly hired to sell off loss-making subsidiaries and manage securities offerings.[9] At meetings with companies, Goldman Sachs suggested the companies should have somebody regularly checking the stock transfer lists. Corporations should change their company bylaws to protect themselves from an unfriendly raid. Board members could be elected to different terms, making it hard for a hostile shareholder to quickly gain board control. The firm, at Whitehead's suggestion, began charging a fee, for such advice. It was initially $40,000 a year.

Sometimes the business of defending companies under attack came to Goldman Sachs in unforeseen circumstances. Sitting in a late-night meeting in Skadden's offices, Joe Flom showed Steve Friedman and Geoff Boisi an advertisement that would appear in the next day's *New York Times*. It said that Colt Industries, a Skadden client, was launching a hostile takeover for Garlock, a maker of leakage control devices in upstate New York. Friedman whispered to Boisi to go and call Mark Green, a new businessman who covered Garlock. Green should wake up Garlock's chairman to tell him he was going to be the subject of hostile takeover and offer Goldman Sachs's services.[10]

Boisi went up to Garlock's offices. He recalled pacing with the company's chief executive, discussing strategy. The management team would also be walking in a pack behind their chief executive. As Boisi and his colleagues needed information, the chief executive would turn and ask the executives for it. It was clearly grating to the managers that a group of young outsiders were now in a position to decide their destiny.

Garlock executives usually had cocktails at 6 PM. Late one night after too much alcohol, the Garlock executives came into the room where Goldman Sachs merger bankers were working and physically threatened them. They were terrified the bankers were going to sell the company to someone they didn't want to sell to and they would all lose their jobs.[11]

Boisi sought out friendly acquirers. He approached Rodney Gott, chief executive of American Machine & Foundry. Gott had served under General George Patton during World War II. Boisi walked into Gott's office. The office's glass doors locked behind him automatically with a distinct click. Boisi asked why. Gott replied the special doors were for "security." Then the West Point graduate took out a large pistol with what looked like an ivory handle, similar to one worn by General George Patton. "If someone came in here, I'd take care of it," Gott told Boisi. Garlock accepted Colt Industries' takeover offer.[12]

■ ■ ■

After its failure to hold off International Nickel's hostile raid on ESB, Friedman and Boisi sought a legal counterweight to Skadden and Joe Flom. Sullivan & Cromwell, Goldman Sachs's usual outside counsel, did not have the necessary experience in hostile takeovers and were slow to build expertise in the business that investment banks craved.

"I remember telling Sullivan & Cromwell, 'Don't tell us about generalists doing this because that's not going to cut it,'" recalled Friedman. 'We need people who have lived through a bunch of these, have done this a bunch of times and know the lore, as opposed to someone who knows the law.'"[13]

Friedman also recognized from his time practicing corporate law that many law firms were confidants of chief executives, closer to a board of directors than investment bankers.[14]

Whitehead and Friedman sought out Marty Lipton. Goldman Sachs and Wachtell shared a philosophy that questioned the long-term benefits of hostile takeovers. Lipton importantly was someone considered to hold much the same intellectual heft as Joe Flom in takeovers. His reputation had been made with his advice to Loews Corporation in its successful hostile takeover of insurer CNA in 1974.[15]

The takeover of CNA was a knockdown, drag-out fight that took six months. The betting on Wall Street was that Loews wouldn't succeed. Loews had to convince six insurance departments as to the merits of the merger and overcome several federal court litigations. In December 1974, Loews was victorious. Wachtell was deluged with calls from investment banks.[16] Salomon Brothers' managing partner Billy Salomon called Lipton and said he urgently needed to see him.

"I thought, 'My god, the firm's most important client and its managing partner wants to see me.' I said, 'I'll come right down,'" Lipton recalled. "No, no, I have to come to your office," Billy Salomon told Lipton. "He came in," recalled Lipton, "and without any introduction said, 'We've decided we want you to become a partner and run our corporate finance operation.' I was so taken by surprise, I said, 'Why would I want to do that? I don't want to do that,'" Lipton said.[17]

Billy Salomon left in a huff. Lipton got Ira Harris to soothe the troubled waters in the wake of his rejection of Salomon Brothers' offer.[18]

Lipton began to appraise a half-dozen investment banks in basic merger techniques, stressing the necessity of very careful preparation of tender offer documents. Bankers were taught what was essential and what was not in a merger agreement, including the covenants and conditions that were considered essential. Bankers had to be careful that financing of an acquisition did not violate margin regulations. Antitrust implications had to be studied. If a large percentage of the stock was traded on a stock exchange, Lipton sought to make the bankers aware of the influence that arbitrage traders would have on any tender offer.[19]

Lipton urged his investment banking clients to take advantage of all of the skills that were present in their firms. It was not just the relationship with the company and the ability to execute transactions that mattered, but the trading issues, and who the institutional investors were and what their attitude would be to a takeover.[20]

The firm that followed his advice almost to the letter was Goldman Sachs. Steve Friedman's vision for a systematic, all-in effort by the firm toward takeovers mirrored the team-oriented approach of Wachtell.

Friedman's approach to business was very much through the eyes of a lawyer. Friedman's approach to analyzing problems was very legal and precedence based. Goldman Sachs's merger department did a lot of comparative analysis, reading prospectuses and legal documents. Bob

Blank had also trained as a lawyer, while Dave Remington and Geoff Boisi came out of business schools that were more about profit and loss, mathematical equations, and the use of technology.[21]

The two sets of bankers complemented one another. Goldman Sachs's merger bankers came up with a very detailed, analytical approach to merger defense that some thought was overkill. So Friedman, Blank, Boisi, and Remington spent a lot of time ensuring that their presentations to chief executives and boards were logical and well written. Friedman would ensure that the merger team kept abreast of the latest legal developments, which seemed to change almost daily and affect the ability of a company to launch or defend against a hostile takeover offer.[22]

If Lipton weren't available for a deal, Goldman Sachs would turn to Arthur Fleischer at Fried, Frank or even Joe Flom and his colleagues at Skadden.[23]

"We started working with a variety of the legal firms because you had to know what the rules were, and figuring out what the rules were and how to deal with them was very legalistic," recalled Geoff Boisi. "Some of the actions we would take to block and slow things down meant we had to work cheek to jowl with the lawyers. If we ended up selling the company, we had to get things documented in a way to protect ourselves to make sure that nobody could gazzump a deal that they decided they wanted to do. It was a lot of late nights working with lawyers. Half the time you couldn't tell who the lawyers were, as they wanted to be the investment banker. We had a lot respect for them."[24]

■   ■   ■

Wall Street's white-shoe law firms largely ignored the Loews-CNA and International Nickel–ESB transactions.

"For some reason, I will never understand, when the hostile deals started, the big Wall Street law firms shunned them like the plague," recalled Skadden partner James Freund. "You could understand why they shunned a raider. But why they would not throw all their efforts into defending their clients against those raiders and become expert will always be a puzzle."[25]

After Skadden's success in the International Nickel hostile takeover of ESB, many companies talked to Skadden because they were worried that the firm may be advising their competitors to take them over. Such a conversation neutralized Skadden attorneys from acting as advisers to any company wanting to acquire the corporation that had spoken with Skadden. Under American Bar Association rules, if a company came in to talk to Skadden about a matter, even if Skadden wasn't hired, it couldn't work on the transaction.[26]

Flom decided to charge a fee, a retainer, to anyone who wanted to talk to Skadden. It was a self-defense mechanism, Flom explained years later.[27] It also garnered Skadden many loyal clients who fell under Flom's spell.

"Joe was able to talk to businessmen in their own language," said Skadden partner Fin Fogg. "One of the most important lessons he taught me was: 'Fin, when you're talking to a client, he doesn't want to hear you say, on the one hand, it could be argued so and so, and on the other hand. . . . He wants to hear the answer. Give him the answer. I don't care if it's wrong.'"[28]

Skadden encouraged those corporations that paid a retainer, good for 12 months, to use it for areas outside mergers. Skadden began hiring lawyers. By 1978, Skadden had grown from 25 lawyers at the beginning of the decade to 160, with two-thirds of its revenue from the retainer.[29] "The retainer was brilliant, as it was the way for a small firm competing with the Cravaths, Sullivan & Cromwells and Davis Polks to build a business," said Cleary, Gottlieb partner Victor Lewkow.[30]

Outside New York, the Skadden lawyers quickly found that the town (anything outside New York, New Yorkers considered a town) lacked the necessary infrastructure to support the work of a takeover. As the takeover practice was often round-the-clock activity, Skadden partners found it difficult in Cleveland or Chicago to get a secretary to work after 5 PM. The firm had to bring its own people or find agencies that would provide temporary staff late into the night or early morning to type up contracts.[31]

After 8 PM, many towns across America closed up. If the Skadden lawyers hadn't eaten by then, they were faced with the problem of getting food to an office building in a deserted central business district. Skadden would have to arrange food and drink deliveries in the dead of the night to its attorneys.[32]

Skadden's burgeoning business made many competitors suspicious that Joe Flom's firm was wooing away their cherished clients. Those law firms that harbored such suspicions found an ally in Wachtell. Lipton had made it a policy that Wachtell would act only as co-counsel with a company's regular law firm.[33] "You had to have two sides to everything, and we had a beautiful time sharing the world at that point," recalled Joe Flom.[34]

Wachtell began to gravitate toward defending companies through the latter half of the 1970s and would do so exclusively in the 1980s. This was partly because Goldman Sachs became an important client to the firm and partly because Lipton shared Whitehead's opinion that many hostile takeovers didn't ultimately benefit the company, its share-holders, or the community. Wachtell worked on trying to repel hostile takeovers through amending company charters to put in shark repellents or classified boards.[35]

Shark repellent provisions in a company charter raise the proportion of votes needed for a takeover beyond a simple majority. Lipton also advised companies guarding against hostile takeovers that its board should be classified so that directors would serve different terms, making it difficult to quickly gain control of a board. Wachtell sought injunctions to slow down a hostile takeover bid that could be consummated in days.[36]

"It was the realization that hostile takeovers were not stoppable through those devices that ultimately led to the poison pill," recalled Lipton. "I thought there had to be some structural device a board could bring into play that would stop a hostile tender offer other than litigation. At the very least I searched for ways to give the target sufficient time to decide what to do, find an alternative transaction, or if the target decided it should remain independent, remain independent."[37]

Companies that got whiff of a hostile offer would call Wachtell on Friday evening or Saturday morning asking for help to defend against a hostile offer. Raiders typically launched their takeovers through a tender offer in a newspaper on Monday morning. Wachtell would have to scramble on the weekend to try and get a temporary injunction by Monday afternoon. "It was very difficult to defend that way," said Lipton.

"Judges aren't prone to sign injunctions. I had to take depositions and serve subpoenas. The whole firm would go to work. We could handle perhaps two at the same time."[38]

Advising on a hostile takeover or defending against them was grueling work, 7 days a week, 16 hours or more a day, at Wachtell, Skadden, and the investment banks. It tested the limits of many. Many burned out. Some stayed because they mustered the energy and because their personalities suited the work. "We're obsessive, compulsive people," said Lipton. "People who come here and are not so compulsive and obsessive and dedicated to doing it don't stay that long. You've got to love doing this. You can't do it otherwise. It doesn't work."[39]

■ ■ ■

Wachtell had fewer lawyers than other firms, yet its merger deal volume was comparable. It also worked on the most challenging takeovers. The firm was adept at getting the most out of people by having a team approach to deals.[40] Skadden, in comparison, had a practice in which its partners did their own deals, with a group of hardworking associates in support. At Skadden, there was a "beast of burden" award. Every month, one associate would be awarded the prize for having worked the most hours during the preceding period.[41]

Skadden partners each had their own clients but shared associates.

"That was Joe's idea," recalled Skadden partner Morris Kramer. "He said he didn't want one mass group of partners. He wanted people to develop their own practice. People ask what is the Skadden, Arps view, and I said I don't know what the Skadden, Arps view is, but I can give you my view, and if you talk to my partners Aaron, Atkins, or Fogg, you may get a completely different view."[42]

Flom had a disdain for consistency, according to Skadden partner Jim Freund. His partners could never figure out what he was going to say next or what position he would take on certain issues. It was tough working with Flom, said Freund, because you're not thinking what's right but "what will Joe think is right?" It could undermine a Skadden lawyer's confidence and judgment.[43]

Flom liked to quote Emerson. A favorite passage is: "A foolish consistency is the hobgoblin of little minds, adored by little statesmen and

philosophers and divines. With consistency a great soul has simply nothing to do. . . . Speak what you think now in hard words, and tomorrow
speak what tomorrow thinks in hard words again, though it contradicts
everything you said today."[44]

Wachtell's personality, in contrast, was shaped by Lipton. He was
responsible for the bulk of the firm's business and imbued in his partners
and associates his philosophy toward business, society and the field of
takeovers.[45]

"Wachtell, Lipton is Marty's firm. No ifs, ands, or buts," said former
Wachtell partner Adam Chinn. "Lipton has a very strong view about
how companies ought to be run, which is that companies are a reflection
of the political system in which we live. We live in a representative
democracy; if someone in the House of Representatives does something
you don't like, you get to throw the person out in three years, but the
electorate doesn't get to micromanage. That's his view of the world.
Companies ought to have the ability to try and fulfill their economic
plans over a longer term that is not just quarter to quarter. Management
ought to be allowed to run companies subject to board of directors
oversight that is not micromanaging."[46]

Flom and Lipton's reputations were such that a simple "yes" or "no"
from them could convince a board of directors to approve a takeover
or decide to battle a potential acquirer. Both men were superb at com-
manding a boardroom with their intellect and presence. Their very status
as pioneers made them much more powerful as advisers than the many
bankers who sought to influence a board. Perhaps only Lazard's Felix
Rohatyn could come close to having such a sway over a group of company directors. Like Flom and Lipton, Rohatyn was a pioneer, at work
on mergers long before Goldman Sachs and Morgan Stanley sought to
formally create departments to deal specifically with acquisitions.

Rohatyn's work as an adviser to ITT's Harold Geenen, perhaps
the most famous serial acquirer in American corporate life, gave the
Lazard partner a mystique that perhaps he had something other bankers
didn't. Rohatyn's reputation preceded him. Listening to Rohatyn for the
first time the impression of many boards were convinced the European
refugee was one of the smartest people they could ever run across in
business.

Like his good friend Marty Lipton, Rohatyn didn't engage in show-biz in front of a board. He almost never stood up in the boardroom when he talked. Rohatyn sat back and delivered his judgment on takeovers relaxed in a chair as though he was one of the board. On the surface Rohatyn was not a striking figure. Elfin, balding and slightly buck-toothed, spoke so softly, people had to crane to hear him. Thus Rohatyn made sure the focus was on him.[47]

Most bankers' egos are insatiable. A 15-minute presentation to a board turns into 45 minutes or an hour of a banker holding forth, enraptured with his own rhetoric. Rohatyn finished his board presentations in five or ten minutes.[48]

"He had a great economy of words, thought, and a laser-like focus on the issues that mattered," a former colleague of Rohatyn's recalled. "There was not a lot of superfluous nonsense. 'I don't need your adulation. I already have it. I'm a busy man and after I finish this I'm going to go off and wow someone else.' After he spoke it was clear there was nothing else to say."[49]

■   ■   ■

By 1976, Greenhill had assumed the role of head of mergers at Morgan Stanley, following Bill Sword's retirement. Joe Flom was an important adviser to Greenhill on many of his takeovers.[50]

"We really liked to take a strong lead role in any major M&A assignment," recalled Bruce Fiedorek, who would later head mergers at Morgan Stanley. "Skadden worked well with our aggressive nature, manner, and demeanor. A firm that didn't work well with us was Lipton's. They always viewed themselves as more than a law firm. Sometimes we clashed."[51]

Most takeovers of the 1970s and 1980s were driven by cost cutting. After the rapid economic growth following World War II, many of the merger bankers thought there were huge inefficiencies and huge waste in corporate America. Takeovers were a tool to address that problem they argued.

The deals were driven by the mathematics of dilution: What would be reported earnings after the deal? How long would it take to recover initial dilution of issuing more shares to acquire a company? There wasn't much thought on how businesses would be integrated or the risks of such a combination. That was left to the companies to figure out.[52]

Greenhill would have Flom and his fellow Skadden lawyers such as Roger Aaron and Peter Atkins bull their way through the psychological, financial, and legal barriers to an acquisition. In terms of sheer stamina, few could outlast Atkins. He would get both sets of company executives in a room, with the condition that no one could leave until a tender offer was drafted and agreed to. Atkins would often be in a room for 50 hours without sleep. Others would come and go, but Atkins wouldn't leave until all the legal documents pertaining to the merger had been drafted. He simply wore others down.[53]

The nonstop pace was part of an effort to ram home approval of a merger amid a tight time frame. Boards leak like sieves, Morgan Stanley's bankers found out. That was a major impediment in efforts to put deals together. Morgan Stanley's merger bankers tried to get a deal negotiated between two chief executives and then hoped they would sell it to their respective boards.[54]

Greenhill came up with the vast majority of Morgan Stanley's merger proposals to chief executives. He was friendly with many of them and would spend several hours on the phone with a number of them, proposing and discussing takeover ideas. Scott Newquist had an office next door to Greenhill's and throughout the day could hear many of Greenhill's conversations or overhear his boss ask his secretary to get one chief executive or another on the line. As Greenhill spoke his own idiosyncratic language, Newquist quickly found he had to master it.[55]

Greenhill would walk into Newquist's office, give a company name, and then bark: "Package. Presentation. Two days. Jet. Cleveland." Newquist would have to figure out whether Greenhill wanted the company sold or to acquire another. He would then get an associate, and together they would prepare a thick booklet full of financial figures and recommendations. Newquist would reserve a jet, and then Greenhill and an associate would fly to Cleveland.[56]

The presentation, or *book* in Morgan Stanley's parlance, would explain the financial ramifications of the deal, the takeover laws, how hard a merger was going to be, and who might be the competitors to the deal. "I'm putting houses together, not plumbing," was how Greenhill summed up his takeover proposals.[57]

Greenhill's credibility meant he hit better than Ted Williams in 1941. At least half of the chief executives he approached investigated his ideas.[58] Greenhill was also successful because once he got a chief executive interested in a merger, he got them intellectually and emotionally committed to success. The chief executives became so personally involved that it was almost a self-fulfilling prophecy.[59]

Greenhill's vast resource of self-confidence also helped. "Bob was able to sit in front of a board of directors and answer questions when there was no answer, and not be worried about it," said one former Morgan Stanley partner.[60]

Morgan Stanley had an accountant on retainer named Steve Key, who worked on two-thirds of Morgan Stanley's deals, checking and helping to calculate the numbers. In a meeting with a client in 1978, Newquist was told that Morgan Stanley was not doing tax recapture correctly in its merger models. Newquist, Steve Key, and Joe Fogg then spent 18 months creating the first purchase accounting software model for Morgan Stanley. By 1979, the firm's bankers could load balance sheets, income statements, and cash flow from two companies; put in 30 or 40 assumptions, such as book value versus tax value; and hit a button. Many firms would take a week to do that analysis. Morgan Stanley could do it overnight once that software was written.[61]

One of Greenhill's ironclad rules was that Morgan Stanley's merger bankers always got paid for time and effort. In addition, the firm always got paid what it termed an *exposure fee* for negotiating a deal, plus a *success fee* if the deal was completed. No other Wall Street firm was that expensive. Greenhill found early on that the merger department was doing a lot of work for clients who didn't pursue deals. In order to get companies committed to the work done by the merger bankers, Greenhill made them sign a time-and-effort contract. Such a contract required senior authorization; its approval indicated that a senior executive was thinking seriously about a deal. Morgan Stanley's time would not be wasted. It would always be paid for the work it did.[62]

As demand for Greenhill's time increased, he would have people fly to different cities to meet him with presentation books. Many times, Greenhill was accompanied to meetings by Barry Allardice, who some referred to as Greenhill's fourth child because of the amount of time the two men spent together. In one meeting, Greenhill swept into the room, made some general points, and then opened the pitch book handed to him by Allardice. The first page was blank, as was the second. Greenhill raised his head and told the company's executives that he was turning over the meeting to Allardice, who thanked Greenhill and made the presentation.[63]

Chapter 7

An Accountant, Feuds, and the Wasserstein Discovery

When Joe Flom advised International Paper on its purchase of oil and gas company International Crude in 1974, a bearded, bespectacled, six-foot-four-inch beanpole banker from First Boston named Joe Perella sat alongside him. First Boston had been at wits' end about what to do with the ex-accountant. In the early months of 1973, it made the 32-year-old, who had just completed the First Boston six-month training program, a one-man mergers department.

Perella knew of Flom's reputation and growing fame on Wall Street. Perella began to be Flom's regular lunch and dinner partner.[1]

Joseph Perella was born September 20, 1941, in Newark, New Jersey, to Italian immigrants. His father, Dominic, was from a poor hill

town in the rugged eastern Italian province of Abruzzo. Children in
Abruzzo went to school until they were 12 or thereabouts, but Perella's
grandfather, Giuseppe, a blacksmith, had a fanatical belief in education. Perella's father moved from town to town to complete high school
and then went to Naples for college, where he got a PhD in economics. Perella's grandfather moved to America during the Depression
and worked as a chef to pay for his son's education.[2]

Perella's father joined the rest of the family in America in the late
1930s and became an accountant. Joe spent his early years in Newark,
New Jersey. When Joe was 10, his family moved to a then German
farming community five miles outside Newark. Perella's childhood at its
heart was Italian, full of the music and the cuisine. Joe was never in a
McDonald's until he was 30. Perella's father brought his three children
up with the understanding that they might want things, but the family
couldn't afford them. He was saving for their college education.

Perella was expected to do well at school. His parents didn't tolerate
bad reports from teachers. For them, there was a hierarchy of sacred
things, beginning with people in religious orders, then teachers and
parents. Perella's mother, Agnes, cooked a meal every year for all of her
son's teachers who taught him during his years at school.

Perella got his first job at 13 as a caddy at Baltusrol Golf Club.
When he was in high school, he got a job parking cars at Club Diana
in Springfield, New Jersey. He would turn over the tips to a guy named
Louis Fiens and get $20 to $25, Friday, Saturday, and Sunday nights.
Perella loved photography and bought his first camera, a Minolta, with
the money and made prints in a darkroom. The job also enabled him to
save to buy his first car, a Buick Century. Perella also made fireworks.
One day, he almost blew up the basement mixing potassium chlorate,
charcoal, and sulfur. A spark from the mortar and pestle ignited the
mixture. Perella suffered second-degree burns. His glasses saved his eyes.
His hands were in bandages for weeks.

The weekend trip for Joe was going to see his grandparents in
Nutley, 15 minutes outside Newark. He was never on an airplane until
he flew to Lackland Air Force Base in San Antonio for basic training
upon his graduation from Lehigh University. Perella didn't know what
a prep school was until he met classmates at college who had been

to one. "I didn't know kids who went on ski trips in the winter or went to exotic islands in the summer," recalled Perella. "When I decided to go to college, Lehigh was 90 miles away. That was far enough for me."

Perella entered Lehigh during the Sputnik era. High school graduates wanted to be rocket scientists. In 1959, there were 700 incoming freshmen at Lehigh. Two-thirds went into engineering, including Perella. He quickly realized the classes weren't for him and transferred to arts and science. Perella found that boring. He took a year off to think things through and returned to Lehigh to try business and graduated with that degree in 1964. He had also taken and passed additional exams to become a certified public accountant.

After his two years of military service in the New Jersey Air National Guard as a crew chief for fighter jets, Perella went to work at accountants Haskins and Sells. He taught CPA review courses from 6:30 PM to 8:30 PM twice in New York to supplement his income. At Haskins and Sells, Perella worked on the Diamond International, First Boston, and Merrill Lynch account. Diamond International was a serial acquirer and Perella perfected his knowledge of merger and tax accounting working on the company's accounts. He was looking for an escape. He remembered being impressed by two friends from his Air Force days, who had both gone to Harvard Business School.

"Until then, I had this image of Harvard Business School as a place for geniuses like Robert McNamara, not the son of immigrants from Newark, New Jersey," recalled Perella. He went to Boston and audited a couple of classes. "A bell went off so loud in my head that I ran down to the admissions office and filled out an application," Perella recalled. In 1970, he entered Harvard Business School. It was not a popular place to be. It was the Vietnam era, and there was a strong anti-business sentiment. "Everybody who was a capitalist was a pig," Perella remembered.

He himself was hardly a conventional business student, with a beard and long hair. Perella referred to himself as the "crazy kid from Newark."[3] In the summer between his first and second years at business school, he worked at the World Bank in Washington. At the World Bank, Perella learned how frustrating it was to work in a place that didn't have a bottom line. Perella remembered an assignment counting pigs per hectare in a part of Colombia to gauge whether a World Bank loan had been a success.

Nearing the end of his MBA studies, Perella sought out Wall Street. Initially, he was disparaged. No one seemed to want a 31-year-old wannabe investment banker, including Dillon Read, Goldman Sachs, Kuhn Loeb, and Salomon Brothers. Once when he was especially discouraged, Perella's spirits were boosted by his fellow Harvard classmate Steve Schwarzman who told him: "Joe, you're going to be the most successful guy in our class." "We all know it turned out to be Steve," Perella would say years later recalling Schwarzman's comment. Oddly, Perella struck pay dirt at First Boston, a blueblood firm with blue-chip clients. The firm's atmosphere was similar to Morgan Stanley, a gentleman's club with pictures of sailing ships on its walls. Its former parent, First National Bank of Boston, financed the first American ships to trade with China. In 1932, First Boston was formed to be the bank's securities firm. Two years later, it became one of the first Wall Street firms to sell shares to the public. After World War II, First Boston acquired Mellon Securities Corporation.[4]

Perella was put into First Boston's six-month training program, where he rotated through the firm's different departments. In 1973, First Boston had 700 employees and capital of $75 million. It chief executive made $175,000 that year, and its investment banking division employed fewer than 50 people.

Perella somehow caught the eye of Greg Doescher, the head of corporate finance. Doescher called Perella into his office one day. "I notice all these guys come into your office when they have accounting questions about mergers," he said to Perella. "Have you seen what Corbin Day is doing at Goldman Sachs? Why don't you think about doing that here?" Doescher asked Perella. Doescher got a one-word response: "Okay."

"Don't you want to think about it?" Doescher asked. Perella replied, "You've been in this business 24 years. I've been in it 24 weeks. I'll do it." The next day, Doescher put out a firmwide announcement, or a *broadcast* in the language of First Boston. It was two sentences: "Perella is going to focus on mergers and acquisitions. He'll get all his assignments from me. Greg Doescher." It was February 1973. First Boston's mergers and acquisitions department was born in less than a five-minute conversation. "Greg was never one for long meetings," recalled Perella.

■   ■   ■

Lehman Brothers' offices in Hanover Square in lower Manhattan were a suitable setting for a firm that spent more time fighting each other than fighting Wall Street competitors. Its headquarters looked like it belonged in Italy. It was a triangular, ornate stone building with lots of marble and iron elevator doors. "It was like a feudal palazzo. If you opened doors, you never knew what was going to be behind them," recalled Steve Schwarzman.[5]

It was often knives. Bobbie Lehman, a descendent of the nineteenth-century founders, fostered such an environment. He ran the former cotton trading and goods trader started in Montgomery, Alabama, in 1850 for more than 40 years until his death in 1969. He was also one of the twentieth century's great art collectors.[6]

Lehman Brothers was a diverse group. There were former CIA spies, ex-lawyers, relatives of senior partners, and business school graduates like Eric Gleacher, Steve Waters, and Schwarzman, who were almost carbon copies of each other, welterweight ex-athletes who didn't hide their intensity and aggression in business.

"It has been described as Lorenzo de' Medici's palace," said Warren Hellman. "All of us were extremely jealous of our clients. It was extremely unbureaucratic. Guys like Schwarzman and Gleacher really prospered in that environment. You got to think for yourself. You got a lot of credit for the business you brought in. It was an atmosphere where you were rewarded for what you accomplished but were jealous of what others accomplished."[7]

The firm was hugely profitable until 1973. Lehman Brothers had grown its trading operation under Lew Glucksman to encompass commercial paper and bonds. None of its partners had any notion of how to run a business. Its executive committee was composed mostly of bankers or dilettantes, according to Hellman. The firm didn't have a back office to track trades. Securities weren't being marked to market. No one knew what the firm's exposure to gyrations in the securities market was. "My secretary came in one day and said, 'It's really wonderful over there in sales and trading; there are whole drawers just full of just wadded up purchase and sales slips,'" recalled Hellman. "People were just executing trades and balling the thing up and sticking it in their drawer."[8]

Glucksman's traders had created a $500 million difference in what Lehman's ledgers said and what the record was. On top of that, the firm discovered it had bet $1.5 billion that government bond prices would continue to rise. The market was collapsing. Lehman Brothers had $15 million of net worth. "By any standard, we were busted," said Hellman. "The Securities and Exchange Commission said, 'We ought to put you guys out of business, but we're going to show you how to run your business.'"[9]

Hellman helped to entice Richard Nixon's former secretary of commerce, Pete Peterson, to become chief executive because the infighting among the firm's partners meant no internal candidate was acceptable. Within four weeks of Peterson's arrival, Lehman Brothers was confronting its worst-ever crisis. Hellman was told by the executive committee he had to fire Glucksman.

"I said, 'Which of you guys knows anything about long governments? Anything?'" recalled Hellman. "'We don't know anything. So you're gonna fire the only guy who has the slightest possible chance to get us out of this? My suggestion is we all go to Lew and say, "All is forgiven, please get us out of this."' He did, and pretty brilliantly, too, as a matter of fact."[10]

Pete Peterson brought in Banca Commerciale Italiana to recapitalize the firm. He sought to restructure Lehman Brothers to make it run on business lines. Peterson picked a committee of what he thought were the brightest people of the firm. They examined each of the firm's businesses and picked ones that they thought Lehman Brothers should continue and discarded others.

Peterson also got personally involved in generating new business. He picked what he thought were the firm's best investment bankers and asked them to invite chief executives to lunch in a dining room hung with the impressionist masterpieces that had once belonged to Bobbie Lehman. Before the two-hour lunches, Peterson would call for his handpicked team to do exhaustive analyses on the company.

"We had to have a good idea what a particular chief executive may be thinking about, his problems as he sees them, so he felt he had a person who could be more than just an operative or technician, but someone who he could trust that could think strategically," recalled Peterson.[11]

Eric Gleacher, a Lehman Brothers partner and adviser to chief executives, wasn't part of Peterson's group. The two men didn't get along.[12] When Gleacher spoke with Peterson about starting a merger department, the Lehman Brothers chairman was skeptical. Peterson doubted that his younger partner had the capability of leading a major new business effort. The sheer nastiness among the firm's partners was accentuated by their demand that Gleacher give up his clients if he wanted to start a merger department. He agreed, much to their shock.[13]

Years later, the animosity between Peterson and Gleacher has yet to cool. Peterson's recollection that he thought the younger man couldn't lead a major investment banking effort rankles Gleacher. He believes Peterson plotted to take control of the merger effort once he saw how much demand there was for the business and how much attention it generated in the media.[14]

Lehman Brothers' merger department was started in the summer of 1977 by Gleacher. He enticed Steve Waters from the corporate finance department to work with him. Waters had worked on the biggest U.S. acquisition at the time in his first year at the firm: the $2 billion takeover by General Electric of miner Utah International in 1976.[15] When Waters told Bob Rubin, the head of Lehman's corporate finance department, that he was going to join Gleacher, he was met with incredulity.

"I don't know why on earth you would want to do that because there's not much business there," Waters recalled Rubin telling him. "You've done a good job for us in corporate finance, but I would advise you not to stay too long because at some point we wouldn't want to have you back."[16]

Waters wasn't intimidated. After graduating from Harvard College in 1968, he served as an officer in the Navy during the Vietnam War. He was on a destroyer giving gunfire support near the demilitarized zone between North and South Vietnam. After two years in the Navy, Waters went back to Harvard and enrolled in its business school.[17]

Gleacher also had the self-confidence to persevere in a new venture. The only child of Joseph and Marjory Gleacher, Eric Jay Gleacher was born in New York on April 27, 1940. Gleacher's father was a construction engineer who, during World War II, went from one Pacific island to another building airfields for the Navy. After the war, Gleacher's father continued job hopping. His son went to nine different schools in the United States and one in South America. Once a job, which usually lasted two or three years, was completed, Joseph Gleacher would move to the next project in another city.[18]

Changing schools made Gleacher self-reliant. It also hardened him. His one solace was his golf. Introduced to the game at age 12, Gleacher began to beat his dad after a year. Sometimes he let his competitive fires get the better of him. After hitting a bad shot one Saturday, Gleacher threw his club in anger. It ended up in the branches of a tree. His dad said, "'You stay here until you get it down,'" recalled Gleacher. "And off he walked. I finally got it down. I didn't throw any more clubs."

Golf got Gleacher a scholarship to Western Illinois University. Gleacher didn't stay at Western Illinois. He left after a year for the more academically prestigious Northwestern University in Chicago's wealthy northern suburbs. There, he also played golf for the college, sometimes against Big Ten rival Ohio State, which was led by a student named Jack Nicklaus. Gleacher graduated in 1962 with a history degree. In 1963, Gleacher chose the Marines to complete his mandatory military service because he thought the corps was "the best." Gleacher was sent to the Marines' Officer Candidate School in Quantico, Virginia.

"They marched us into an auditorium," he recalled. "A guy came out, a general, in uniform with a lot of medals. Everyone was told to stand at attention. It was very brief. He said, 'I'm here to welcome you to Officers Candidate School at Quantico. Look to your left, look to your right. One of those two men will not be here at the end of this course.' And he walked off. It was very tough, extremely tough. Fifty percent make it through. They push you mentally and they push you physically. They see who quits or who can't take it."

The Marines gave Gleacher a big jolt of confidence. On the second day of initial training, Gleacher and other members of his platoon hadn't been issued their equipment. Gleacher had on a pair of dress shoes, as he was forced to run outside up and down the barracks stairs, which were wet from an overnight sprinkling of snow. Gleacher slipped. He reached back and grabbed a banister to prevent himself from falling. He felt a sharp pain. Gleacher had dislocated his right shoulder. The next morning, he couldn't move his shoulder.

Gleacher faced a dilemma. He could go to the doctor and tell him what happened. He would be taken out of the course and made to wait six months for the next course, occupied on base by picking up cigarette butts. Or he could stay in and try and make it through with his damaged shoulder. He chose not to see the doctor. Despite his damaged shoulder, all but one of the physical training exercises came easy to Gleacher. The exception was pull-ups from a horizontal bar. Gleacher could manage only three. He took a lot of abuse from the drill instructors because he couldn't match the average of 10. Every morning when Gleacher woke up, his shoulder was completely stiff. Eventually, he had to have his arm repaired, as his shoulder was coming out of joint in his sleep.

After he passed the initial three-month training program, Gleacher faced another six months of training in the classroom and the field. He was then put in charge of a rifle platoon—45 men, who were mostly teenagers, 17- and 18-year-olds from New York's Spanish Harlem, the Bronx, and Newark. For Gleacher, it was the best part of being in the Marines. His goal was to do things just as well or better than they did. If he could do that, Gleacher felt he could gain their respect and the platoon wouldn't begrudge his issuing orders. "It was the ultimate training in how to be a leader, if such a thing exists," he recalled.

Gleacher got out of the Marines in May 1966, after three and a half years without seeing any combat. He counted himself lucky not to have gone to Vietnam. By June, Gleacher was attending MBA classes at the University of Chicago's business school. He got a fellowship after a couple of terms, which paid his tuition and some expenses. He also had a part time job as a counselor for the MBA evening program to help support his wife and child. He had married his college girlfriend in 1964.

Gleacher studied for six straight quarters and graduated in December 1967. Golf would play a role in getting Gleacher jobs on Wall Street. Don Perkins, chairman of the Jewel supermarket chain and a golfing acquaintance, offered Gleacher a job. Gleacher told Perkins he wanted to work on Wall Street. Could Perkins introduce anyone to him? Jewel had a partner from Goldman Sachs and a Lehman Brothers partner on its board. Perkins said he liked the Lehman Brothers partner more. The Goldman Sachs partner seemed just to want to make a fee for his firm. Gleacher got a meeting with Lehman Brothers in New York and started there on January 3, 1968. He was hired to do corporate finance and worked in the firm's buying department. Among his colleagues were Warren Hellman and Peter Solomon. Roger Altman joined in 1969, and Schwarzman in 1972.

Gleacher worked for the firm's partners, doing general investment banking work. Although he did the regular number-crunching work, he disdained it and instead concentrated on giving broad recommendations to clients. By 1973, he was a partner. "I did feel back in the mid-1970s the hostile takeover was going to become an accepted medium of transacting business in the United States," said Gleacher. "It wasn't then. I felt businessmen wanted to grow their companies. If they wanted to build their companies, one of their options was to acquire other companies."[19]

Gleacher sought out Marty Lipton for advice when he started Lehman Brothers' merger department, aware of the Wachtell partners' growing reputation in acquisitions. Simpson, Thacher, Lehman Brothers' usual outside counsel, complained when they heard about it. Gleacher ignored it. Lipton tutored Gleacher and Steve Waters on Saturdays on takeovers. "It was unbelievably helpful," recalled Gleacher. "I don't know whether he did it because he liked me or because if I was going to do this with Lehman Brothers it was going to be a great source of business for him, which it was."[20]

Gleacher didn't get any business referrals from his Lehman Brothers colleagues. It was Schwarzman who in 1980 would be hailed by the *New York Times* as "Lehman's Merger Maker."[21] In the late 1970s, the merger profession was so new, the well-known professionals so few, and the marketing by Wall Street so bad that even an investment banking associate such as Schwarzman could break into the deal business in a big way and create a name for himself.

One Friday afternoon in 1978, Schwarzman was called while he was working in Chicago. On the line was Ken Barnebey, president of orange juice maker Tropicana Products. Barnebey wanted Schwarzman to fly down to Florida that afternoon. There was a Tropicana board meeting scheduled for the next morning, and a sale of the company was the main topic for discussion. Schwarzman didn't arrive in Florida until 4 AM Saturday morning because snowstorms delayed his plane. At 7 AM he met Barnebey and was given three sheets of paper with the price three bidders were willing to pay for Tropicana. The price was the same on all three sheets, $488 million, but the three bidders would pay using different combinations of securities and cash. Schwarzman was supposed to give Lehman Brothers' view in one hour. Then a 29-year-old Lehman Brothers associate, Schwarzman had never done a merger.[22]

"I started dialing any person who was senior at the firm to ask what the heck I should do," recalled Schwarzman. "I reached Pete Peterson, Lew Glucksman, Bob Rubin, and started giving them information. At 8 AM I went to a board meeting. I had never been to a board meeting in my life. Anthony Rossi, Tropicana's founder and chairman, had me sit next to him at the end of the table. They had a small board of six or seven people, including the governor of the state, who had just retired. I had never met a governor. I was being tape recorded, and there was a stenographer. Rossi introduced me and said, 'Now we're going to hear from our young friend at Lehman Brothers as to what we should do with our company.'"[23]

Beset by internal hurdles to develop the merger business, Gleacher and Waters took a leaf out of Joe Flom's book. They charged a buy-side consulting retainer to companies looking for acquisitions in order to get some cash flow into Lehman Brothers' new merger department. When they got deals, they publicized their role in every merger they were involved in. The *Wall Street Journal* was the beneficiary of Gleacher and Waters' advertising largess. Soon, other firms would start copying Lehman Brothers' tombstone advertisements, so named because they looked like the headstone of a grave. Bankers started to do a tombstone tally, comparing the number their firm had in the paper with a competitor's.[24]

Interestingly, for an ex-Marine, Gleacher shunned what he saw as the machismo Wall Street culture of working around the clock seven days a week. By his own admission, he "wasn't some guy hanging round the office every night till midnight." If he wasn't working on a deal, Gleacher took the train from Montclair, New Jersey, and got into Lehman Brothers at 8:30 AM. He would take the 6:30 PM train home.[25]

"I wouldn't work on weekends unless I had to," Gleacher said. "A lot of people end up doing that, but that doesn't mean they're more productive. I never wanted people to do anything at all unless it was productive. If things were slow and there wasn't anything to do, I told them all to get out of there. There would always be periods where it was extremely intense."[26]

■ ■ ■

Joe Perella had spent the first couple of years as First Boston's head of mergers trying to convince the firm's senior bankers who had the relationships with corporations to work with him. Many tried to do mergers by themselves. "When they fucked up, they would call me in," recalled Perella.[27]

In 1975, First Boston's board went outside the firm and hired the president of Merrill Lynch to be its chief executive. George Shinn spent nine months studying First Boston, walking around, talking to people. One day he made a presentation to the investment banking division. "You know, First Boston's a little bit like a sailing ship," Perella recalled Shinn's saying. "It's very quick and nimble but needs auxiliary power. We've got to build up certain parts of it." Shinn then went through different initiatives for the corporate finance department. "One more thing, Joe. We're going to get you help," Shinn said. "I sat there and my jaw dropped. My voice had been heard," recalled Perella.[28]

Shinn put Jack Hennessey in charge of investment banking. Hennessey told the investment bankers he was betting on mergers' being a big business. He told Perella he could start hiring. Moreover, First Boston's investment bankers should cooperate with him.[29]

Perella's first recruit was in May 1975. He was a Harvard College graduate named Charles "Chip" Baird. Baird's father had been the chief financial officer of International Nickel when it made the hostile offer for Electric Storage Battery. Baird, like Perella, had sported a ponytail at Harvard. They enjoyed working together. Baird, by his own admission, couldn't initially do much of anything as an investment banker. He had majored in sociology and psychology. Perella would tutor Baird on Saturdays in accounting.[30]

Perella pushed Baird into assignments, including him in meetings Baird felt he shouldn't be part of. Everything was still done by hand on huge spreadsheets. There were no computers smaller than the size of a small refrigerator. The two men cranked away on merger analysis, trying to come up with ideas for mergers that First Boston's coverage bankers could take to their clients. "Joe had a wonderful combination of analytical and interpersonal skill," recalled Baird. "He understood how to tackle a problem. He quite naturally was participative in his leadership style, always asking others what they thought. He was incredibly fun to be around."[31]

In 1976, Perella tapped Harvard again and hired Brian Young, a philosophy major. Perella was on a budget, so Young was hired as a secretary. Young worked so much, he made more than an entering associates. He could charge overtime. First Boston promoted Young to an associate so it could pay him less. It was Young's first lesson that title and compensation weren't necessarily linked on Wall Street.[32] Soon after Young joined, a group of Harvard Business School students, guided by Professor Michael Porter and Michael Lovedahl, were hired by First Boston to do a study on what it took to be a successful merger department on Wall Street. After looking at Robert Greenhill at Morgan Stanley and Felix Rohatyn at Lazard, they recommended that First Boston begin to frame Perella as a "merger star." It was all the encouragement Perella needed.[33]

In 1976, Marjorie Yang became the first Harvard Business School graduate to be hired by Perella. Great with numbers and people, Perella said, she left after two years to run her family's clothing business in Hong Kong following her father's illness. In 1977, Perella enticed J. Tomilson Hill III (who thankfully went by the simple Tom Hill) and Chris Beale, an Australian, to the department.[34] When Hill joined Perella after working in Jeddah, Saudi Arabia, for First Boston, Baird felt it was a vote of confidence in Perella. Hill was a prized recruit. "He was the whole package: smart, well-educated, well-dressed, ambitious, competitive, technically capable," Baird recalled. "People just knew Tom was going to be successful at whatever he chose to do. He chose Perella and M&A."[35]

When First Boston's merger group got to be five people, Chris Beale left. He said there were too many people. "The upside's gone out," Beale told Perella. Beale went into project finance.[36] Perella recruited Jim

Maher, who was doing mainly project finance in First Boston's corporate finance department. "Joe's personality was somewhat magnetic," recalled Maher. "I remember saying to myself, let's see if I like M&A or not." Maher's first job was to watch the Dow Jones tape machine and tell people breaking merger news, such as who had been the subject of a hostile takeover offer. First Boston's merger bankers would then start calling the company that had received a hostile takeover bid to offer their services.[37]

In 1977, Perella hired Sam Butler of Cravath as a legal adviser on a takeover bid by Combustion Engineering. Butler brought Bruce Wasserstein, a young associate, to the meeting. Wasserstein proceeded to take over the meeting. "I was at the meeting with Tom Hill. I said to Tom, 'I don't know who this kid is, but he's one smart guy,'" recalled Perella. "I called Sam up and told him how impressed I was with the job they had done and said we ought to have a special relationship with Cravath. He sent me a letter outlining how we should work together. In the letter, I noticed Bruce's name wasn't mentioned. So I called him up and said, 'What happened to Wasserstein? I thought he was part of the team.' Butler said, 'No, he has to transfer to municipal finance. If you want to make partner at Cravath, you have to work your way through the system.' I said, 'Jesus, Sam, that's not very commercial.'"[38]

Bruce Wasserstein, born December 25, 1947, was a native New Yorker. He was one of Morris and Lola Wasserstein's five children. His father, with his two uncles, had a ribbon business and dabbled in property investments. Bruce grew up in Midwood, Brooklyn, a predominantly Jewish area.[39] From a young age, Bruce Wasserstein had a confidence that many of his peers envied. When he was a child, his sister Georgette recalled riding the subway with her brother, who proclaimed while looking at the Manhattan skyline, "One day, this is going to be mine."[40] Bruce was a stand-out student, graduating from high school at 16 and the University of Michigan at 19.[41] Wasserstein enrolled at Harvard Law School and its business school. After completing his law and business degrees, a scholarship sent Wasserstein to England's Cambridge University for further study. He joined Cravath in 1972.[42]

Cravath was one of the blue-chip Wall Street law firms. It liked to boast that it recruited only the top 10 percent from America's best law schools.[43] Cravath associates went through a rotation system in which they spent time with different partners who specialized in different areas of corporate finance. As part of the rotation, Wasserstein was assigned to work with Sam Butler, the firm's most experienced partner in mergers. "Bruce even then was brash, obviously very intelligent, outspoken," recalled Butler.[44]

The Cravath partner had been one of the first lawyers Perella had contacted after being appointed First Boston's sole merger banker in February 1973.[45] Butler had worked on mergers since the 1950s. "Joe said, 'Sullivan & Cromwell are Goldman Sachs's lawyers and First Boston's lawyers, and I don't want them representing my group. I've got to be imaginative to compete in this new area of mergers,'" Butler recalled Perella saying.[46]

After meeting Wasserstein, Perella had an idea of contractually integrating him into First Boston's merger department. In frustration that he couldn't get Wasserstein onto his team because of the Cravath system of rotating young associates through different areas of corporate finance, Perella called Wasserstein to ask whether he had to call a partner or could he call an associate if he wanted to hire Cravath on a project. Wasserstein said he didn't know and promised to find out. He called Perella back and said that anyone could call an associate if they wanted to hire one. "I said, 'I want you to work on a deal. Let's clear a conflict,'" Perella recalled.[47]

First Boston had been hired by Cities Service. The oil company was thinking about being a friendly acquirer of Otis Elevators during a time in the late 1970s when oil companies thought about buying anything but natural resources. Harry Gray, United Technologies' chairman, had launched a hostile bid for Otis. Perella and Wasserstein flew to Tulsa, Oklahoma, where Cities Service was headquartered. On the plane, Perella told Wasserstein of his frustration from his failure to get a deal with Sam Butler whereby First Boston could use Wasserstein exclusively. "All of a sudden, I turned to Bruce and said, 'Would you ever think about coming to work for us at First Boston?'" recalled Perella. "He said, 'Gee, I don't know.' I said, 'Do me a favor. Think about it. If you're favorably disposed, I'll set you up with a bunch of interviews, you'll meet the team, senior people, we'll talk about it.' He calls me up a few days later and says, 'I'm willing to think about it,'" said Perella.[48]

Wasserstein went to talk to Butler about Perella's offer. "It is not as though you're not going to be a partner here; you might very well, as you're a very, very bright, imaginative guy," Butler told Wasserstein. "I think from your very own personal preferences, you would be better off on the business side of things."[49]

On July 1, 1977, Wasserstein started in the First Boston merger group as a vice president. He had six other colleagues.[50] From the start, Wasserstein cultivated an image that ran counter to the carefully tailored one that many on Wall Street prided themselves on. Rotund, thinning mane uncultivated, he sometimes wore jeans to work without a jacket or a necktie. He would enter meetings eating a sticky bun and let loose a torrent of words and ideas. At a party, he might pass the night in the corner. He was, according to a competitor, "as odd as a $3 bill."[51]

"What set him apart was his legal training," said Jim Maher. "Young lawyers are taught to control things, and how you do that is to control the documents. You don't let anyone else do the drafting. If you do the drafting, then you're more in charge. When Bruce came, he had a good sense of how ultimately to control things. Make sure the lawyers working on the transaction were our lawyers. Make sure they're loyal to us because they are going to control some part of the transaction. That sort of thought process Bruce brought to the table early on."[52]

In 1978, George Shinn committed to move First Boston uptown saying that Park Avenue was the Wall Street of the future. He created the managing director equity incentive plan, which resulted in a quarter of the firm being owned by its employees. He took over White Weld's venture with Credit Suisse in London. It became Credit Suisse First Boston. For Wasserstein, 1978 was also the year of his first large, public merger transaction. He advised Chicago conglomerate IC Industries on its acquisition of food producer St. Louis's Pet Inc. IC Industries was also advised by Joe Flom and Marty Lipton, an unusual situation where one company had retained both the leading merger lawyers of their day. Wasserstein benefited from working with both attorneys, who helped get approval for a deal that required the go-ahead from antitrust authorities.[53]

In 1979, Tom Hill, Perella's erstwhile deputy, left First Boston to become head of Smith Barney's merger department. Perella realized Wall Street had awakened to the importance of the merger business to their bottom line. First Boston's competitors wanted to hire people, and Perella felt vulnerable. Wasserstein could be lured away, he thought.[54]

"I sat down with Bruce and said, 'I know you could have your own group at this point somewhere else on the street,'" Perella recalled. 'I'm the kind of guy who believes having half of a big loaf is 100 percent better than having the whole of a small loaf. You can have the psychological and real equivalent of having your own group somewhere else on the street if we join forces as partners and become co-heads.'"[55]

Perella went to see Jack Hennessey, First Boston's head of investment banking. "I said, 'I would like you to make Bruce my co-head,'" recalled Perella. "Jack frowned and said, 'This doesn't usually work on Wall Street.' I said, 'It doesn't because it is usually imposed on people. I'm imposing it on myself. I can't come and bitch to you, ever.'" From May 1979 until Perella and Wasserstein resigned in February 1988, Wasserstein and Perella ran M&A and later investment banking at First Boston as co-heads.[56]

Others in First Boston's corporate finance department waited for the phone to ring. Perella and Wasserstein, eager to catch up with Morgan Stanley and Goldman Sachs in business and reputation on mergers, decided to go on an outreach program to get new clients. They divided up the country between themselves. Wasserstein took Los Angeles, Perella took San Francisco. They both took Chicago. Perella went to Dallas. Wasserstein went to Houston and London. Perella went to Europe.

Both men would go out and talk about their group of merger bankers, their resources, and track record. They would always try to go to a meeting with an idea. Perella's merger bankers would boast they won business through their smarts, not because they were members of the same country clubs as chief executives. "We're not winning clients on a golf course" became something of a maxim of the group.[57] Sometimes First Boston won deals at wedding celebrations.

When Brian Young married in May 1978, the whole merger team was at his Boston wedding. That month, Seven Up had hired First Boston to defend it from Philip Morris's hostile bid. During the weekend of Young's marriage, Philip Morris tried to reach First Boston's merger department in New York. No one was answering their phone. They were all in Boston. Philip Morris, alarmed that First Boston may be trying to do a deal with a friendly acquirer for Seven Up, raised their bid by nearly a third on Monday.[58]

Perella and Wasserstein moved to create industry specialists within the merger department. Arthur Reichstetter was a specialist in oil and gas companies. Randall Caudill was an adviser to food and beverage companies. John Lathrop, who would leave First Boston to try and earn a living as a country-and-western singer, concentrated on providing advice to insurers. Bill Lambert, a former analyst of conglomerates, was dubbed "creative director" and wheeled out to provide advice on what businesses companies should buy or sell.[59]

Perella and Wasserstein got First Boston's offices outside New York staffed with their merger bankers. That caused friction with First Boston's other bankers, who didn't want the merger men to take over the relationship they had built with chief executives. "They played with real knives at Lehman Brothers and rubber knives at First Boston," said Jim Maher. "Greenhill fought the same battles at Morgan Stanley."[60]

Chapter 8

The Cult of Greenhill, California

B y the time Bruce Fiedorek joined Morgan Stanley out of Columbia Business School, the firm had moved from lower Manhattan to midtown. Morgan Stanley employed about 200 people on three floors at 1251 Avenue of the Americas. The firm was still almost exclusively an investment banking business with a very small trading function. After three months, Fiedorek was assigned to Bob Greenhill's merger department, which had about 15 professionals and revenue of about $15 million.[1]

Morgan Stanley's reputation was still riding high, and it was regarded as the most prestigious investment bank on Wall Street, even if associates such as Fiedorek did price studies by looking through stacks of newspapers. There were no personal computers on desks. Instead, enormous units on each desk fed figures into a central processing unit. That was the calculator of the day.[2]

"M&A was chosen for me. I didn't like the personal life and the dimensions that were imposed on your personal life. It was a very tough business from that vantage point," recalled Fiedorek.[3]

The merger department's aggressive, no-holds-barred culture was still controversial at Morgan Stanley. Its bankers kept to themselves, recalled Scott Newquist, who joined in 1977 from J. P. Morgan. "Within the merger department it was highly collegial, as everyone was working horrendous hours because there was so much to look at and do," recalled Newquist.[4]

Morgan Stanley was a place that, while demanding long hours, also insisted the work was of the highest quality. "It had to be insightful, perfectly accurate, and perfectly up to date," one former Morgan Stanley managing director recalled.[5]

Bob Case was forced by Bob Greenhill to work through his appendicitis. Case ended up in the hospital and in surgery. Doctors removed several feet of intestine.[6]

Greenhill was also a perfectionist. "Every number needed to be scrubbed down perfectly," another former managing director recalled. "In finance, if you get 80 percent of the numbers right, it tells you the right answer. That's about as accurate as you can be. Every number needed an explanation behind it, even if the client didn't ask, because you always wanted to be buttoned up for the client."[7]

Greenhill was also a very quick study and very impatient. He always wanted things to be done yesterday. "In deal situations, he could see ahead to the next several stages and envisage possible countermoves by other parties with a clarity and quickness that was quite exceptional," recalled Fiedorek. "Greenhill, in his own way, was just as smart as Wasserstein."[8]

Morgan Stanley's merger bankers were "midway between a fraternity and a cult," according to one who worked there. If they were a cult, it revolved around Bob Greenhill. "If you were in Greenhill's camp, he was in your camp," said Scott Newquist.[9]

The Greenhills would have the whole merger team to their Greenwich, Connecticut, house almost every Saturday and Sunday morning for breakfast during the warmer months. After breakfast, there would be marathon games of tennis involving the three Greenhill children, dips in the house swimming pool, a barbecue lunch, and then, of course, work. Associates and partners headed back to Manhattan to Morgan Stanley's office on Saturdays and Sundays.

Like the practical commercial man he is, Greenhill turned his love of tennis into merger assignments. Every year, he took about 30 chief executives and Morgan Stanley bankers to James Gardner's tennis ranch in Carmel Valley, California. There would be tennis instruction, guest lecturers to talk about the issues of the day, informal discussion about business, and after-dinner plays and skits. It was a rule that a Morgan Stanley banker could attend only if accompanied by a chief executive. Bob Lessin, a young associate, was in charge of organizing the week.[10]

Lessin contracted cancer while working for Greenhill, who was advising insurer Marsh & McLennan on its efforts to acquire the United Kingdom's C. T. Bowring. Marsh & McLennan's chairman, Jack Regan, used to wonder why Lessin was leaving his Bowring strategy meetings at 4 PM. Lessin was getting radiation treatment. Later, Lessin would have surgery. While he was recovering in the hospital, his regular visitors were Bob and Gayle Greenhill.[11] When Robert Niehaus's two brothers died in a car accident in Charlottesville, Virginia, Greenhill chartered a plane so he could attend the funeral with five other Morgan Stanley partners.[12]

"Greenhill was exceptional," said Bruce Fiedorek. "There is a really human side to him. You can learn a lot about someone from their marriage partner. Gayle is four stars on a scale of four, a wonderful person."[13]

Early in the takeover battle for Bowring, Lessin remembers being called to London, as often as twice a week, for talks with Bowring. Lessin and Greenhill would dutifully take the Concorde to London and wait for Bowring's investment bankers, Goldman Sachs and Rothschild, to turn up at the offices of S. G. Warburg, who had also been retained by Marsh & McLennan. Many times, Bowring's bankers wouldn't show up.

"They tried to wear Bob down, but you can't wear down Greenhill," said Lessin.[14]

Jeff Williams, another Morgan Stanley associate, took over Lessin's role in the Bowring battle while Lessin underwent surgery and recuperated. Williams, too, would fly to London with Greenhill. When Bowring and its bankers failed to show up for yet another meeting, someone among the Morgan Stanley bankers, Skadden lawyers, and Marsh & McLennan executives suggested they all go to Monaco for dinner. That's when Jeff Williams learned you could charter a plane on an American Express card.

In London, the Americans would stay at Claridge's. Williams called the hall porter and told him he needed to hire an airplane. The hall porter said that Claridge's doesn't usually charge airplanes to a room. Marsh & McLennan's chairman, John Regan, overheard the exchange and said to the hall porter, "Oh hell, you can use my American Express card."[15]

It is no wonder that Greenhill's merger bankers, fostered by their leader, felt that they were the best. "To all of our colleagues throughout the firm, it was 'Get out of the way; we're coming through, and if you don't, we'll run you over,'" said one. "We played by our own set of rules."[16]

Morgan Stanley's merger bankers had, in effect, because of their high-profile deals and revenue-generating ability, created their own firm within Morgan Stanley. They didn't depend on their colleagues in corporate finance, as the merger bankers did their own business development.

Morgan Stanley's equity and debt departments were the organizational enemy to the firm's merger bankers. If the equity or debt departments felt they added anything to the success of the merger business, then part of the merger department's revenue and thus compensation pool had to go to the other areas. Many merger bankers fiercely resisted sharing their bounty. Joe Fogg once advised his merger bankers: "Don't waste your time on 50-cent dollars." In other words, don't deal with colleagues in other Morgan Stanley departments when originating a deal as they could claim half of the fees crimping the compensation of the merger bankers.[17]

"It was silos, and that's why John Mack [Richard Fisher's protégé in the bond department] and Bob [Greenhill] hated each other. They ran independent businesses with the same brand name on them, or tried to," said one former Morgan Stanley managing director. "Bob was the most important reason why Morgan Stanley had a shitty research department for many, many years because he didn't think research paid. When he was sitting on the executive committee he wouldn't approve spending a lot of money on high quality equity research."[18]

What Greenhill and John Mack didn't know was that some of their junior people were cooperating. Barry Allardice had started the risk arbitrage department at Morgan Stanley. Allardice would help the merger department engineer their deals by helping the bankers understand how the marketplace would react once the deal became public. He would bring someone in from equity or debt. They and the merger bankers would all sit around the table and talk.[19]

Scott Newquist sought to bridge the hostility between the rest of corporate finance and the merger department by setting up a transaction development group. A merger banker or a corporate finance banker could come to the group when they decided to call on a company. After three days of analysis by the transaction development group on the corporation, the corporate finance and merger partners and associates would reconvene. The corporate development group would suggest the major issues to raise with the chief executive and make suggestions on how to solve his problems or grow his business. There would be debate and finally an agreed strategy and presentation to be made by a corporate finance banker or a merger banker, depending on the course of action.[20]

■ ■ ■

Like all competitive men, Greenhill was loath to share credit or cooperate with others he viewed as rivals.

Hambrecht & Quist was started by Richard Fisher's Princeton friend, William Hambrecht, and his partner, George Quist, in 1968 in San Francisco. When Hambrecht came to San Francisco in 1965 for then one of the country's largest securities firms, F. I. DuPont, there were more than a dozen small local firms, including J. Barth, Dean Witter, Blythe & Company, and Irving Lundborg. These firms were doing well because of their distance from the East Coast rivals. It was a major effort to travel from New York, and telephone expenses were very high.[21]

Hambrecht & Quist wanted to be a merchant bank, a firm that invested in companies and managed their securities sales. In the 30 years of its existence, about 40 percent of H&Q's earnings came from its portfolio, and 60 percent came from its investment banking fees, primarily underwriting.[22]

"We were fortunate that we started H&Q the same month Intel started when they spun out of Fairchild," recalled Hambrecht. "Intel changed everything. I'd like to tell you I really saw it coming, but I remember our original business plan said we thought there might be as many as six really outstanding companies that will spring out of technology. I think we ended up investing in 500 of them. We built our business largely on technology. Robertson Stephens then did the same thing. But the local firms were bought out by the big New York firms."[23]

A young Smith Barney investment banker named Sandy Robertson, who was a friend of Ira Harris, thought about joining H&Q but couldn't work out the partnership interests with Quist and Hambrecht. He started an investment bank of his own, Robertson Stephens.[24]

"The East Coast didn't understand the industry; it looked like a mystery to them," recalled Robertson. "The thought was technology companies leapfrogged each other, so you may have the leader today, but someone else leapfrogged you and was the leader the next day and you were on the wrong horse. The companies were sometimes too small for the East Coast firms. The big investment banks were certainly interested in Hewlett Packard. But they were the only ones getting the attention."[25] Mergers were never a large part of H&Q's business except for long-established clients such as Salt Lake City's Huntsman Packaging, which made the original McDonald's Styrofoam package for hamburgers. Huntsman sought to acquire another company and turned to H&Q for advice.[26]

The lawyers advising on the deal advised that another outside party should give a legal opinion, a comfort letter, on the takeover. Bill Hambrecht and George Quist went to see Morgan Stanley where Richard Fisher introduced them to Greenhill. He looked at the Huntsman acquisition and told the two west coast bankers that the merger agreement needed to be renegotiated by professional investment bankers.

"You guys step out of the way and we'll do it," Hambrecht recalled. "George being a very forceful guy said no. If you guys are going to do that we want half the fee. Take your pick. Greenhill refused to do it."[27]

Hambrecht and Quist went to Goldman Sachs and saw John Weinberg, who agreed to split the Huntsman fee with H&Q 50-50. H&Q brought several other merger deals to Goldman Sachs. "It became reasonably clear that Goldman was not a great partner firm, either," recalled Hambrecht. "They all had the instincts, 'We can do this better than you guys. Maybe you guys are a decent finder, but you don't add anything to the equation.'"[28]

H&Q ended up signing an agreement with Lazard, and for 15 years, whenever H&Q smelled a merger, they would do it jointly with Lazard and split the fee.[29]

"M&A lagged in Silicon Valley, as it was seen as the consolation prize as opposed to the real prize of going public," said Sandy Robertson. "Company CEOs would be so fixated on going public that they would turn down a merger even if their business was doing poorly and deteriorating, as they wanted to do an IPO so badly."[30]

Sandy Robertson said the best merger he ever did was to introduce Eugene Kleiner and Tom Perkins to one another. Kleiner Perkins Caufield & Byers would become Silicon Valley's foremost venture capital firm, backing companies such as Google.[31]

Hambrecht would later again go to his college friend, Fisher, at Morgan Stanley to seek cooperation on underwriting initial public offerings. In 1981, during a two-month period, H&Q and Morgan Stanley co-managed the IPOs of People Express and Apple, splitting the fees 50-50. It put H&Q on the cover of *Fortune* magazine and won it national attention.[32]

"It was always contentious at Morgan Stanley because there were an awful lot of their aggressive bankers like [Frank] Quattrone and others who didn't want to carry us along," Hambrecht recalled. "They thought they could cut us out."[33]

Chapter 9

Stovepipes

At Goldman Sachs, contrary to myth, everyone "wasn't totally ecumenical," said Steve Friedman. There were, in Friedman's words, "plenty of stovepipes." As in any large organization, people had loyalties to their own line of business. Goldman Sachs was able to bridge most of it only with a lot of effort.[1]

"We probably started better than Lehman Brothers or Lazard on their best days, but we weren't where we ought to be," recalled Friedman, who always thought it instructive to read military history for lessons on how to get people to cooperate. He began to build a substantial library on the subject, including biographies on Wellington, Napoleon, Grant, and Patton.[2]

"If you're trying to lead people in a competitive enterprise, what's a more competitive enterprise than warfare?" said Friedman. "My view is that everything managerially you want to know is in military history. Military leaders had lots of stovepipe arms and units. If you couldn't get them to cooperate, you had all kinds of unfortunate things."[3]

One of Friedman's heroes was an American admiral, William Moffett. In the 1920s, Moffett shepherded through a program of building aircraft carriers. He declared to suspicious and hostile colleagues
that these new types of ships would aid the Navy by giving it another
weapon—airpower. Moffett's efforts proved crucial to the Allied success
in World War II.[4]

In Goldman Sachs's small merger department, where the team could
all gather at Friedman's apartment for chili dinners, cooperation was
never a problem. They faithfully followed a menu devised by Friedman.
The template, written by the swimming pool of a colleague, included
checking to ensure there were no conflicts for Goldman Sachs defending
the company, getting buyer ideas and a team together quickly, as well as
freezing trading in the company's stock by the arbitrage department. If
Goldman Sachs represented a company in a deal, it couldn't bet whether
a deal would succeed or not.[5]

Friedman was fortunate the firm's arbitrage department under Gus
Levy and later Bob Rubin recognized it was sometimes more valuable
for Goldman Sachs's long-term success to represent a client in investment
banking than to trade the stock. Some in the firm wanted the matter to
be decided by arbitration. By the mid-1970s, Rubin and Friedman had
formed a close relationship. "You can have an arbitration committee, but
Bob and I are going to decide the matter," Friedman recalled telling his
fellow Goldman Sachs partners. Still, Friedman recognized that sometimes it was better not to offer Goldman Sachs' advice to companies that
had been the subject of a hostile raid. He would decline assignments,
and Rubin and his team continued to trade.[6]

The thought process the arbitrage area brought was very valuable to
the bankers. It wasn't just market intelligence the arbitrage area provided,
but also an insight into an understanding of how the market would
approach a merger. The bankers would frequently come down to the
arbitrage department and show the traders a merger they were about to
announce and ask how the market would react.[7]

In order to prevent violations by employees privy to inside information on deals the firm was working on, Goldman Sachs had a restricted
list that listed stocks that nobody in the firm could trade. In addition
to that, there was a gray list that had a very limited distribution. The
gray list was anything that banking was involved in but hadn't yet been

made public. That gray list prohibited bankers and traders from talking about any of the companies in the list, let alone trading their securities for the firm or personally for their own account. It was quite clear what the guidelines were in the case of proper behavior. For many, it was a cruel irony that Goldman Sachs, after paying so much attention to ethics, would have a partner, Bob Freeman, go to jail after pleading guilty to insider trading.[8]

The firm's merger department also sought help from Goldman Sachs's research department. Friedman wanted specialists who were able to ascertain whether a company that offers stock as part of a takeover offer was offering something of value and what the dilution of a stock offer would do to the target company's share price. The merger bankers also wanted cooperation with people in the debt area to assess, for instance, whether the company making a hostile bid could raise the money it needed for the takeover, how long it would take them, and what would be the likely terms. Goldman Sachs's merger bankers, as they sought to put together a list of friendly acquirers of a company subject to a raid, needed their new businessmen colleagues to tell them who of their clients would be most interested in an acquisition.[9]

"We came to the conclusion that if we could improve our cross-stovepipe communications, we would be far more formidable than anyone else," recalled Friedman. "That wasn't handed to us. We had to work to make that happen. It wasn't something that came with the nameplate. We worked real hard to persuade people that their careers depended on cooperating with each other. It got easier as I got senior. On a scale of 1 to 10 on internal teamwork and cooperation, no one ever got to a 10, but we improved dramatically. M&A was a catalyst for the whole firm's teamwork."[10]

The teamwork would pay off in the 1980s as Goldman Sachs would be involved in some of the biggest and most complex transactions of the decade.

In 1981, the firm marshaled its traders, bond department, analysts, and investment bankers in the merger of health insurers Connecticut General and INA. The merger utilized zero-coupon notes in a deal and developed collars, two interest rate options combined to protect an investor against wide fluctuations in interest rates, during a period of high inflation.[11]

In trying to work out exchange ratios for the Connecticut General and INA merger, Geoff Boisi turned to his merger colleague Chris Flowers, who had studied mathematics at Harvard. Flowers, for the first and only time in his career at Goldman Sachs, used the quadratic equation to solve the problem.[12]

Flowers went with Boisi to John Whitehead's office to talk about the deal and discuss what the merged company should be named. Whitehead suggested CoNiner. Flowers was asked his opinion. He replied that it was "charming" but perhaps it rhymed infelicitously . CoNiner was rejected in favor of Cigna.[13]

Boisi was at the center of many of the 1980s' biggest takeovers, having taken over running the merger department from Friedman at the beginning of the decade.

"Raid defense or merger negotiation was kind of round-the-clock work. You had no free time," recalled Friedman. "One night, after just getting back from a raid defense, I was in the kitchen of our apartment with my wife preparing dinner when I got a phone call. So-and-so had been raided and I had to be on a plane. I don't remember what I threw against the wall. You need a little R&R between these things."[14]

In one of the most famous mergers of the 1980s, Goldman Sachs was hired for the Getty Oil sale and asked to give a fairness opinion on Pennzoil's $112.50-a-share offer. Boisi told the Getty board the offer was too low and pointed to analysis done by the firm that valued it at $125 to $128 a share. If given the opportunity, Goldman Sachs could find a buyer in that price range, Boisi told the Getty board.[15]

Larry Tisch, a Getty board member, was infuriated at Goldman Sachs's analysis. He began screaming at Boisi, saying he was going to sue the Goldman Sachs banker personally for billions of dollars if he didn't support the Pennzoil deal. Boisi ignored Tisch's tirade. In a week, through a worldwide effort by the firm, Goldman Sachs went back to the Getty board with three bidders, including Saudi Arabia's national oil company and Texaco, who all offered to pay more for the company than Pennzoil did. Texaco agreed to pay $125 a share.[16]

During the auction of RJR Nabisco in 1988, Goldman Sachs pioneered an approach to pledge capital alongside that of clients in a proposed acquisition of the food and tobacco giant. One Saturday afternoon, Goldman Sachs raised $18 billion at Chemical Bank and put together bidders, including buyout firm Fortsmann Little, consumer giant Procter & Gamble, and food companies Ralston Purina and Castle & Cook, who would each take multibillion-dollar tranches of an RJR acquisition. A bid by a Goldman Sachs–led consortium would not eventuate, but it foreshadowed a future strategy by the firm to marshal its own and its clients' resources for takeovers.[17]

Sometimes the concept of teamwork was extended to Goldman Sachs's competitors. One day, the firm's merger department got a call from two people who said they were writing a book on mergers and acquisitions. Geoff Boisi and Mike Overlock took the two out to lunch and told them the keys to building a merger department on Wall Street. "It turned out to be Wasserstein and Perella," recalled Boisi. "Here we were spilling our guts to these guys. About a year later, they show up as a competitor."[18]

Boisi first spied Wasserstein in a deal after flying to California. He was with two merger department colleagues and Bob Freeman, who worked in the arbitrage department and was a friend of Daylin's chief executive, whose company had received a hostile takeover offer from W. R. Grace. As was the case with many a raid on a company, the phone call requesting investment banking help and the next airline departure hadn't given the four Goldman Sachs employees time to pack clothes or a toothbrush. They had rushed out of their homes in order to catch the last plane from New York to California.[19]

When they all got to their hotel room, it was 2 o'clock in the morning. Freeman was assigned to find provisions. He came back after finding a five-and-dime store. In his arms he had silk underwear and shirts with ticker symbols running down the front of them, toothbrushes, toothpaste, shaving cream, and disposable razors.[20]

When Goldman Sachs's bankers went to present their strategy for takeover defense to Daylin's board on Saturday morning, they kept slipping down under the table because of the silk underwear. A board member told them he had asked his secretary to get all the Goldman Sachs bankers new clothes "because I cannot sit here with a straight face and look at those ridiculous shirts anymore," recalled Boisi. Later that morning, a heavyset man shod in untied boating shoes with his shirttail out sauntered into the room. It was Wasserstein.[21]

■   ■   ■

Scale became very important to Goldman Sachs as business became more global in the 1980s. After Friedman and Bob Rubin were named vice chairmen of the firm in 1987, they accelerated a push begun by John Whitehead and John Weinberg to consolidate a network of offices around the globe.[22]

Rubin also developed the firm's proprietary trading business. Geoff Boisi revamped the firm's client coverage model. He and others set up a global finance department to coordinate investment banking efforts. They promoted promising investment bankers with local contacts, such as Henry Paulson in the Midwest, to lead efforts to consolidate corporate relationships. Few firms outside the United States recognized the threat of the American investment banks to their home business.[23]

"The British merchant banks said Goldman just put people on the Concorde with a computer and they think they can do business. I used to choke. They had no idea what they were up against with Goldman," said Dillon Read's Fritz Hobbs.[24]

Within Goldman Sachs, Friedman and Boisi were keen to create an environment where people didn't hesitate to express an opinion. They also wanted people to think differently. As part of an effort to get people to think differently and find new ways of solving problems, Goldman Sachs's merger department brought in specialists in brain functions. One English expert trained Olympic athletes. He taught the merger bankers how to get both sides of their brain working. There were exercises of how to excite your brain so it didn't do things conventionally. The firm would later institute innovation awards to encourage new ideas.[25]

Goldman Sachs's merger department was the first in the firm to institute 360-degree reviews twice a year, where everyone from analysts to partners would comment on each other. Teamwork was stressed and factored into compensation and nominations to the management committee to appoint someone partner. Those who were overtly political, self-promoting, and not team players found that their compensation had been affected. Those who demeaned others were disciplined. If such behavior continued or an employee's self-promotion was thought not to mesh with Goldman Sachs's approach, pay was docked. If the lack of teamwork persisted, they were fired.[26]

Even clients were warned about their use of language or tone in front of women and minorities. Geoff Boisi, who competitors acknowledged placed an unusually high degree of stress on ethics during his career, remembers clearing the room of his bankers and clients apart from the chief executive after a comment was made toward a female employee of Goldman Sachs. "I warned the CEO if he ever made that kind of comment again in the presence of a Goldman Sachs employee we would resign the account and the firm would refuse to conduct business with the company again," recalled Boisi.[27]

Boisi's high moral tone in business didn't prevent him from being ruthless as a manager. Friedman and Boisi felt the merger department was only as strong as its weakest link. The two men would ultimately decide to cut what they perceived as the bottom 10 percent of their merger bankers each year. Goldman Sachs would later follow that example on a firmwide basis. The two men would sit down and evaluate everyone in the department. Both men tried to hire people they felt would become a partner of the firm, and when they thought they were not going to become partner, the person was told that he or she "had got off track." Typically, employees had six months to fix their errors, and if they didn't, they had three to six months to find another job.[28]

Friedman began to assign merger bankers to industries. After being embarrassed by Goldman Sachs's lack of knowledge of the industry in a presentation to a chief executive, Friedman appointed Peter Sachs the chief oil and gas merger banker. Mike Overlock took over responsibility for the timber industry.[29] Chris Flowers was put in charge of dealing with mergers among financial institutions. Friedman also dispensed practical advice to his bankers when confronted by a chief executive hell-bent on going against what Goldman Sachs thought was against the best interests of the corporation.

"Steve had a rule," recalled Chris Flowers. "If your client is doing something stupid, you warn them three times and after that if they still want to do it get it done. You had carried out your responsibilities to your client."[30]

Friedman felt that teamwork started with hiring. He placed an immense effort on recruitment, initially concentrating on the top half-dozen business schools in America. Boisi and others would talk to the professors at the leading business schools and ask them to identify their brightest students. At the advice of his merger colleagues, Friedman decided to conduct interviews on Saturdays. On the weekend, the merger group was less likely to be interrupted by a ringing telephone. Each member of the merger group would talk to each potential hire. The discussions would be extended through to lunch.[31]

Initially, it was hard to recruit people to the merger area because it was not considered mainstream in the firm. When mergers began getting written about in the newspapers, a career as a merger banker became popular. Potential recruits were divided into two groups. There were those who didn't graduate from business schools but who had "a bit of the Green Beret mentality." Then there were the traditional Harvard Business School types who confessed to a lifelong desire to be investment bankers.[32]

The new recruits who would go to work in Goldman Sachs's merger department would suffer a mixture of culture shock and sleep deprivation. The firm demanded absolute commitment from its employees. "Gus Levy or John Weinberg said, 'You've got a commitment to God, your family, and Goldman Sachs, and it's up to you to determine what order they are in,'" recalled Geoff Boisi.[33]

A Goldman Sachs associate in the merger department typically got into the office at 8 AM and left at 2 AM the next day. On weekends, the hours were perhaps only a little shorter.[34]

"You had been working all week and think on Friday night at 8 PM you're going to go home and finally get a good night's sleep," recalled a former Goldman Sachs associate. "Just when you are about to head out of the office, another raid assignment would come in. Mike Overlock, who later ran the merger group, would walk around in his stocking feet and see someone, a young associate, and go 'You. Come here.' And you would go, 'Oh shit, I've got to do a raid. This is terrible.'"[35]

When given an assignment, the first thing a Goldman Sachs merger banker tried to do was learn about the company subject to the hostile takeover offer. Associates scrambled to study all they could about the company, pulling figures from annual reports, visiting the library looking for newspaper articles, and reading call notes from colleagues who may have visited the corporation. "It was time-consuming, brute-force stuff that now you can do at the press of a few buttons," recalled one.[36]

Once all the different material was pulled together for the presentation, it had to be typed into the correct Goldman Sachs format on an Artek machine, a giant typewriter. The pages, which often ran into the hundreds, then had to be bound, a process that itself took hours. A number of hard-pressed women at Goldman Sachs's investment banking department formatted the merger bankers' presentations using the Artek. Unfortunately for Goldman Sachs's associates, who were forbidden to touch the Artek, the machine's operators stayed only until midnight.[37]

"There would be seven of us at midnight around the Artek who would be insane, as we couldn't get our projects done in time if the operator didn't stay," recalled the former associate. "Everyone is wheedling with her, cajoling with her, begging her to stay. 'Please stay,' we would say. 'Make it through the night.'"[38]

"I personally pulled only two all-nighters," recalled Chris Flowers. "I tried to be very efficient. Don't bother doing anything early because a deal might get canceled, the meeting might get canceled, or I might die, you may die, don't waste your time. Wait until two days before something and then get really focused on putting the information together."[39]

Even after the necessary information had been painstakingly gathered, it was sometimes disposed of inadvertently. Flowers recalls sifting through garbage with his girlfriend outside the firm's headquarters at 3 AM after a panicked analyst, Frank Brosens, had called him at home at 2 AM, saying he had thrown out presentations that had to go to with him on the first flight out of New York that morning.[40]

After the 120-hour workweeks when associates thought they had a free Saturday morning, their hopes were dashed by football practice. Every year, there was a football game between the merger department and the rest of Goldman Sachs's corporate finance division in Central Park. One former merger banker remembers breaking another's rib during blocking practice. One year, the game produced a fight between a partner and an associate.[41]

Goldman Sachs required its employees to keep their work on takeover defense confidential. Some compared their life to one of a spy. A former associate recalled leaving town to defend companies that had been raided and not telling anyone where he was or what he was doing. "I was dating this girl and I said to her one day, 'What would you say if I told you I was in the CIA?' She said, 'You're in the CIA?!' I said, 'I didn't say I was in the CIA. I said, "What would say if I told you I was?" She said, 'That explains it—you are in the CIA!'"[42]

Chapter 10

Fall and Rise

At the end of the 1970s, many of Wall Street's most famous names had been subject to takeover, their proud heritage and name soon to be a memory, subsumed by an aggressive upstart. White Weld had a reputation on par with Lehman Brothers. As Goldman Sachs, Morgan Stanley, and First Boston sought to professionalize and organize their merger teams, other firms such as White Weld, Kuhn Loeb, and Loeb Rhoades continued their idiosyncratic practices.

What passed for a merger department at White Weld in the early 1970s was an old partner named Harmon Remmel, the firm couldn't figure out what to do with. The firm's entire merger database consisted of two boxes—one for buyers and another for sellers. According to Jeffrey Rosen, they were similar to the boxes in which his mother kept her recipe cards. "They would hear reports from people and would write on recipe cards what someone wanted to buy and what someone wanted to sell," recalled Rosen.[1]

In 1978 Merrill Lynch bought White Weld. Its storied name, like Kuhn Loeb and Loeb Rhoades, would disappear.[2] Lazard's New York practice, to many observers, seemed to be on its last legs in the late 1970s. The firm was rudderless. Andre Myer was dying in his suite at the Carlyle Hotel. Felix Rohatyn, its biggest revenue producer, had no interest in running the firm.[3]

Rohatyn and Don Petrie, another Lazard partner, got on the telephone and called Michel David-Weill, whose family had helped run Lazard since the nineteenth century. David-Weill had left New York for the protection of his father in Paris in the 1960s because he couldn't bear being under Andre Meyer's thumb. Rohatyn and Petrie said to David-Weill that he must come to New York and run its New York office, in addition to his duties of running the Paris branch. "Michel supposedly said, 'Not so long as Andre Meyer is still alive,'" recalled a former Lazard partner. "Felix and Don said, 'Well, he never comes to the office. He stays in his hotel suite at the Carlyle. He's almost dead.' Michel said, "Almost dead isn't dead enough.'"[4]

When David-Weill established his reign at Lazard, everyone, perhaps only excluding Rohatyn, was an employee under his will. "Michel owns it, Michel runs it, and I'm an employee at will and I'll always be an employee of will," one former Lazard banker remembered explaining to a friend who congratulated him on being made partner. David-Weill did not bring a lot of business to the firm except in mergers involving an American and French company because of his contacts in Paris.[5]

One crucial ally for Lazard, especially for Rohatyn, was Marty Lipton. He referred business to the firm as he did to others. Gerald Rosenfeld, who worked as an investment banker at Salomon Brothers in the 1970s and 1980s, said Lipton and Joe Flom created two keiretsu of merger bankers. Each was largely allied to one or the other man. Flom's keiretsu was Morgan Stanley and First Boston. Lipton's was Salomon Brothers, Goldman Sachs, and Lazard.[6]

"It became a kind of joke around town that in every deal Joe was on one side and Marty was on another," said Skadden partner Jim Freund. "Joe had a niece that was getting married and he was giving her away in Westchester. At the hour for the nuptials, Joe was nowhere to be seen. Someone said, "Where is Joe?' Another said, "Don't worry; if he doesn't show, we'll get Marty.'"[7]

Flom and Lipton would often breakfast together at the Regency Hotel. "We didn't discuss grand philosophy," recalled Flom. "When we talked cases, it was specific things. This is my position and this is your position. We could talk to each other because we trusted each other. That was the key in getting a lot of transactions done."[8]

The Regency attracted others from Wall Street who would make the short commute from their grand Upper East Side apartments to meet over scrambled eggs and coffee. Rohatyn was a regular. He negotiated with union leaders and politicians at the Regency during New York City's financial crises, sometimes sketching out financing agreements on napkins with his pen.[9] Lipton traces his friendship with Rohatyn back to the height of the city's financial crises in 1975.

"When people ask me, 'How did you and Felix become so friendly?' I say, 'Well, we slept together on a wooden bench outside the blue room in City Hall,'" recalled Lipton. "It was for three days. But we went day and night negotiating the various agreements that solved the city fiscal crises, and we'd catch naps on this old wooden bench that was outside the blue room. Most of the people who evolved into friends did so through some intense activity such as the defense against a hostile takeover. At the conclusion of these intense deals, you either never wanted to see the person again or you become fast friends."[10]

Rohatyn's work and growing reputation as a savior of New York City attracted clients. He became more than a mere banker. He became a financial statesman. To his delight, New Yorkers—from garbage truck drivers to the city's most famous comic, Woody Allen—would recognize him in the street or stop by his restaurant table to talk. Through his work with the city, the former refugee later said he felt he "became part of America."[11]

In business, Rohatyn was still European at heart. He didn't walk into a room and demand to know the opposite side's position. He was an old-world person with considerable savoir faire. A 30-minute meeting would begin with coffee and 15 minutes of talking about the issues of the day. Then there was five minutes of working into an issue, five minutes of working out what was the bottom line, and then five minutes of goodbyes, recalled Morris Kramer, a Skadden partner.[12]

There were a small number of associates at Lazard, constantly harried by senior partners to do the mind-numbing calculations and forecasts for mergers. They toiled away in little recognition or appreciation. Luis Rinaldini recalled that at least once a week he would work 24 hours at his desk without sleep during his first few years at Lazard.[13]

"Lazard historically hired big guns from outside the firm who were established in the investment banking industry and had big rolodexes," said one former Lazard partner. "You had a bunch of junior people who did their work and were expendable."[14]

Rohatyn picked his support staff from inside and outside the firm. Bankers at Salomon Brothers often worked for Rohatyn if both firms were on the same side of a deal. "Lazard had nothing beyond the Wizard of Oz curtain," said Gerald Rosenfeld. "Whenever we did a deal together, we always did the analytic work. I was Felix's VP all the years I was at Salomon."[15]

Rohatyn used various aides-de-camp—Luis Rinaldini, Bob Lovejoy, Gerald Rosenfeld, somewhat dismissively described by some as "bag boys"—to coordinate and help analyze the work he was hired to do.

"There was no better career path at Lazard than being Felix's bag boy," a former Lazard partner said. "It may have not been a lot of fun, but you did well. By association with Felix, you got to meet the corporate CEOs. The fact that he brought you along as his bag boy was instant credibility. This must be a bright young spark, the next big thing, because Felix doesn't pick dummies. People coveted the position."[16]

The Lazard partner described Rohatyn's presence in the Lazard office as a lighthouse. "He had a beam of light. It would go from deal to deal. You would be in your office and all of a sudden the beam would shine on you. Life would be miserable because he would want to focus, be brought up to speed, give his views on things. Then the beam of light would move on and you would emit a great sigh of relief. If you screwed up for Felix, your career would not be long. You wanted to look good in front of Felix. Rohatyn would be very calm. He never shouted. The bag boy lived in fear of screwing something up. When the spotlight was coming, those guys panicked and would dump a lot of things on you."[17]

Still, compared to the legions that staffed the larger merger departments on Wall Street, Rohatyn was sometimes starved of the financial information as his workload increased in the 1980s. Just before one meeting with Rohatyn, Bob Greenhill asked his young associate Jeff Williams to bring along "the books." Williams hadn't thought to bring any material. The analysis was preliminary. The meeting with Rohatyn wouldn't involve a presentation.[18]

"I said, "Why do we need the books?"" Williams recalled. "Bob said, 'Felix will want one.' I said, 'What?' Bob said, 'Felix will want one. At least bring one for him. Tell you what—bring one for each of us.'" The two Morgan Stanley bankers walked into Rohatyn's office in Rockefeller Center. It wasn't grand. Rohatyn's office had linoleum on the floor. He had a simple metal-framed desk. At a small conference table, Greenhill took out Morgan Stanley's book and began the discussion. "Felix said, 'Do you have an extra one of those?'" Williams recalled.[19]

Lazard had no new business or marketing department. It did not sell itself, let alone go on road trips to pitch mergers as did Greenhill, Perella, and Wasserstein, or explain its expertise in takeover defense as did Steve Friedman and Geoff Boisi.

"We didn't have new business presentations, or go out with teams of people with black books pitching ideas," recalled Lazard partner Louis Perlmutter. "Whatever happened, happened because someone had heard about, met, or sat across the table in a transaction from a Lazard banker and was impressed. The next time he had something to do, he picked up the phone and called the Lazard banker who impressed him. That was the Lazard way of doing business. Very, very individually oriented. Lazard was a bumblebee, something that wasn't supposed to fly but figured how to."[20]

Rohatyn was not only superb with people, but he was regarded as brilliant at summarizing and focusing on what matters in a merger to a chief executive. "Lots of people can analyze information and prioritize it," said former Lazard partner Luis Rinaldini. "But they just don't distill it or prioritize it the way a CEO responds. The CEO is going to listen to an adviser who is anticipating his concerns. Felix had an absolutely uncanny way of doing that."[21]

Ken Miller, the head of Merrill Lynch's merger department, recalled walking into a meeting and finding Rohatyn already there with the chief executive. Miller's team had been up most of the night preparing their presentation to the chief executive. "Felix said that's not what he's interested in. He knew and we didn't. We looked like jerks," recalled Miller.[22]

Like many successful men, Rohatyn jealously guarded his business relationships. He would not let other Lazard partners get too close to chief executives he had cultivated and advised over the years. "In high-profile situations, Felix wanted to be high profile himself," one former Lazard partner said.[23]

One exception was Steve Ross. Rohatyn had known Ross since the 1960s and advised him as he transformed a funeral parlor business into the world's largest entertainment and media company that was to become Time Warner. Ross worked very well with young people. He would call a Lazard associate and ask them to come over to his office saying he needed to work through some numbers and didn't want to bother Rohatyn with such mundane matters. The associate made sure, of course, to check that it was okay with Rohatyn.[24]

■   ■   ■

Salomon Brothers was a firm like Lazard wherein investment banking business was largely based on individual effort. Long-term planning at the firm was never in vogue.

"At Goldman they had Steve Friedman and Bob Rubin thinking about the long term. We had John Gutfreund and Ira Harris thinking about what's for lunch," said one former Salomon Brothers executive.[25]

It was not until 1978 that Salomon Brothers formed a merger department. Its founder was Harris's former Chicago deputy, Jay Higgins.

"At Salomon everything existed to support Ira," said one who worked there.[26] As head of investment banking at Salomon Brothers from 1977 to 1981, James Wolfensohn was careful to pay due deference to what he saw as Harris's "idiosyncratic practice that was individually oriented and hugely profitable."[27]

Harris's efforts to broker mergers were also helped by his relationship with Marty Lipton. The two men were very close, talking on the phone dozens of times a day about business or family. They had complementary abilities. Harris had a great sense for deals and who would fit would whom. He was a great door opener in getting a deal started. Harris would initiate transactions, get negotiations started, and then Lipton would join in the negotiations. The execution of the transaction became the Wachtell partner's prime responsibility.[28]

"Any second-year MBA student can take two companies and tell you within 10 percent where they should trade, where the deal should be done," said Sandy Roberston, who founded the investment bank

Robertson Stephens. "What makes or breaks a deal are the psychological aspects of it. Who's going to run what afterwards. Maybe someone internally is trying to scuttle the deal because they are going to lose their job and is whispering in the ear of the seller, 'This is terrible.' It's all psychological. You, as a banker, really have to stay cool. You don't want to burn a bridge."[29]

Harris, like Rohatyn, had an extensive list of acquisitive chief executives. One was David Mahoney, who ran conglomerate Norton Simon. Mahoney was looking to buy an international consumer products company. Harris proposed that he buy Avis. "I said to David, 'This is a consumer products company, a brand; it's international. Most people probably rent a car more times a year than they buy bottles of ketchup,'" Harris recalled.[30]

Harris benefited from a paucity of competition from Wall Street rivals. Talented Chicago investment bankers were moved by their firms to New York. There, they found it hard to compete with Harris, who had remained by Lake Michigan, for business in the Midwest. "They (chief executives) could pick up the phone and say, 'Hey, come over for a cup of coffee,'" said Harris. "A guy in New York would have to go and get on the plane. You might get five calls for coffee before they would even want to call the guy in New York."[31]

Don Kelly, president of Esmark, once called Harris over to his Chicago office for a cup of coffee. Both men hadn't decided on what Salomon Brothers would be paid following an Esmark acquisition. Kelly told Harris to take a piece of paper and write a number on it and he would do the same. They put both papers face down in front of them. When Harris turned his paper over, his had a number. Kelly's was blank. "I said, 'Whaddya mean?'" Harris recalled. "He said, 'You never screwed me before. I trust you.' I have this love of thirteens, and the fee turned out to be $1,313,313.13. The only thing the lawyers did was knock off the 13 cents."[32]

Harris was also friendly with other bankers. "It was much more a gentleman's business in those days," Harris said. "It wasn't as dog eat dog. People trusted each other."[33]

Lazard's Louis Perlmutter recalled negotiating past the hurdles to a merger in Chicago with Harris in five minutes. Harris then said to Perlmutter: "What are they paying us for? We gotta do something here." Harris undid his tie and rustled his hair. "We gotta make it look like a wrestling match," he added. "We hung around for two hours bullshitting," Perlmutter recalled. "Ira took his shirt and pulled it out. He emerged from the room telling the two sets of company executives, 'I think we might have something here.'"[34]

Harris once surprised the patriarch of Chicago's Pritzker family, Abram Nicholas Pritzker, on his 75th birthday by sending a woman to his office dressed in a harem costume. She had a sign that said, "Happy Birthday A.N." Harris told the woman to spend the day with Pritzker. "She sure wasn't wearing a helluva lot for a January 6. When I turned 80, I told Ira I was disappointed he didn't send her sister over," Pritzker said.[35]

Chapter 11

"The Genius Franchise"

The patron saint of Wall Street in the 1980s was Ronald Reagan. His administration, which took office in 1980, had a laissez-faire, open-market philosophy. Reagan's advisers believed mergers would cause the repositioning of assets to their best use. Under John Shad, the Securities and Exchange Commission shifted to a pro takeover stance. In the 1980s, it went to court to fight those like Marty Lipton who sought to create measures that inhibited takeovers.[1]

If Reagan was the philosophical father of the 1980 takeover boom, Paul Volcker, as Federal Reserve chairman, laid the fundamental groundwork. Volcker choked inflation, thereby restoring the confidence of chief executives in asset values. He raised the Fed's prime rate to as high as 21.5 percent. Volcker would later become chairman of former Salomon Brothers banker James Wolfensohn's boutique merger advisory firm.[2]

At the beginning of the 1980s, the value of the assets of U.S. corporations was considerably larger than their stock market value. Chief executives smelled a buying opportunity. In 1980, there were 97 announced deals worth $18.3 billion. Just eight years later, there were

more than 3,500 mergers worth $366 billion. The Dow began a dizzy-
ing climb in 1982. Despite a hiccup or two, most notably in 1987,
the stock market boom lasted 18 years.[3] The greatest bull market in
Wall Street history installed confidence among chief executives to acquire competitors in the belief that a combination would substantially
bolster the value of new combined entity reflected by a rising share
price.

The oil industry started the takeover wave. Oil as a commodity
had gone up. The share prices of major U.S. oil producers hadn't. A
barrel of oil was cheaper on Wall Street than was drilling for it. Mergers
among industrial companies were done for the same reasons. Inflation
had caused factory values to go up. The stocks of these companies had
remained flat. A chief executive could be convinced by a merger banker
that he could buy value by an acquisition.[4]

First Boston became the hot hand on mergers on Wall Street at
the beginning of the 1980s. The firm defended lead producer St. Joe's
Mineral Corporation when it was attacked by Edgar Bronfman Sr.'s
Seagram. It successfully brought in Fluor Corporation as a friendly acquirer. Wheelabrator-Fry played white knight to Pullman on the advice
of First Boston. The maker of railroad cars was raided by offshore engineering firm J. Ray McDermott, whose bankers at Smith Barney were
led by Perella's former number two, Tom Hill.[5]

First Boston perfected the front-end-loaded takeover offers. Cash
was offered to shareholders of the target company, often for the first
50 percent of the company's stock, and shares were offered for the
remainder. It was a tactic that sought to take advantage of the fact
that traders who bet on takeovers—arbitrageurs—had accumulated the
target's shares.

Perhaps First Boston's most significant victory using this strategy
was its advice to chemicals giant DuPont in its successful acquisition of Conoco, then the ninth-largest U.S. oil company, advised by
Bob Greenhill. The front-end-loaded offer enabled DuPont to outfox
Seagram, advised by Felix Rohatyn, and America's number two oil company, Mobil, advised by Salomon Brothers. Seagram was outflanked in
tactics. Mobil was defeated through efforts in Washington on antitrust
grounds. Mobil was willing to pay $125 a share for Conoco. DuPont
bought the company for $97 a share.[6]

DuPont's success was in large part due to Bruce Wasserstein. Joe Perella said his colleague had the best understanding of the Williams Act, the Federal takeover law, than any of his banking peers. In the 1980s, the Williams Act was constantly changing. Other bankers may have understood the consequences of changes in the takeover law. Few understood the second- or third-order consequences of the changes like Wasserstein did.[7]

"Wasserstein thought through much of the technical aspects of the takeover law as it evolved," said Bob Lovejoy, who was an attorney at Davis Polk and later a partner at Lazard. "His mind permitted him to game theory out. When you were trying to get an advantage over a target or another bidder, understanding how rules worked was very important. You would have coercive tender offers. The front-end bid would be worth much more than the back end. It was important to put your money where it mattered in those days because the guy who bid the most didn't always win. The guy who got to 51 percent first did."[8]

The Securities and Exchange Commission had modified its rules in the late 1970s declaring that a takeover offer should remain open for 30 days. Previously, it was just seven days for all cash offers and 10 days for partial offers. Companies complained that seven days was too short for their shareholders to make a life-or-death decision. When the SEC changed the length of time an offer had to remain open, they ignored other rules. The law said that in a partial offer for a company, after 10 days it was first come, first served.[9]

First Boston advised DuPont to make partial offers for Conoco. Seagram's and Mobil's higher offers for Conoco had to remain open for 30 days. DuPont's lower offer went first come, first served after 10 days. That attracted arbitrage investors. Wasserstein correctly predicted that they would be attracted to DuPont's lower offer because they could sell nearly all their shares for cash. Arbitrageurs also figured out DuPont would probably improve its offer.[10]

Arbitrageurs knew that DuPont would improve their offer. They also knew that, under the law, once they accepted DuPont's first offer, they were included by law in any improved bid. DuPont's bid, despite being lower, had the advantage in that it promised investors a premium for their shares before Seagram's and Mobil's higher bids.[11]

DuPont was baffled by First Boston's advice. The company thought it counterintuitive that their bid for a company they wished to acquire was lower than their rivals'. Wasserstein went to Wilmington, Delaware with Perella and used beakers to explain to DuPont's chemists and engineers how partial tender offers filled up with stock from arbitrageurs.[12]

First Boston's strategy was a combination of cash and DuPont stock for the first 50 percent of Conoco and DuPont shares for the remainder of the oil producer. First Boston dubbed their strategy "Big Rube," named after American cartoonist Rube Goldberg, who drew complicated devices that performed simple tasks in an indirect, convoluted way.[13]

"Bruce was very clever at this stuff, and no one could keep up with him—no one. He ran circles around people," said Joe Perella.[14] Rival merger departments began to call First Boston somewhat derisively the "genius franchise."[15]

Wasserstein was very good at convincing clients they should follow his advice. There were bankers in the 1970s and 1980s who wanted to appear to be conservative and not make extravagant claims. Not Wasserstein. If he had an idea he thought was right, Wasserstein sold it and he sold it hard. He more often than not was opposed to passing an opportunity by. His view of the economics of the world was that you could end up overpaying, but you were much more likely to get something you couldn't buy otherwise.[16]

He cultivated an image that was always counter to the traditional, button-down, immaculately tailored investment banker. Wasserstein played that up with his studied sloppy dress and the air of an absent-minded academic. Wasserstein would sit down with a pencil and a piece of paper and sketch out a decision tree of how to get from A to Z and the decisions a chief executive would need to make. He could be mesmerizing when he had finished.[17]

Wasserstein realized chief executives were lonely in their executive suites. They needed a friend who could double as a therapist. They also needed someone supremely confident in themselves who would, in turn, gird their loins to embark on acquisitions.

Traditionally, bankers had always talked conservatively. They also didn't say a lot. Wasserstein was a torrent of words. He could overwhelm a chief executive. He could switch themes in midsentence if he had to.

If he saw that his pitch wasn't working, he could go off on another tangent. There were few people in a room who wanted to say, "Bruce, that's wrong." The smart director or businessman would let Wasserstein finish up, thank him, and, after he departed, oppose his advice.[18]

When Cities Service, the 19th-largest oil company in the United States at the time, became Mesa Petroleum's first takeover target of the 1980s, it hired First Boston. Mesa's Boone Pickens made a partial tender offer on the suggestion of Joe Flom in the hope that the premium offered for the stock would cause a flood of acceptances that would enable Pickens to buy more than 51 percent of Cities Service. Wasserstein advised Cities Service to make a counter tender offer for Mesa.[19]

Pete Peterson, who sat on Cities Service's board, recalled, "I looked at John McGillicuddy from Chemical Bank and said, 'This is an interesting ploy, John. If it doesn't cost us anything, I guess we ought to see if it scares them off.' It didn't scare them off. We go to this meeting. Bruce is up there, and he says, 'Well, I propose you do a counter tender offer.' John says, 'Just wait a minute; this was supposed to be a ploy, not something we would do.'

"We called a meeting of the finance committee and looked at our finances, and for us to acquire the other company would have put our debt levels up to 85 percent and resulted in a serious dilution of our debt rating and required us to sell a lot of our oil fields at prices we didn't know. It would have been just a hazardous thing to do.[20]

"I said to Bruce, 'You're so brilliant in the same way as a high diver, and you do these magnificent twists and turns no one has ever done before, but most of the rest of us look at the pool and want to make sure it's deep enough to handle this. I'm not entirely sure, in this one at least, you've looked at the depth of the pool," recalled Peterson.[21] Gulf Oil rescued Cities Service from Pickens but then dropped the company on antitrust grounds. Occidental Petroleum would end up buying Cities Service.

Wasserstein was a master at using the press to signal or smokescreen his takeover tactics. He cultivated selected journalists at the *Wall Street Journal* and the *New York Times*. It proved to be a far more sophisticated tactic to garner good press and signal or confuse the other side in a deal than the use of a public relations firm.[22]

Food maker Anderson Clayton hired Wasserstein to fight off a hostile bid for the company by rival Ralston Purina. Wasserstein turned the defensive assignment into a sale assignment. He got Anderson Clayton management to consider a leveraged buyout. The company's executives would buy Anderson Clayton at a higher price than Ralston Purina was offering for its stock. Anderson Clayton's management may not have known it at the time, but once it considered the buyout, it had put the company into play. "For an M&A guy, loyalty was not to the client. The loyalty was to the deal," said one former Anderson Clayton executive.[23]

Secretive, emotionally icy Wasserstein would deal only with Anderson Clayton's chief executive. Isolated from their chief executive, Anderson Clayton's treasury department would follow First Boston bankers into a photocopy room where they retrieved shredded spreadsheets and glued them together, eager to find out what Wasserstein was thinking.[24]

Anderson Clayton's finance department sought to keep the company independent by selling $270 million worth of high-yield bonds. The proceeds from the bond issue would be used to pay a large dividend to the shareholders. In return, the shareholders would vote for Anderson Clayton independence and remain publicly listed, albeit with its debt far outstripping its equity.[25]

But Wasserstein orchestrated a series of press leaks that started a controlled auction among the major food makers for Anderson Clayton. Kraft and Quaker Oats joined with Ralston Purina to bid for the company. Kraft was after Anderson Clayton's salad dressing business, Quaker was after the dog food business, and Ralston Purina was after the animal feed business.[26]

Wasserstein leaked to the press that Anderson Clayton was negotiating seriously with Ralston Purina. He knew full well that Quaker would never allow its rival to buy Anderson Clayton. If Ralston Purina acquired Anderson Clayton, the company's number one pet food business combined with Ralston Purina's number three pet food company would wipe out Quaker's number two dog food product.[27]

Quaker Chairman Bill Smithburg had used Bear Stearns to mask his interest in Anderson Clayton. Wasserstein had identified that Quaker was behind Bear Stearns. Smithburg turned to Goldman Sachs in desperation. Unbeknownst to Quaker, Kraft and Ralston had dropped out of the auction. Quaker, because of Wasserstein's orchestrated leaks to the press, raised its own bid twice when there was no one bidding against it.[28]

In September 1986, Anderson Clayton's finance department closed the $270 million high-yield bond issue. They retreated to a Houston bar, where they celebrated saving their jobs. One executive came back to the office and found a press release on his desk. The Anderson Clayton board had recommended the sale of the company to Quaker. He hurried to Anderson Clayton's chief executive Fenton Guinee: "Fenton, you sold the company?" "Bruce has convinced us this is in the best interest of stock holders," Guinee said. "Between this morning and this afternoon?" the executive asked.[29]

Anderson Clayton was sold for $63 a share after trading at less than $20 two years previously. "Wasserstein played a brilliant chess game," said the former Anderson Clayton executive. "If management had said, 'No, we're not going to sell to Ralston,' it would have ended. But management bid through a buyout. Wasserstein, as an M&A guy, threw the hook into the water. He was able to look at the competitive motivation of all the players and knew exactly which buttons to press to get the maximum bid out of Quaker's Smithburg. Quaker was happy to let Anderson be independent but would never allow the company to be purchased by Ralston."[30]

Nowhere in Anderson Clayton, a Fortune 200 company, was there any knowledge of how mergers were decided. The great advantage of merger bankers in the 1980s was that they knew what was going on in the marketplace and most of their clients didn't. As a result, there wasn't fresh knowledge of values in the marketplace, tax codes, or how terms and conditions on mergers may have changed. Companies were reliant on the banker. Some argue that it is the same today.

The community of merger bankers and lawyers in the United States was small at the beginning of the 1980s. Business was done mostly in a collegial environment. Many became friends because it helped to do business. "It was almost impossible to go to a dinner party and not have someone get up from the dinner table to take a phone call on a live deal on the weekend," recalled former Lehman Brothers partner Steve Schwarzman.[31]

Wasserstein and Schwarzman formed an unlikely friendship. They met during an abortive deal for the United Kingdom's Oriel Foods in 1978. Two years later, Schwarzman had a house constructed for himself in East Hampton, one of the traditional summer retreats on Long Island for Wall Street. Wasserstein and his wife showed up one Saturday morning on their bicycles, covered in dirt, peddling onto Schwarzman's lawn which had just been seeded.

"I thought to myself, 'I don't know this person,'" recalled Schwarzman. "They introduced themselves. I asked, 'Where do you live?' He said, 'West Hampton.' I asked, 'Did you just pedal 20 miles?' 'Oh yes. We always take long bike rides on the weekends,' he said. I offered him some water. Bruce ended up having a house just down the road from me in East Hampton. We would see each other every weekend and play tennis. Bruce is not a particularly good tennis player. He didn't like to play because he would lose. We played one time and I beat him very badly. So we would just hit the ball for an hour and then sit and have a cold drink and talk about the world. We did that for years and years."[32]

Chapter 12

Stagnation and Implosion

Morgan Stanley had no concerted new business effort unlike First Boston. Greenhill's merger bankers lived off their franchise's reputation. First Boston was "new business, new business, new business," said Perella.[1] Morgan Stanley's complacency was never more demonstrated then in 1979 when IBM asked the firm to co-manage a bond offering with Salomon Brothers. Morgan Stanley's chairman, Bob Baldwin, refused, citing its long-standing policy of not co-managing deals. IBM went ahead with the securities sale using Salomon Brothers and didn't do business with Morgan Stanley for years.[2]

The same year of the IBM debacle, Morgan Stanley's adherence to its motto of "first-class business in a first-class way" was publicly questioned. Kennecott Copper had been forced to divest a coal mine by antitrust authorities in the late 1970s and had received about $700 million in cash. Morgan Stanley advised Kennecott to spend the cash by pursuing a merger. A company sitting on that amount of cash would attract a raider who would use the cash to fund the acquisition. Morgan Stanley approached conglomerate Olin Corporation and received confidential information on its forest products business, Olinkraft.[3]

Kennecott decided against buying Olinkraft and purchased industrial products manufacturer Carborundum. Panhandle Eastern made an offer for Olinkraft. Morgan Stanley had retained the confidential information on Olinkraft and persuaded a client, Johns Manville, that it could pay more than Panhandle Eastern for Olinkraft and still not overpay.[4]

A courageous Skadden lawyer made Johns Manville disclose that it had access to confidential information on Olinkraft courtesy of Morgan Stanley, which had also put 7 percent of the firm's capital into Olinkraft stock, betting on a takeover of the company. The *Wall Street Journal* disclosed all this in a story and added in the wake of such revelations: "Many on Wall Street are questioning Morgan Stanley's integrity." It prompted an angry denial by the firm in a letter to the newspaper.[5] In 1979, Morgan Stanley's long-time client Shell Oil was shocked to find itself shunted aside by its traditional Wall Street advisers. Shell had hired Morgan Stanley to help it buy Belridge Oil from the descendants of the founders who wanted to sell their majority stake. Shell planned to negotiate with Mobil and Texaco to buy their minority stakes in the California oil producer. After talking to Belridge management Bob Greenhill and his colleague in the merger department, Joe Fogg decided there was more money to be made representing Belridge than Shell. Greenhill and Fogg ran an auction in which Mobil, Texaco, and Shell all participated. Shell won control of Belridge by agreeing to pay $3.6 billion. When Shell found out it had won by agreeing to pay more than $500 million for Belridge than Mobil and Texaco, "the shit hit the fan at Morgan Stanley."[6]

After these scandals, Greenhill was promoted to director of investment banking and made a member of Morgan Stanley's management committee with the orders to bring his merger bankers firmly under the firm's umbrella by making them formally part of the investment bank. Joe Fogg became head of mergers but was junior to all other department heads at Morgan Stanley because of his partnership year.[7]

But Fogg continued the antagonistic tradition that the merger department had with other Morgan Stanley departments.

"There was a bit of we versus them at Morgan Stanley," recalled Scott Newquist, referring to the merger bankers and the rest in corporate finance. "We were paid a lot better. There was definite resentment around that. Greenhill fought the battles. There was lobbying to even the pay scale between M&A and corporate finance. The solution was to put all of it together. The only one in a position to do it was Greenhill."[8]

But Greenhill did little to heal the divisions within the firm. He didn't curb the independent nature of the merger department that he himself fostered. Moreover, Greenhill continued to do deals and created an independent merger effort that centered around himself.

Meanwhile, Fogg's tenure as head of the merger department was not a happy one. Fogg insisted on reading every book before it went out to a client. A stack several feet high soon accumulated on his desk and floor. Potential deals stymied. Calls to clients were not made. Coupled with all this, Fogg's personality didn't endear him to many inside or outside Morgan Stanley. A charitable assessment of his personality was made by Boone Pickens, who called him a "sourpuss kind of guy."[9] Another who worked with Fogg at Morgan Stanley said, "He was a complete asshole."[10]

In a private plane with a Morgan Stanley colleague and two Skadden lawyers, Fogg was reviewing for the first time forecasts made for a client they all were flying to see. He didn't like the assumptions. When the Morgan Stanley associate defended them, Fogg's ire only increased. "To this day the two Skadden lawyers, whenever they see me, say, 'Remember the time when we were in a plane and Joe Fogg got so mad at you, he would have thrown you out of the plane if he could,'" recalled the associate.[11]

■ ■ ■

Eric Gleacher, who had been hired by Morgan Stanley chairman Parker Gilbert, from Lehman Brothers, was waiting impatiently in the wings. He wanted another chance to run a merger department. Gleacher's departure from Lehman Brothers had been acrimonious. He had fallen foul of Lehman Brothers' chairman, Pete Peterson. Many at Lehman Brothers say Peterson removed Gleacher as head of mergers, something a proud Gleacher denies. As a result, Gleacher and Peterson didn't talk to each other. They communicated through Gleacher's deputy, Steve Waters, who remembered it as "a totally thankless task."[12]

"Gleacher was always the kind of an operative who was not much into an organized marketing effort. He loved to played golf and he admitted it. He could connect with certain people and I guess would do a good job. He was not a person that could organize a major effort, in my opinion and in the opinion of others," said Peterson.[13]

Gleacher's role as head of mergers at Lehman Brothers was diminished by Peterson. Gleacher seethed but soldiered on. In 1983, Allied Chemical's chairman called him to represent the company in a deal Gleacher would call the most "mind-blowing" of his career.

Bendix, a conglomerate with aerospace, electronic, and automobile businesses, made a hostile offer for arms maker Martin Marietta. Martin Marietta's chairman in turn made an offer for Bendix in a "Pac-Man" defense. Such a defense was made stronger by an alliance with United Technologies to acquire Bendix and split its assets. Allied Chemical would ultimately buy Bendix and also end up owning 40 percent of Martin Marietta. Bendix chairman Bill Agee brought Allied in as a friendly acquirer following the "Pac-Man" tactic.[14]

Gleacher and Allied chairman Ed Hennessy went over to the Helmsley Hotel to talk with Bendix chairman Agee at his suite. After greeting both men, Agee took a seat on the couch next to Mary Cunningham, his former executive assistant and new wife. He held her hand and began talking business. Agee and Cunningham had previously drawn scrutiny over the nature of their relationship when they had been married to other people. Hennessy, a Jesuit, couldn't stand Agee and Cunningham's hand-holding. He asked for a break and went out in the hallway with Gleacher.[15]

Hennessy turned to Gleacher and said: "'What am I going to do about this fucking guy?'" recalled Gleacher. "I said, 'You're going to make him president of the company.' 'What?! You gotta be kidding. I can't do that,' said Hennessy. I said, 'You got to.' 'Why?' asked Hennessy. 'It will make him happy, and you know if it doesn't work out, you're the boss.' And so he did. It lasted one week. Then Hennessy fired him."[16]

■   ■   ■

Gleacher's role in the Bendix battle bolstered his credentials. Morgan Stanley's Parker Gilbert had heard that Gleacher was unhappy at Lehman

Brothers. Golf once again played a part in Gleacher's career. Over 18 holes, Parker Gilbert asked Gleacher whether he would like to join the firm. If he joined, Gilbert said, it wouldn't be long before Gleacher would again be running a merger department. Fogg's divisive reign and the subsequent loss of business to First Boston and Goldman Sachs had hurt Morgan Stanley.[17]

"There was an uprising that ended Fogg's reign," recalled one merger banker in the firm at the time. "He was just very hard on people. Everybody thought he was as smart as they come, respected him, but they just didn't like being beaten up on a regular basis. If he didn't agree or thought something should have been done better, he would let you know. Joe managed by fear and bullying, and it didn't work."[18]

Gleacher was appointed head of mergers in 1984. After the diversity of Lehman Brothers, Morgan Stanley seemed bland. "They had one Jewish guy there, the only one that was important, Lewis Bernard," recalled Gleacher. "A lot of Yale, Harvard, Princeton. Everybody had suspenders. It was a very homogeneous-type culture, which I think hurt them because everybody was so conformist."[19]

Gleacher was different. In 1985, Gleacher persuaded Parker Gilbert, over much opposition within Morgan Stanley, to back Ronald Perelman in his bid for Revlon. The cosmetics maker had been a client of Morgan Stanley. Revlon's chairman Michel Bergerac had been frustrated at Revlon's stock price and had wanted to sell its other businesses such as health care and pharmaceuticals. His approach to other companies to buy Revlon units had sparked Gleacher's interest. "We said, 'If we don't do anything, something's going to happen here,'" recalled Gleacher. "That's what investment banking is, and we found someone to buy the company."[20]

Gleacher spoke to Perelman, who had raised a war chest in high-yield bonds from Drexel Burnham Lambert for acquisitions. "There was huge internal resistance at Morgan Stanley," recalled Gleacher. "This guy is a Milken guy. Parker Gilbert one day called me in and said, 'Eric, we're going to do this.' I trust you completely; just don't get us in trouble and don't embarrass us." Perelman succeeded in buying Revlon.[21]

"If that deal had blown up, it would have ended my career," said Gleacher years later. "I was willing to do it because I felt if you came to Wall Street and you weren't willing to take risks, then you weren't doing what I wanted to do. I didn't come to New York to do investment banking just to play it safe all the way through and never make a mistake. I wanted to do things that were interesting only if I thought they were right, only if they were done by the rules. It didn't need to be a sure thing."[22]

However, to many, Gleacher failed to bring harmony to Morgan Stanley's merger department after Fogg. "He was divisive," said one who worked with him. "You were either in his camp or not. He picked his guys and girls. They were mostly girls."[23]

Part of Gleacher's problem was that there were three merger departments at Morgan Stanley. One was run by Gleacher, the firm's official head of mergers, another by Fogg, who was promoted to head of worldwide corporate finance while Bob Greenhill largely abrogated his management responsibilities to pursue deals.[24]

Gleacher and Greenhill didn't like each other.[25] They failed to work together and were competitors rather than colleagues. Many felt it was because they had been rivals for nearly a decade at competing firms and were men who always felt they should be the leader of any team or deal. Gleacher didn't engender the same empathy others who worked for Greenhill felt with the older man. Greenhill's gruff manner masked a genuine warmth, many felt. In contrast, Gleacher's personality struck many at Morgan Stanley as cold.[26]

Still, within Morgan Stanley and outside the firm Greenhill was known to have "very, very sharp elbows" when it came to business.[27]

In 1985 Sandy Weill, marginalized as an executive by Jim Robinson at American Express, sought to buy the Fireman's Fund Insurance from American Express and go into business on his own. Weill approached the private equity firm Warburg Pincus for capital and used Greenhill to try and hammer out the acquisition.[28]

"I listened to a presentation that Greenhill gave to Jim Robinson and then went to Lionel Pincus and told him 'I'm going to get us out of the deal,'" said a Warburg Pincus partner. "Lionel asked 'Why?' I said 'I don't want to be a triple loser. I think Greenhill is going to screw up the deal therefore it isn't going to go through. If I'm still in the middle of it he's going to blame me. If by some chance the deal goes through he's going to take credit for it. Finally if the deal goes through and it's a good deal he will see to it that Morgan Stanley gets to invest in it and not Warburg Pincus. So I don't see how we can win and I see three ways we can lose.'"[29]

      ■   ■   ■

Gleacher resented Greenhill's continued role as a merger adviser to chief executives, believing he should be Morgan Stanley's point man on acquisitions. The two men would battle to be on the most high profile deals. Throughout the 1980s the discontent among Morgan Stanley's top executives would hamper the firm's planning and erode its standing as the predominant Wall Street investment bank.[30]

    Parker Gilbert was a compromise candidate to lead Morgan Stanley following Bob Baldwin's retirement in 1983. The stepson of Harold Stanley, the firm's co-founder, Gilbert was appointed chairman after the partners couldn't decide between Lewis Bernard, the strategic thinker and planner for the firm; Richard Fisher, the architect of its trading initiatives; and Bob Greenhill, its leading investment banker.[31]

    "M&A into the mid-1980s was the bad boy group because we were beginning to make a lot of money and flew in the face of traditional investment banking," recalled one former Morgan Stanley managing director. "We called on other people's clients within the firm and had a group dedicated to that. That ruffled a lot of feathers."[32]

    Greenhill's candidacy to become Morgan Stanley's chairman suffered because his personality, so successful in the deal world—unrelenting, aggressive and demanding—was not appreciated among his peers. He had built a profitable and powerful business and wielded the power associated with that, which upset some. There was some personality clash, a lot of it due to jealously. Greenhill has a strong personality and doesn't suffer fools gladly. Morgan Stanley had a lot of dead wood, Greenhill thought, and wanted to get rid of it to make the firm as cutting edge as possible in terms of who was recruited and rewarded for performance.

    Morgan Stanley partners at the firm elected someone as chairman, said a Greenhill loyalist, "who leaned into the wind"—Parker Gilbert.[33] The rivalries at Morgan Stanley between the senior partners were never allowed to flare in the open in the 1980s, as would happen after Richard Fisher's death in 2004.[34]

The firm that would gain notoriety for its public self-destructive class battles was Lehman Brothers. It imploded following the departure of Pete Peterson in 1984.

Lehman Brothers' profitability, as other firms discovered at the same time, had started to shift to the trading side. The investment bankers owned more of the firm than did the traders. Lew Glucksman, who had always been resentful of the bankers, directed his hostility at Pete Peterson and forced him to resign from Lehman Brothers where he was chairman and co-chief executive with Glucksman. Glucksman was afraid Peterson would sell the firm and the bankers would reap most of the gains. When Glucksman took control of Lehman Brothers, he redistributed the partnership interests from the bankers to the traders. That only served to cause a steady erosion of banking talent that included men who liked Glucksman, such as Gleacher.[35]

"Pete was a very highly involved guy, and he made friends and he made enemies," said Steve Waters. "There was a camp that really liked Pete, and there was a camp that really didn't like him. That's what enabled Lew Glucksman to ultimately take control of the firm. The camp that didn't like Pete got to be big enough that Glucksman ended up being sole CEO. Of course, Lew tried to right imbalances he thought existed and lost the trust of the firm within a year."[36]

Glucksman was forced out the door. Ironically, Glucksman's departure enabled Steve Schwarzman, a Peterson ally, to do what Glucksman feared Peterson would do—sell the firm. Schwarzman sold Lehman Brothers to American Express in 1984 and, in a further twist, started a merger boutique with Peterson, the Blackstone Group, the next year.[37]

"My first day at Lehman Brothers was Schwarzman's last day," recalled a banker. "We had breakfast at the Old Mayfair Regency. I said to Schwarzman, because I was in awe of the firm and its heritage, 'How could you leave?' And he said to me, 'How could you join?'"[38]

Lehman Brothers' internal sniping didn't stop with the sale to American Express. When Peter Solomon was appointed head of the merger department in 1984 the *Wall Street Journal* wrote on July 26 that "Mr. Solomon's appointment was criticized by investment bankers inside Shearson Lehman/American Express. Mr. Solomon, while recognized as a talented investment banker, has little mergers and acquisitions experience."[39]

"The new M&A group on the street was asking themselves, 'Who is this guy?'" said Solomon, who framed the Wall Street Journal article and hung it in his office. "Yes, he's been in the business for 25 years, but what does he know about M&A? I had more M&A experience than anyone except for Felix [Rohatyn]. We all knew about M&A. We just didn't do it in an M&A department. M&A guys found it too difficult to separate what they wanted to accomplish from the facts. I assiduously stayed away from M&A bankers. They were marketing tools that were very important as the 1980s started, as people believed you were smarter if you arrived with an M&A guy."[40]

"In 1986, I had to call Tom Hill who worked with Lehman's M&A department at 11 PM. My wife, when I mentioned I was going to call Tom, said, 'Don't; it's too late.' I said to her, 'If I call him at 11 he'll think it's great. If I call him at 3 AM, he'll think it's even better.' M&A bankers viewed themselves as Green Berets, the warriors who saved the day. It was Perella and Wasserstein's influence," said Solomon.

What changed mergers in the 1980s was not only the specificity of the marketing of the expertise but the use of capital to achieve it. The American Express and Lehman Brothers merger was supposed to be the merger between the capital of the former and the brains of the later to compete with Drexel Burnham Lambert. Previously, capital had never been an issue in the merger business. Drexel's high-yield bond business changed that.

Chapter 13

The Rise of Drexel

D rexel's origins were impeccably white shoe. Anthony Joseph Drexel was J. Pierpont Morgan's partner in the nineteenth century. Drexel was absorbed into J. P. Morgan. It reclaimed its independence in the mid 1930s after the Glass-Steagall laws separated commercial and investment banking. Drexel struggled in the post–World War II years. A merger with Harriman Ripley in the 1960s didn't bolster its business. The firm also failed to capitalize on an investment by a large client, Firestone. Burnham acquired Drexel in 1973.[1]

The takeover was a culture clash. Burnham was essentially a Jewish brokerage firm. Drexel was an elegant WASP investment bank that had fallen on hard times.

"Coors Brewing was the big offering in 1974," Fred Joseph recalled. "Drexel had been giving opinions to the Coors family for years on the value of the Coors stock for tax purposes or arranged private family transactions. I asked the fellow who covered Coors at Drexel if we had called them and asked if we could be in the underwriting. 'No. They know we're here. If they wanted to invite us, they'd call us.'" Belgian's

Groupe Bruxelles Lambert added its name to the firm in 1976 when it took a stake.[2]

Joseph joined Drexel in September 1974 from Shearson Hammill as co-head of investment banking. The firm's investment banking revenue that year was $1.2 million. Most of it was retainers. There were 19 corporate finance bankers. Joseph whittled the number down to 12 after finding out many didn't want to work as hard as he demanded.[3]

As an investment banker and later as a chief executive, Frederick Harold Joseph seemed to be from the central casting department on a movie lot. He possessed an easy, down-to-earth charm and retained somewhat the build of an amateur boxer into his 50s. His father drove a Checker taxi in Boston until he was 71. His mother, who attended college in the 1930s on a scholarship, was a dental hygienist. She encouraged her two sons in their studies, and both would end up working at Drexel. Joseph won a scholarship to attend Harvard and drove trucks and cabs at night to pay his way through college, where he boxed competitively. After two years as a naval officer as part of his mandatory military service, he went to Harvard Business School. Joseph worked first at E. F. Hutton and then at Shearson.[4]

After working at two second-tier investment banks, Joseph wanted to transform Drexel into a top-tier firm. He admired Goldman Sachs. Joseph sought to emulate Goldman Sachs's senior partners, John Whitehead and John Weinberg, who were remaking the firm into an investment banking powerhouse. Joseph recruited many of his former Shearson colleagues, who shared his zeal and ambition. Joseph knew after more than a decade on Wall Street that trying to woo companies away from their established investment bankers was a venture fraught with failure. Joseph sought out entrepreneurs. He had his bankers go out and pick a strong management team in a particular industry.[5] In its search for the next great American entrepreneurs, Drexel got tips from lawyers and accountants. The future large fee payers to Wall Street were not the behemoths of the day. They were the recently planted acorns, and the key was finding the next mighty oak.

Joseph had statistics to back his strategy. Of the companies on the Fortune 100 in 1955, 12 companies were no longer on it in 1960. Another 27 dropped off in the decade between 1960 and 1970, and nine more from 1970 to 1980. By 2006, 84 companies that were in the Fortune 100 in 1956 were no longer part of it. "I loved Bill McGowan, who built MCI right in the face of AT&T," said Joseph. "Actually, fanatically dedicated to doing what he wanted to do. We talked about it. Our clients often had to be fanatics."[6]

■ ■ ■

Joseph met Michael Milken soon after he joined Drexel. Milken had become fascinated with companies whose credit rating was not investment grade after reading economist W. Braddock Hickman's *Corporate Bond Quality and Investor Experience* (Princeton, NJ: Princeton University Press, 1958). Hickman's study of the bond market from 1900 to 1943 found that an investor was better off with a non–investment-grade portfolio rather than an investment-grade as long as it was diversified and the bonds held until maturity.[7] Milken's view of high-yield bonds was expressed succinctly by a former colleague: "Buying bonds in companies rated highly was a loser's game. Things couldn't get better. They could only get worse."[8]

Michael Robert Milken was born in Los Angeles on July 4, 1946 and grew up in Encino, just north of his birthplace. His father was an accountant, and from the age of 10, Milken helped his dad sort checks and reconcile checkbooks. Later, he helped with tax returns. At the University of California at Berkeley, one of the centers of protests against the Vietnam War and the gathering place for the 1960s counterculture movement, Milken studied business. "I asked him once why he wasn't picketing and he said you can accomplish more if you can get good grades, get a good job, make a lot of money, and contribute to things that interest you," Milken's friend from childhood, Harry Horowitz, said. After graduation from Berkeley, Milken went to Philadelphia to study at Wharton to do an MBA.[9]

Milken created a real high-yield bond market by assuring buyers that they could always sell their securities through him. What had hindered the development of the high-yield market before Milken was that buyers had no one to sell to if they decided that the company whose bonds they had bought were indeed junk. Milken not only assured junk bond buyers he could get them out of a position, but also convinced them that they didn't need the traditional covenants placed on the securities Drexel underwrote.[10]

"Internally, you had a certain trepidation in dealing with Milken because he was so smart," said a former Drexel managing director. "He had more command of 50 deals going on at the same time than you felt you did on your own deal. He could get to the heart of the matter like no one I've ever seen. Having said that, he was a guy who never raised his voice, ever."[11]

Boone Pickens, after years of dealing with Milken, couldn't fathom the man. "Milken's not a guy you want to spend a weekend with," Pickens said. "He's strange, kind of. You can't get to know him. He just isn't knowable. He's an okay guy. Very bright."[12]

■ ■ ■

Drexel had identified cable companies as a perfect industry for Milken's junk bond machine to fund. Once a company had gotten through the first few years of losses as they laid cables in the ground, they were cash machines. Many were effectively monopolies. Drexel's clients included Ted Turner, John Malone, Chuck Dolan, and Ted Rogers in Canada.[13]

Drexel broke a taboo on Wall Street by financing gambling companies. Its first client was Steve Wynn. Milken pushed Joseph to finance Wynn. Joseph had his reservations. "There are always stories about the mafia and gambling," Joseph said. John Kissiack, an investment banker who served as a go-between between Joseph and Milken, investigated. "He said, 'Fred, you're going to love this. You can do more analytical work on the numbers in gaming than you have ever seen. I can show you what the win per hour, per seat, per slot machine is,'" Joseph recalled.[14]

Drexel decided to finance Wynn, but it wasn't easy. It took 12 months and three tries to sell the high-yield bonds. After this inauspicious start, Drexel dominated capital raising for casino operators. From 1979 to 1989, Drexel, by its own reckoning, had done 85 percent of the financing for the gambling industry.[15]

"Drexel had a renegade approach to the business," said a former Drexel managing director. "A lot of what I had seen on Wall Street previously was a thought process that if you had a new idea and talked to the senior guy about it, the senior guy would say, 'That's smart, but if it's so smart, why didn't someone else think of it first?' Drexel's aggressiveness, innovation and willingness to take risk was so monumentally ahead of everyone else."[16]

Years later, Goldman Sachs's former senior partner, John Whitehead, believes Drexel's ultimate demise was inevitable. "We always thought that Drexel Burnham was taking risks that we didn't want to take selling bond issues that we wouldn't have done," said Whitehead. "But they had a certain place in the world of investment banking for a few years. I think their ultimate downfall was destined to happen. We simply would have never taken those risks."[17]

Wall Street has moved more toward the Drexel model of business, risk taking, rather than the considered approach implemented by men such as Whitehead.

Initially, Joseph and Milken discussed every high-yield issue. As the transactions by both the high-yield and investment banking departments grew so dramatically in the 1980s, the two men couldn't liaise as they had done in the past. They also weren't sitting in the same office. Milken had moved his high-yield department from New York to Los Angeles in 1978. Drexel set up a capital markets group to intermediate and communicate between New York and Los Angeles. Peter Ackermann was put in charge as the expert for the investment bankers on how to structure a deal and price it.[18]

Drexel's initial efforts in takeovers were leveraged buyouts: Kohlberg Kravis Roberts, Thomas H. Lee Partners, Westray, and Forstmann Little, who were beginning to do buyouts in the late 1970s and early 1980s. Most were very small because insurance companies did the private placements for the mezzanine piece of the capital structure. The buyout firms were putting up the equity at the bottom, banks on a secured basis were putting loans on the top, but the middle piece, the unsecured piece, the glue that was the leveraged buyout, was the tough piece. It was a perfect piece for high-yield bonds.[19]

Drexel sent Leon Black to KKR to convince Jerome Kohlberg, Henry Kravis, and George Roberts that Drexel could sell high-yield bonds quickly, in amounts never seen before, and with little guarantees. All the buyout firms with the exception of Forstmann Little would use Drexel to raise money for takeovers. Ted Forstmann, in the pages of the

Wall Street Journal, famously compared high-yield bonds to "wampum," beads made of shells used for money by Native Americans.[20]

Black had visions of Drexel's becoming a great merchant bank. He thought the firm should own the cash-rich cable TV and Coca-Cola bottling franchises the firm was arranging financing for others to buy. Black pushed for Drexel to get warrants attached to buyouts the firm backed. The firm would use these small equity components to attract investors to buy the high-yield bonds and to keep some in anticipation of a profit.[21]

Black could have ended up battling Drexel at Goldman Sachs. He had spent the summer at Goldman Sachs between his first and second year at Harvard Business School. In 1975, his father committed suicide. He had been involved in acquiring companies during the conglomerate craze of the 1960s and was chief executive of banana grower United Brands, which was under investigation for trying to bribe the Honduran president. Black recoiled from business. He mulled over what he wanted to do while working for a year and a half as a consultant and then as an assistant to a publisher. Black decided he didn't want to go to a traditional investment bank. He had met Joseph while at Harvard. Joseph told Black that if he joined Drexel, he would get responsibility early.[22]

■   ■   ■

In 1983, Joseph complained that the merger bankers weren't keeping up with the firm's high-yield operation. Joseph's complaint led to a fateful decision. Drexel decided to finance hostile takeovers using its high-yield department, "thereby leveling the playing field between large and small companies," said Joseph.[23] Drexel's bankers were not into soft sell.

"I got a phone call one day from the CFO of General Foods, who said, 'I've just had a visit from Drexel today,'" recalled Steve Waters, who was at Lehman Brothers. "I said, 'What did they say to you?' He said, 'They gave us their analysis of what we were worth if we were broken up and asked to be signed up as their investment banker. They said if we didn't sign them up, they were going to take this to their raider clients and have someone make an offer for us.' I said, 'That's a hell of a new business pitch, isn't it?'"[24]

Other firms looked at the burgeoning business of Drexel's high-yield practice and tried to compete. Milken wasn't prepared to give an inch.

"They were quite the extortionists," recalled a banker who headed a merger department at a competing Wall Street firm. "I remember representing the Pritzkers and Marriott, who were looking to buy United Airlines. We had a very good relationship with both of them, as we had the leading research analyst in the lodging area and a very capable banker in that space. We did an enormous amount of work. There was no way we were going to raise $11 billion of junk financing. Nobody on the street could have done it except Milken.

"We went to Milken to see if we could jointly do this. We fully expected to have a minor role relative to Milken. We would get a quarter of the bonds and he would get three quarters of the bonds. We would get an M&A fee. The total fees would be $200 million. Fee negotiation went like this: 'We'll take $199 million, and you'll take $1 million.' We said, 'You've got to be kidding.' And they said, 'No. We control the market and you're irrelevant. Here's a tip.' We resigned. We decided not to pursue. The deal never happened. They had that kind of market power."[25]

Boone Pickens was introduced to Drexel by Sunshine Mining chairman Mike Boswell. "I could not justify going out and looking for oil and gas because I had proven in the 1970s it was too expensive to find," said Pickens. "I kept looking over at Cities Service, and the management was so goddamn dumb. The managements were all dumb at these companies."[26]

He was equally dismissive of bankers. "An investment banker, it's a business that'll hunt with anybody who's got a gun," Pickens said.[27] Still, it didn't stop Pickens from hiring them.

Tony James, head of mergers at Donaldson Lufkin & Jenrette, flew so frequently to Mesa's headquarters in Amarillo, Texas, on Saturday evenings from New York that it seemed to him he was there almost every weekend.

"I would go into Mesa's office on Sunday morning," recalled James. "Boone, his top cronies, and his key advisers from DLJ and Merrill would sit around. Boone would tell off-color stories for half an hour and then he would say, 'Boys, I need to go play racketball. But it's time to make a deal.' He didn't have a target. It was just time for Boone to make a deal. We'd kick around different targets, analysis on companies we had done before we had come down. Eventually, we'd pick a target and off we'd go."[28]

After Pickens failed in his attempt to acquire Cities Service, he dumped Donaldson Lufkin & Jenrette and Merrill Lynch as advisers in favor of Drexel. Asked years later what attracted him to Drexel, Pickens replied: "Money. They said they could get the money." Gulf Oil had become Pickens's next target.[29]

Drexel's oil and gas banker, John Sorte, went to Amarillo to examine the analysis done by Mesa on Gulf. Sorte concluded the proposed takeover of the sixth-biggest U.S. oil company was a perfect transaction for Drexel to lead a hostile leveraged buyout.[30] Gulf's stock was very undervalued compared to its assets. Drexel pledged to raise $1.5 billion in high-yield bonds for Pickens's attempted takeover. In the days before e-mail, multipage purchase documents for the securities had to be faxed page by page to investors. Not surprisingly, word leaked of Pickens's plans.[31]

"Milken was cavalier about leaks," said Bob Lovejoy, who worked as an attorney for Pickens at Davis Polk. "He would send out documents marked 'Confidential—do not open until Mike Milken tells you.'"[32] At the same time, Milken guarded his list of high-yield buyers closely.

"I said, 'Let me see a list of the people who you've offered the private placement to,'" recalled Lovejoy. "Drexel said, 'We can't do that—that's confidential.' I said, 'Mesa is gonna ask our firm to say this is a valid, privately placed issue. To do that, I have to know who's buying and who's offering.' They said, 'It's impossible. We can't disclose it.' I said to Drexel's Cahill Gordon lawyer, 'How do you give an opinion? Do you get the list?' He said, 'I don't.' 'Then how are you giving an opinion that it's a good private placement?'"[33]

The problems of fund-raising among 20 Drexel clients and then coordinating the tender offer for Gulf made John Sorte despair. In desperation, Drexel went to Carl Lindner of American Financial and closed on $300 million to do a partial tender offer for Gulf.

"Then Gulf was acquired by SoCal who bought Pickens out along with all other shareholders and gave rise to the argument that all Pickens was in the takeover business for was greenmail and all Drexel was in it for was to help its raider clients do greenmail," recalled Sorte.[34]

■   ■   ■

In 1985, Drexel decided to hire a proven merger banker for its hostile takeovers, as it had none of its own. Several prominent merger bankers were approached; all turned the firm down.

"I had a recruiting offer to run M&A for Drexel," said Steve Waters. "I was at Lehman, and the pitch was, 'We want someone who will do anything to get a deal done.' They attracted people who found that an attractive pitch. I think they did get carried away. They got some folks who went beyond where the lines were."[35]

Drexel hired Dennis Levine, Waters's junior, from Lehman Brothers. Levine was a crook. He had been betting on takeovers on the basis of confidential information since the late 1970s.[36] Levine did so on his first deal at Drexel.[37]

Oscar Wyatt's Coastal Corporation, which had made several attempts to take over other companies, had another target and talked to Drexel. Coastal wanted to buy another pipeline company, American Natural Resources, linking its East Coast pipelines to American Natural's in the Midwest.[38]

Drexel raised $600 million for Wyatt and launched an all cash, hostile takeover offer for American Natural which entered into talks with Wyatt and agreed to a takeover by Coastal. It was a big step for Drexel, Sorte thought. During the deal, Dennis Levine had been talking to an arbitrage trader named Ivan Boesky. Levine had leaked word on the deal to Boesky.[39]

Ivan Boesky was a publicity hound. He hired a public relations firm to broadcast the returns of his fund.

"It was in all the newspapers. Ivan this, Ivan that," recalled Alan "Ace" Greenberg, who had worked as an arbitrage trader since he joined Bear Stearns in 1949. "Ivan took risk arbitrage from a semi-secret society and into the mainstream."[40] Boesky was invited to speak at conferences and at universities. At Berkeley's business school graduation in 1986, he famously remarked: "I think greed is healthy. You can be greedy and still feel good about yourself."[41]

"If you studied Ivan's track record, the things he did on his own research were lousy and the things he based on his bribery were terrific," said Greenberg. "It was all horseshit."[42]

After Dennis Levine was arrested and pleaded guilty to insider trading, Oscar Wyatt came to Drexel and said he believed he might have bought American Natural at a lower price if Levine had not been employed by the firm. Drexel worked out a drilling program where Drexel gave the equivalent amount of money Coastal Corporation had paid extra for American Natural in a drilling fund that Coastal used to drill for oil and gas. In return, Drexel got less than an economic return for the money it gave Coastal. Drexel set up an entity, Double Oil and Gas, a play on DBL, and it was successful. Drexel broke even.[43]

After a couple of deals, Fred Joseph and John Sorte had figured out that Dennis Levine was not in the pantheon of merger bankers. Drexel sought another merger specialist. It hired Marty Siegel. "Too bad it turned out he was a crook as well," said Sorte.[44]

Chapter 14

Crime and Punishment

Most of the insider trading scandals of the 1980s involved clear-cut examples of people who knew in advance of mergers or who knew of something terrible that was going to happen to a company. They then went out and traded or tipped others to trade. Wall Street's view of insider trading was that it was someone else's problem. Compliance officers were viewed as a drain on profits. When profits went up, compliance was fine. As the profits started to narrow, people viewed it as a cost center.[1]

By the 1980s, the economics of the markets had suddenly made it much more attractive to grow or expand or build by acquisition. "It got very heady for people," said Harvey Pitt, one of America's foremost experts on securities law, who represented Ivan Boesky when the arbitrageur pleaded guilty to insider trading charges. "There were people like Dennis Levine and others who fancied themselves as phenomenal deal makers. It became easy for some people to lose sight of their moral compass. They tried to find ways to take advantage of this information."[2]

As investment banks had expanded their business, their employees could utilize nominee accounts and foreign accounts to look for places to secretly put money based on confidential information. Levine opened bank accounts in Switzerland and the Bahamas. Marty Siegel, while at Kidder Peabody, accepted suitcases of cash from Ivan Boesky in the Plaza Hotel.[3]

When Siegel was hired by Drexel, the firm felt it had at last hired a bona fide merger star. He had been tutored by Marty Lipton. He had been involved in a string of high-profile takeover battles, including Martin Marietta's successful "Pac-Man" defense. He was, moreover, sexy.[4]

"He was like a movie star," said Lipton. "The girls in the office used to line up, not overtly, when they knew he was coming, to look at him. They just wanted a peek at Marty Siegel. He was a brilliant salesman, maybe the best among the M&A bankers. Prior to his being arrested, people would say, 'It's very suspicious about Marty Siegel and Ivan Boesky. Boesky seems to trade well in connection to Siegel deals.' I said, 'You must be nuts. He would never do that. He's making a fortune. Why would he do anything like that?' I have the same question today."[5]

Wachtell itself would be caught up in the insider trading scandals. Two young partners, Carlo Florentino and Ilan Reich, would be convicted within five years of each other. Like Siegel's crimes, Lipton could not fathom years later what motivated the two men. "We had two people, and in each case it was inexplicable," he said.[6]

The passing of confidential information among a ring of bankers and traders corrupted the market.

"I remember one Smith Barney deal where we represented Browning Ferris, and my old colleagues at Merrill were representing Waste Management; it was the takeover battle for SCA Services," said a former merger banker. "Kidder Peabody and Marty Siegel were representing SCA. We had a week of back and forth, Waste Management and Browning Ferris upping their bids. Siegel ran it like a Ping-Pong match. It was odd because I remember going to the airport in Boston, Butler Aviation, at 1 o'clock in the morning after all the bidding was over, and I got a call from Ivan Boesky. 'Are we going to up your bid?' he asked.

"I said, 'I don't know how you got my number, found out where I was, but I'm not going to respond to you,' and hung up. We walked out to the private plane. Waste Management pilots were there, and they realize Browning Ferris is leaving. They gave the CEO the finger. We got on the plane to go back to New York and the CEO turned to me and said, 'Call Marty Siegel to up the bid. We're not going to lose.' I got back to New York. It was three in the morning. I woke up Marty's wife and said to Marty, 'We're going to up our bid.' And he said, 'That can't happen.' I said, 'Yeah, it can happen. We're putting a 20 percent increase on our purchase price.' It was all because the Waste Management pilots pissed the CEO off.

"Siegel said, 'If you do everything I tell you to do, I'll accept your bid.' I agreed. We had a deal. We worked all weekend. Monday morning came and we thought we had won it. All of a sudden, radio silence. We get a call. Siegel has tipped the bid to Waste Management, who got them to up their cash price. So we lost. Ivan Boesky had a 10 percent position in SCA, and he gave Siegel about $700,000 in cash. Siegel was helping a client win, putting cash in his pocket while giving Boesky the information. Many years later, I had to take a plane from Florida to Chicago and the Waste Management CEO gave me a ride on his jet and said, 'You cost me half a billion dollars that day.'"[7]

Jack McAtee, the Davis Polk partner who was a close friend of Bob Greenhill's, remembers seeing Siegel the day after he was charged. "He showed up at Davis Polk the next day on a deal. Siegel was in denial," recalled McAtee.[8]

Wall Street knew what was going on. Before a merger announcement, there would be huge run-ups in prices of stock. Between 1981 and 1985, there were 172 run-ups in stock prices on the New York and American Stock Exchanges just prior to a takeover offer.[9]

"Wall Street at the time did what many in business do and have done forever—people sit back and wait for the government to tell them what they are doing is wrong," recalled Harvey Pitt, who later became chairman of the Securities and Exchange Commission. "Instead of saying, 'Let's focus on this stuff; let's see if we have a problem.' More could have and should have been done."[10]

In stepped the U.S. attorney for the Southern District of New York, an aggressive prosecuting attorney with political ambitions named Rudolph Giuliani. Giuliani went in to meet Steve Waters and Tom Hill, who jointly ran the merger department at Lehman Brothers. He had evidence that one of their best young bankers, Ira Sokolow, had been caught up in insider trading. Giuliani added that he thought everyone in the department was guilty of the same crime. "I said, 'If you've got a guy, we'll cooperate any way we can, and if you've got anything more than one guy, we're happy to hear about it,'" Waters recalled.[11]

John Weinberg, Goldman Sachs's senior partner, was furious following the arrest of Goldman Sachs partner Bob Freeman in 1987 on insider trading charges. Weinberg went and protested the arrest personally at Rudolph Giuliani's office.[12] Goldman Sachs was investigated by a Grand Jury.

Geoff Boisi was the first Goldman Sachs partner asked to testify because of the interaction between the merger and arbitrage departments. Boisi was told his testimony would set the tone as to whether the grand jury would look at Goldman Sachs and whether Goldman Sachs would be brought in as a co-defendant in Bob Freeman's trial. Prosecutors wanted to know what the merger department and the arbitrage department did together during takeovers.

Bob Freeman ran Goldman Sachs's arbitrage department. His conviction stemmed from his efforts to get information on the takeover of Beatrice Foods by Kohlberg Kravis Roberts. Freeman had bought shares and options for Goldman Sachs and for his personal account, betting on a takeover by KKR.[13]

When Beatrice stock fell and another arbitrageur sold his shares, Freeman was unnerved. He called KKR's Henry Kravis. Kravis told him nothing. From Kravis's hurried manner, Freeman decided to start selling his family's and Goldman Sachs's Beatrice shares. After receiving a call from Bernard "Bunny" Lasker, Freeman called Siegel, who was advising KKR. "I told Mr. Siegel I had heard there was a problem with the Beatrice leveraged buyout. He asked from whom I had heard that. When I answered, 'Bunny Lasker,' Martin Siegel said, 'Your Bunny has a good nose,'" said Freeman.[14]

The trading Freeman engaged in after he spoke with Siegel was considered insider trading. Prosecutors viewed Siegel as someone with privileged information. Freeman avoided $930,000 of losses on Beatrice but not 109 days in prison.[15] It was a stain on Goldman Sachs's reputation, exacerbated by an earlier jail sentence given to one of the firm's former investment bankers David Brown, who sold takeover information to Dennis Levine.[16]

For former Goldman Sachs partners John Whitehead, Geoff Boisi, Steve Freidman, and Robert Rubin, Robert Freeman's arrest and subsequent investigation by Rudy Giuliani smacked not of a considered examination of the facts but of the urge by Giuliani to win headlines and popularity by prosecuting rich Wall Street figures. Freeman said his name was unfairly tarnished by Siegel who invented conversations with the Goldman Sachs arbitrageur to falsely implicate him and deflect public wrath away from himself. "I was arrested on Siegel's totally uncorroborated accusations," said Freeman. "I passed a lie detector test. I never tipped Siegel, he never tipped me." In a 143-page document prepared by his lawyers, Freeman said he pleaded guilty to one count of insider trading because of the poisonous atmosphere in the late 1980s surrounding anyone on Wall Street accused of a crime. Writers such as James Stewart were repeating Siegel's allegations, making it impossible to get a fair trial, Freeman said. "In an era of Siegel, Levine and Drexel, the public thought an arbitrager was lower than a rapist," said Freeman.[17]

The reputation of the merger bankers too were not spared. After all, one of their own, Siegel, went to jail. "When my eldest daughter was in high school, she was asked, 'What does your father do?'" recalled Steve Friedman. "'He's an investment banker,' was her reply. 'What's that?' When she was in college, she was asked the same thing. But the response was 'Where is he?' As best we could tell, everyone about to graduate from Yale wanted to be an analyst at Goldman Sachs. At another point she was asked, 'What does your father do?' 'He's an investment banker,' she replied. The response was 'Yuck.'"[18]

■   ■   ■

The insider trading convictions raised the perennial broader question of where did the loyalty of Wall Street lie? Was it to their clients or themselves? The answer was, as trading and principal investments became a more important profit center for firms, sometimes the client and sometimes themselves. Henry Kravis and George Roberts had protested mightily when Goldman Sachs set up a unit to do leveraged buyouts in 1981.[19]

"Henry Kravis always felt he was one of the deans of private equity and was always uncomfortable with new entrants, particularly new entrants that were his service providers, vendors like Goldman," recalled a former Goldman Sachs partner. "I was asked to cover KKR. I was there almost every day. It was the biggest fee-paying client in the world. The first time I went to see Henry, it was in the paper that Goldman Sachs was buying Westin Hotels & Resorts. We had a signed engagement letter that we were advising KKR on the purchase of Westin. Henry said, 'What are you doing? Get out of here. This is the most atrocious thing I've ever seen.'"[20]

John Whitehead, until he retired as Goldman Sachs's senior partner in 1984, had resisted efforts by others to grow the firm's principal businesses. "We had lots of opportunities to make money by investing our capital," Whitehead recalled. "But I leaned against that all the time."[21]

After Whitehead's retirement in 1984, there was a gradual shift away from the client-first mentality at Goldman Sachs. Many former partners at the firm felt that this retreat from a client-first mentality was pushed by Steve Friedman and Geoff Boisi.

For a long time, Goldman wouldn't represent anyone on the acquiring side; they wouldn't do any unfriendly transactions and would only represent clients in friendly transactions. "I believe that specialization of hostile takeovers was very important to Goldman Sachs's general success and large market share in the M&A business," said John Whitehead. "We didn't do unfriendly offers. That policy has softened I would say." That shifted a little bit under Friedman's and Boisi's tenures as heads of investment banking. On the private equity side, both men saw the potential of leveraged buyouts and sought to find a way to participate as a principal and not just as an adviser.

Under Friedman and Boisi, Goldman Sachs's defense-only principal in takeover battles shifted. Both men wanted to grab more business for the firm and sought to advise companies on acquisitions. They also wanted to invest the firm's capital as both men saw the potential of private equity and sought to participate in deals not only as an adviser, but also as a principal. That raised questions of conflicts-of-interest.

Friedman believed conflict-of-interest questions could be solved by disclosure. The very nature of Wall Street, he argued, meant that conflicts were unavoidable. It was how you dealt with such conflicts that was important. By being open and truthful, clients would understand and either make a decision to hire or not hire Goldman Sachs. The firm also had a choice as to whether they wanted to work with a company.[22]

"You can solve conflicts with sunlight and disclosure," said Friedman. "Even clients who are comfortable with a conflict of interest may give the banker or the firm pause, and they may not decide to represent a company. A good banker knows what is going on in the industry and knows all the executives and the issues facing the industry. If a banker doesn't know these things, then perhaps he or she isn't in the flow. You want a banker who knows what is going on."[23]

■　■　■

Many former Drexel bankers believe their firm's collapse was partly engineered by overzealous prosecutors and paranoid chief executives who wanted the firm shut down because it was leading a destructive hostile takeover wave.

When Drexel financed Nelson Peltz's tiny Triangle Industries' successful takeover of National Can, many at large corporations became worried that Drexel's high-yield bond machine could finance raiders that were worth only a couple hundred million dollars and go after sizable companies. There was a backlash. In May 1985, *Fortune* magazine's cover story was entitled "Have Takeovers Gone Too Far?"[24]

Eric Gleacher at Morgan Stanley was hired by Union Carbide and Gillette and successfully defended them against Drexel and its raiders, Sam Heyman and Ron Perelman. He had a more sympathetic view of Drexel.

"It was Milken and his money machine and Drexel against the American establishment," said Gleacher. "People kind of faced off. Milken provided the money for these takeover artists, who shook this economy up and did a lot of good. Many of the companies restructured because they had to or did in anticipation of having to. I think it made the whole business landscape more efficient.

"He used to tell me how in his kind of funny voice, 'I don't understand why all these people from Morgan Stanley hate me. I made you all rich.' He was right. He was very, very smart, and I had lots of dealings with him and they were all good business dealings. I might not have wanted to do what he was doing, but I also felt economically it was better having a free market with someone who wants to do that and keep some of these other people on their toes."[25]

Part of the hostility that Drexel endured was backing takeover artists who seemed to want more of a payoff for their stock, greenmail, more than the prize of acquiring the company. Bob Lovejoy of Davis Polk warned Pickens that he would need to acquire a target or risk losing any credibility as someone genuinely interested in running a major oil company.

"Boone, the next time you do a deal, you're going to have to buy the company," said Lovejoy. "You can't do this a couple of times more, as you're going to have no credibility."[26]

Pickens sought to take over Phillips Petroleum. Many bankers thought Pickens wasn't serious about an acquisition of the oil producer. He didn't raise financing and took greenmail. Phillips's stock tanked after Pickens was bought out.[27] Drexel's merger group was charged with trying to find a buyer for Phillips. The stock was in the hands of arbitrage traders who all had big losses. Leon Black spoke to Carl Icahn, with whom he had a close business relationship. Icahn, who knew nothing about the oil and gas business but knew about undervalued companies, was interested in acquiring Phillips.[28]

Icahn did not want to pay for the commitment letters to finance a takeover. He wanted to do something cheaper. Takeover specialists had assumed that to do a tender offer for shares, there had to be committed financing. On closer examination of the law, there didn't. Icahn or any other simply had to believe they could get the financing. The "highly confident" letter was born out of all-night negotiations between Black, Sorte, and Icahn and his lawyers.[29]

Drexel couldn't state that it was committed to raising the financing for Icahn because that would be a capital charge. A broker-dealer such as Drexel could not afford a capital charge for funding acquisitions.[30]

"We told (Icahn), 'We're sure we can raise the money, we're confident we can raise the money, we can give you a letter saying we're confident we can raise the money,'" said Sorte. "He said, 'Nah, that's not good enough.' At some point, it became, 'We're highly confident,' and he said no and the deal seemed to be off. The next morning, he called up and said, 'Okay, I've talked to my lawyers, and I think the street will believe you. If Drexel says it's highly confident they can raise the money, they'll believe you, and I think that's good enough to go on a transaction.'"[31]

Drexel's "highly confident" letter of 1985 was a watershed. It was the first serious commitment of capital in modern times by a securities firm for a merger. Icahn launched an $8.1 billion tender offer for Phillips with Drexel's "highly confident" letter. Phillips argued that the "highly confident" letter was fraudulent in a lawsuit. As Sorte was being deposed in court, Drexel put out a statement that it raised $1.5 billion to finance part of Icahn's offer, quashing Phillips's lawsuit. A proxy fight ensued, which Icahn lost. He took $25 million from Philips for "expenses," another form of greenmail.[32]

■   ■   ■

The same year as the birth of Drexel's "highly confident" letter, Ralph Roberts and Julian Brodsky, the two top people at Comcast, were trying to buy Storer Broadcasting. KKR had locked up Drexel. Roberts and Brodsky went to see Ken Miller, the head of mergers at Merrill Lynch. They needed $1.2 billion, fast. Miller went to Merrill Lynch's executive committee. The firm agreed to lend Comcast the money. Comcast would lose out to KKR in acquiring Storer, but Merrill Lynch awoke to a new line of business, the "rent-a-balance-sheet" program called bridge loans.[33]

Bridge loans would prove a highly profitable business for investment banks when married with their advice, and would foreshadow the strategy of the financial supermarkets such as Citigroup and J. P. Morgan, offering financing for a takeover along with advice. Bridge loans would eventually trump Drexel's highly confident letter because it was a real rather than "highly confident" commitment to use a balance sheet.[34]

Pickens came back to Drexel one last time. He decided to try to take over Unocal. It proved to be the beginning of the end for hostile, junk-bond takeovers. Pickens's offer was two tiered—the front end was cash and the back end was paper.[35]

"The big issue with Unocal was the fact we had this two-tiered offer which caused lots of lobbying against the offer in Washington, 50 percent cash, 50 percent junk bonds, to the extent that little old lady in Omaha would only get the back end and the arbs would, of course, tender their shares and get more cash and less junk bonds," recalled Sorte. "Those offers were viewed as not being very fair, and I would agree with that. It was certainly something that was used against us."[36]

Unocal and its Dillon Read banker, Fritz Hobbs, and Steve Friedman of Goldman Sachs came up with a self-tender offer that excluded Pickens.[37] Mesa filed suit. The Delaware Court ruled in favor of Unocal. It was a shattering disaster for Mesa. Pickens's career in the takeover arena had ended.[38]

For Unocal, its triumph in the Delaware courts was a short-lived celebration. The oil and gas producer took on $4.1 billion in debt from issuing debt securities to pay shareholders to support incumbent management instead of Pickens.[39] Fritz Hobbs, who had thought of Unocal's successful defense on an airplane flight to Los Angeles with Steve Friedman, was not welcomed back to Unocal as a conquering hero.

"They hated us," recalled Hobbs. "The survivors felt we loaded up with all this debt. I continued to go after Unocal from 1986 to 1996. I was determined to change that. I never did. There was DNA in their body that these guys put us in that position and for seven or eight years our hands were tied."[40]

Goldman Sachs fared little better. In 1987, the firm and partner Bob Freeman in Goldman Sachs's arbitrage department were sued by Unocal for insider trading.[41]

Five years after Pickens's raid on Unocal, Drexel filed for bankruptcy in 1990. The firm was mortally wounded by a three-and-a-half-year investigation into its activities. Drexel pleaded guilty to six counts of mail and securities fraud in 1989. The next year, Milken pleaded guilty to six felony charges of securities fraud and conspiracy.[42]

"He did break the law," said Sorte. "There is no question about it. He did things that he didn't have to do. It's one of those things you just never understand about people. He was so successful. He was making a lot of money. At the time, I was really pissed off when I found out he did it because he ruined a good thing for a lot of us. Drexel would be around today if it weren't for that," said Sorte. "He [Milken] did things he didn't have to do. It's one of those things you just never understand about people. He was so successful. He was making a lot of money."[43]

Milken was paid $550 million in 1987 alone.[44] Even Boone Pickens found that outrageous. "That's totally out of the question. That's unconscionable. Nobody should be allowed to make $500 million on an idea."[45] Between 1977 and 1989, Drexel's high-yield bond unit had raised more than $98 billion. Milken personally got 35 percent of the commission on each transaction.[46]

"Fred [Joseph] was head of a firm where Milken was making probably 10 times what Fred was making and was the total powerhouse," said a partner at a New York law firm who was involved in the Wall Street scandals of the 1980s. "It's like criticizing the coach of a professional basketball team, where the superstar does all kinds of bad things. The superstar feels he doesn't have to answer to anybody. I kind of feel that is what was going on at Drexel.

"I dealt with Milken during that period of time. I don't think I've dealt with anybody in business who I found so scary. I didn't know what his limits were. I couldn't find out what his limits were. What would he not do? He had unbelievable power. There is nobody now who is like Milken. Nobody has been like Milken. He is the most interesting guy in corporate finance in the last 50 years, and his influence has been lasting."[47]

Joseph was forced to resign as Drexel's chief executive and barred from running a Wall Street firm again. Sorte was appointed the chief executive of Drexel to work the firm out of bankruptcy with Joseph and a few others.[48]

"At the time of Drexel's bankruptcy in 1990, you were on either the Milken team or the Fred Joseph team," said Sorte. "I was on the Fred Joseph team. We weren't friendly with Milken for quite a while, especially going through the bankruptcy where we were still having to deal with some of the aftermath of some of the things he had done. As we've all gotten older, we've forgiven each other our past sins. But it's a shame that he did that."[49]

Joseph, for one, thought Drexel's role as the leader of hostile takeovers in the 1980s partly spelled its downfall. The Business Roundtable had identified Drexel and Milken as its enemies.

"I'm not entirely sure it was smart of Drexel to finance unfriendly takeovers that worried the Roundtable," said Joseph years later. "We would have done better in troubled times if we had not developed the constituency of people that didn't like us. I haven't discussed it with him, but I think Michael has reached the same conclusion."[50]

Marty Lipton once flew to Los Angeles on behalf of newspaper publisher Gannett to see Milken. Drexel backed Carl Lindner's attempt to take over Gannett. Lipton warned Milken that there were political and public concerns about Drexel's financing a raider seeking control of a major newspaper.

"I expressed those concerns," recalled Lipton. "He rejected them out of hand, showed disdain for my views. It's always difficult to say in retrospect what you thought of somebody. I felt sorry for him in that I thought his disdain of the other banks and his imperiousness were going to cause the problem that ultimately led to his downfall."[51]

Chapter 15

A Voice in the Wilderness

Almost alone in the merger world, Marty Lipton mused, warned, and wrote on the costs of hostile takeovers. Jobs and income lost. Communities who relied on the income earned by those employed in the company that ceased to exist. Lipton was especially critical of the Drexel-backed raiders.

"The goal of such bids was not to improve the management of the target's assets or to reap synergies from an existing rival, but to 'bust up' the corporation and sell the pieces for a quick profit. The bidders were often seeking quick returns, not improved enterprises," Lipton and his Wachtell colleague Paul Rowe wrote.[1]

Many scoffed at Lipton's views, considering them an anachronism in the modern, cutthroat, free-market world. Rivals poked fun at his injection of moral tone into debates on takeovers. They preferred to do business and leave such questions aside. "I tended not to get involved in the philosophy. I just enjoyed doing what I was doing," said Skadden partner Fin Fogg.[2]

Lipton dared to publicly point out how hostile takeovers enriched bankers and lawyers, including those at Wachtell, notorious for its high fees.

"The new breed of hostile bids was, one the one hand, wreaking havoc with expectations of managers, employees, and communities, and, on the other hand, enriching the raiders and a new class on Wall Street: the bankers who advised, financed, or arbitraged takeovers," wrote Lipton.[3]

By the late 1970s, the merger department was the biggest revenue generator for Goldman Sachs's investment banking department. Fees were based on the size of the transaction, a low percentage of the asset value of the merger, but a very high total amount because the firm was advising bigger and bigger companies.[4]

At Smith Barney at the time of the firm's sale to Primerica in 1988, 80 percent of its firm's profits came from the merger and arbitrage departments.[5]

Compensation for merger bankers skyrocketed from the late 1970s. Ken Miller and Carl Fernbach made half a million a year running mergers at Merrill Lynch. By the 1980s, managing directors at merger departments on Wall Street were earning $3 million a year. Bruce Wasserstein and Joe Perella made more than $4 million annually. Felix Rohaytn earned between $5 million and $6 million, and Eric Gleacher by the late 1980s made about the same.[6]

A merger banker's compensation, both salary and bonus, was based on the amount of business they brought to the firm. They had a natural incentive to initiate mergers even if they made little sense from a long-term business point of view. In proposing mergers, many who sat alongside bankers questioned their optimistic assumptions. Forecasts to justify an acquisition, some believe, are estimates compounded by a guess.

"I personally have a great problem with valuation methodologies," said Harvey Miller, who was a vice chairman for more than four years at Bob Greenhill's firm Greenhill & Company, advising bankrupt companies before resuming his law career. "I get a real kick out of discounted cash flow analysis where the entire value is in the terminal value. What are you guys talking about? Five years out is all the value and it's there till all eternity. It's a fiction."[7]

Marty Lipton, despite his early ambitions to be an investment banker, questioned not discount cash flow analysis but the economic orthodoxy of the time. Proponents of free markets, which struck a rich vein of support during the Reagan years, wanted little interference by the courts, boards of directors, and antitrust oversight in takeover matters. Markets were the best guide for decision making and for law courts. Short-term shareholder value maximization was the only criteria that Delaware's law courts should take into account in their judgments.[8]

In 1979, Lipton wrote a seminal article, "Takeover Bids in the Target's Boardroom."[9] In it, he argued that it was often in the best interest for shareholders to reject a takeover. Between the end of 1973 and June 1979, the shares of more than half of the 36 companies that rejected a takeover offer were higher than what the raider was prepared to offer.[10]

Lipton successfully helped defend McGraw-Hill against a bid by American Express in 1979, and within two years McGraw Hill's stock price was higher than American Express's $40 a share offer. Twenty-six years later, Lipton could point out, the publisher's market value had climbed from $806 million to over $17 billion.[11] Moreover, the stock market crash of 1987 and the later collapse of the technology-heavy Nasdaq in 2000 undermined the philosophical underpinnings of efficient market theory.

Lipton argued for what would become known as the business judgment rule. Companies should not have a permanent "for sale" sign on their headquarters. Boards of directories had responsibilities to employees, customers, suppliers, and the community. The long-term interests of the corporation were more important than the raider or group of arbitrage traders seeking short-term profits from takeovers. Lipton argued that if shareholders were unhappy with the way a company was managed, they should conduct a proxy fight to change the management, sell the company, change the strategy, or change the business.[12]

Lipton's views provoked a storm of academic counterargument. Believers of efficient market theory and raiders such as Boone Pickens accused Lipton of trying to protect management.[13] Lipton shot back. In testimony before Congress in 1984, he said there had been takeover abuses. Raiders like Pickens can demand a premium in exchange for their shares, greenmail, if they want their hostile attempts at taking over a corporation to stop.

Greenmail discriminates against other shareholders, Lipton said, as they aren't offered a premium for their shares, unlike raiders such as Pickens or Carl Icahn. Lipton also inveighed against two-tier front-end-loaded takeovers such as the one that Pickens launched for Cities Service and Gulf Oil. They are, Lipton said, "devices through which unsophisticated shareholders are taken advantage of by professional investors. They are devices by which a target's own balance sheet is used to finance a raid. They create highly leveraged companies with enormous debt."[14]

■ ■ ■

Lipton had been trying to prevent hostile takeovers through litigation and the use of state antitakeover statutes and classified boards, where directors serve for different periods. None of his tactics proved effective. In 1982, he wrote a memo called the "Warrant Dividend Plan." It would change takeovers and corporate law forever.[15]

Lipton's plan entailed a dividend being issued to shareholders of the company under threat from a raider. The dividend was one warrant to buy shares of the raider's stock after a merger between the raider and the company. The exercise price of the warrant would be substantially less than the market price of the common stock. The warrants could be created and issued as a dividend by the company's board of directors to prevent a raider from gaining control of a company as it made a takeover too expensive.[16]

The raider's shareholding and power was effectively diluted by the issuance of the warrants. Lipton also created a flip-in provision in the warrants. If the raider purchased more than 15 percent or 20 percent of a company's stock, all the other shareholders would get a dividend of one share for each owned, but the raider therefore would suffer major dilution. This made it virtually impossible to do a hostile takeover of a company that had adopted a "warrant dividend plan."[17]

Lipton's goal was to enable directors of company under a hostile takeover threat to create time for them to consider and respond to a raider's bid. Previously, directors had only a matter of days to decide the fate of a corporation. In 1983, an investment banker interviewed in the *Wall Street Journal* dubbed Lipton's "Warrant Dividend Plan" the "poison pill." It stuck.[18]

In 1984, Lipton was at home one weekend when Household International chairman Donald Clark called. "He said, 'I understand you have something called a poison pill. I think that's just fabulous. I do hope it works,'" recalled Lipton. Clark was worried that John Morant, who was on his board, would attempt to take over the financial services company. The company adopted the pill and was sued in the Delaware courts by Morant.[19]

Most of America's biggest corporations had incorporated in Delaware. The state's courts had the reputation of being the most sophisticated in their corporate law judgments. Their rulings set the tone for corporate law in the United States. Few gave the pill much chance of survival.

"I remember thinking, 'This is the stupidest thing I have ever heard of. There is no way this makes any sense,'" said a former Goldman Sachs merger banker and partner.[20] The Securities and Exchange Commission filed an amicus brief that argued against the pill.[21]

In the end, the Delaware court ruled in favor of the pill. It was a triumph for Lipton as the Delaware courts reaffirmed his central argument that boards could exercise their business judgment to decide the future of a company.

"I felt great relief after the ruling because, in large measure, we had bet the firm on it," recalled Lipton. "If we had lost that case, it would have been an enormous embarrassment. Major companies, investment banks, they don't want to be associated with a loser. It would have hurt us dramatically.[22]

Delaware's ruling in favor of the pill, as Skadden partner Morris Kramer said, "was a seminal event."[23] Skadden, which had argued against the poison pill, paid Lipton the ultimate compliment after the Delaware judgment by becoming pill experts themselves. "We had all these clients," recalled Skadden partner Jim Freund. "They all wanted the pill, so we became expert in the pill. You had to be light on your feet. You couldn't be left behind, and so we sold it."[24]

In 1985, the Delaware courts also made three other crucial decisions that would prove to be the bedrock of American corporate law. In *Van Gorkham*, the courts rejected the efficient market theory and required directors to make takeover decisions based on the "intrinsic" value of the company rather than the stock market value. In *Unocal*, the courts accepted the appropriateness of "takeover defenses," but they would be reviewed under an objective "reasonable in relation to the threat posed" test. In *Revlon*, Delaware required directors, once they decided to sell the company for cash, to maximize the return to shareholders. At the same time, the court ruled, directors could agree to friendly stock mergers without putting the company into play or auctioning it to the highest bidder.[25]

■ ■ ■

Following the Delaware court rulings, companies rushed to put the poison pill into their bylaws. Merger bankers had to adjust their tactics. "Before, a bidder always wanted to buy cheap and always came to the lawyer and banker and asked, 'How do I buy this at the cheapest possible price by buying the fewest possible shares?" said Morris Kramer of Skadden. "The genius was the guy who could figure out how to get 51 percent of the stock, paying no premium. The pill eliminated that as a possibility. So the genius became 'What's the highest price we can pay? How do I put my offer on the table in the best light?'"[26]

The greenmailers did not die after Drexel's demise. If anything, they got stronger and their activities more accepted.

Icahn inspired a new generation of imitators, activist investors. These activist investors are accepted and even lauded in parts of the investment community, as they are perceived to play a positive role in keeping management lean, healthy, and focused on improving the bottom line. Many wished they had been more numerous in the 1970s and 1980s to put pressure on certain sections of the American business community that had been either complacent or incompetent or both. The U.S. automobile industry perhaps is the best such example.

But an activist investor has no special expertise or insight into a company's business except an analysis that the stock of a target corporation is undervalued. The broader constituencies that a business serves are of little interest, at least initially, to raiders and greenmailers such as Carl Icahn until they have to run the business. Icahn succeeded in acquiring Trans World Airlines in 1985. Financier Lester Crown sat on TWA's board, which voted to approve Icahn's offer for the airline. "Icahn had no experience running an airline," Crown said. "To make a company operate well, someone has to really understand the operations."[27]

Icahn owned TWA until 1993 and failed to stem its long decline into bankruptcy in 1995.[28] When Icahn made a last-ditch attempt to acquire TWA again in 2001 with a brief set of terms, a Delaware judge called it "almost a joke."[29]

Lester Crown is equally dismissive of Icahn and other greenmailers such as Boone Pickens. "Their motivation, Pickens, Icahn, was all money," said Crown. "Their motivation wasn't to make the company better. If the motivation is merely to make money, then get out of it and leave it to someone else to run the company."[30]

Lipton argued that if activist investors are dissatisfied with the management, they can conduct a proxy fight to change the board of directors. Companies should not be pressured into making fundamental changes in their business strategy by minority shareholders that could damage the long-term health of the corporation in order for the greenmailer to profit from a stock position.[31]

Like his concerns about hostile takeovers, Lipton's campaign against activist investors has been met with some derision. Many have also cast aspersions on his support for management and boards of directors under attack from activists such as Relational Advisers, founded by Boone Pickens's former colleagues David Batchelder and Ralph Whitworth.[32]

Batchelder and Whitworth forced out Home Depot's former chief executive, Robert Nardelli, because they disagreed with his strategy of building a wholesale supply business for the home improvement retailer.[33] Despite the fact that Lipton represented the board of Home Depot and not Nardelli, a reporter from the *New York Times* called Lipton an "unapologetic apologist for the days of the Imperial CEO."[34]

"Very few people have been willing to stake out the positions that he and others in the firm have staked out," said Adam Chinn, a former Wachtell partner. "There is almost no one who shares his view of the world. Those who do are too scared to say it, as it's against the tide of history and they're worried they're going to get criticized. It says something for Marty's stature that he can do it."[35]

Chapter 16

Intrigue and Resignations

F elix Rohatyn never used a calculator. Rohatyn worked on calculations using a slide rule throughout his career at Lazard, an irony when one considers that some of his best known merger deals were in telecommunications and media.[1] His personal instincts on technology may have been like a Luddite, but his deal instincts were in demand. Lazard was involved in more mergers because of Rohatyn, partly because his reputation had skyrocketed as a result of his help in saving New York City from bankruptcy in the 1970s. This brought Rohatyn accolades and invitations from the powerful in Washington.

"Everybody took his call," recalled former Lazard partner Bob Lovejoy. "Rohatyn was not just an investment banker but a public person. If he called, he could be calling about politics. You didn't need to take a lot of investment bankers' calls. You needed to take Rohatyn's call."[2]

By 1988, Rohatyn had turned 60, and he had turned his attention to his next career: politics. Some at Lazard said a banker working on

Wall Street in his 60s, even of Rohatyn's stature, has to face the fact that their network of loyal chief executives are retiring or have already quit or died.[3]

"Your influence wanes after a while," said a former Lazard partner. "The new generation came in, and they wanted their own advisers. If you're a CEO and you're in your mid-40s, you don't want a 70-year-old or a 60-year-old being your adviser. That's your dad. You want your peer. If you're 48 years old and you're taking advice from a 70-year-old, it is probably an admission you haven't got what it takes, you haven't been around long enough."[4]

There was a feeling at Lazard in the late 1980s that if Rohatyn retired, it might not have the rainmakers necessary to successfully continue. Lazard chairman Michel David-Weill always felt that the firm needed a star. He was always looking for the next Rohatyn. David-Weill spoke with Roger Altman, Bob Greenhill, and Bruce Wasserstein. David-Weill lived in fear that once Rohatyn was gone, there was no one who could sustain the franchise.[5] In 1988, David-Weill scored a coup by hiring Ira Harris and his colleague Gerald Rosenfeld from Salomon Brothers. In 1989, Steven Rattner joined Lazard from Morgan Stanley, and the next year Kendrick Wilson joined. The future of Lazard's franchise seemed secure.[6]

Lazard had a spectacular reputation partly because of its French mystique. David-Weill was a very good recruiter. He would invite some he wanted to work at the firm as a partner to lunch at his house on France's Cap d'Antibes.[7]

Bob Lovejoy remembers David Weill's house overlooked the Mediterranean. Lovejoy looked out at cigarette boats full of gorgeous people alighting or clambering on board their vessels. Over lunch, David-Weill went through the whole firm and what everyone did. It was clear to Lovejoy that Lazard and its people were not only outstanding, but that David-Weill had an extraordinary grip on exactly what everyone was doing. "At Lazard, there are an infinite number of ways to succeed and only one way to fail," Lovejoy was told by David-Weill.[8]

At the end of the lunch, David-Weill quoted a percentage of the firm's profits Lovejoy would be entitled to if he joined as a partner, which was vastly more than he was making as a partner at Davis Polk. David-Weill gave a further piece of advice: "When you're a lawyer, you don't really need a point of view; you just explain the pros and cons. When you're an investment banker, you have to have a point of view on everything. So when your client calls you up asking if the market is going to go up or down today, you have the answer and a reason."[9]

Typically, by the end of January, Lazard would have covered all its costs for the year. The money made by the firm from February on was partner profits.[10] All partners were not equal in compensation or status. The only person at Lazard who David-Weill felt was a peer was Rohatyn. On conference calls, the two would converse with each other in French to the bemusement and annoyance of others.[11] To be a partner at Lazard was economically remunerative, said one, but it did not bring you closer to David-Weill or the running of the firm.[12]

One associate recalled going to see David-Weill, who offered him a Lazard partnership.

"David-Weill's office could be split into four sections," recalled the banker. "His desk was in one section, a conference table in another; there was a sitting room and a dining table. I sat in the sitting room with him. As we began to talk, he had food delivered for his lunch. He did not offer any food, nor did he excuse himself while he ate in front of the new partner. You were clearly subservient."[13]

Ira Harris left Salomon Brothers disillusioned with the leadership of John Gutfreund and his own inability to dampen an aggressive trading culture he felt would lead the firm into trouble.[14] Gutfreund and Harris didn't like each other. Gutfreund dismissed Harris years later as "a pretty good salesman; not a brilliant man."[15]

"Deal guys are great seducers," said Gutfreund. Harris is "generous. Everybody is his friend."[16]

Steve Friedman at Goldman Sachs spoke with Harris about joining Goldman Sachs. Fritz Hobbs wanted him to join Dillon Read. He settled on Lazard. Rohatyn had become a friend, and both men as dealmakers were similar in style.[17] "Ira and Felix were old school, lovers not fighters, relationship M&A," said Peter Solomon.[18]

Lazard agreed to open a Chicago office for Harris, and he took three Salomon associates to stock the firm's first Midwest office.[19]

One former Lazard partner recalls going to board meetings with Harris in which mergers were contemplated. Harris would not have read the presentation book choke full of financial analysis his younger Lazard partner had put together. He simply comported himself like a member of the board, asked questions that a director would ask, and then with a flourish bless the transaction.[20]

Perhaps only a figure such as Harris could get away with such behavior. Chief executives relied on him to tell them how to put a merger together. He was the trusted go-between who had the confidence of both sides and ensured neither would perhaps feel aggrieved in a deal. Harris was a generalist, like Rohatyn. Their pioneering reputations were such that no one demanded the industry expertise lesser merger bankers were increasingly expected to provide.[21]

Information was a scarce commodity in the 1970s and 1980s. There were very few live news feeds. Sophisticated financial analysis was not available to everyone via the Internet. Bankers such as Rohatyn and Harris had power because they had information that was not available to their rivals or the public. Now publicly listed companies are under increased regulatory scrutiny. They are constantly under pressure to disclose more information and hold conference calls with analysts and investors. Remarks of a chief executive at a conference are disclosed on a company's Web page. There is no information arbitrage as in Rohatyn and Harris' day.

Becoming a confidant to a chief executive in the mold of Harris or Rohatyn is now immeasurably more difficult for a banker. Chief executives are more suspicious of bankers. Many prefer to keep merger decisions in-house and not to rely so much on a banker except to give a fairness opinion on a transaction. The free-for-all days which characterized Lazard in the days of Rohatyn and Harris are long gone.

"I once heard Andre Meyer or Michel (David-Weill) described as the Indian tribe leader who sends the braves out each day to go hunting and see what they could bring back," said Harris summing up Lazard's business strategy.[22]

On the surface Lazard's way of business seemed to suit Harris perfectly. In practice he clashed with Rohatyn who undermined Harris by taking his long-held clients or exaggerating his role in high-profile assignments.

"Most of the time at Lazard was good," said Harris. "Felix was a great salesman. I thought Felix and I working together on stuff was something we could leverage. We did for quite a while. We developed a lot of business by selling ourselves to clients, making a lot of calls together. Eventually, with Felix you realize it's a one-way working relationship. The river flowed one way, which never bothered me because for me the key was to get things done."[23]

Rohatyn shunted aside Harris, a traditional adviser to fellow Bronx native Marty Davis, in advising Davis on the sale of Paramount.[24] In the auction of RJR Nabisco, Harris secured Lazard's assignment to advise RJR's board on the basis of his long relationship with chief executive Ross Johnson. Dillon Read's Fritz Hobbs, who also advised the RJR board, said Harris was plainly the main Lazard banker, notwithstanding Rohatyn's presence on the deal.[25]

Lazard "brought Felix in because Felix wasn't missing this deal," recalled Fritz Hobbs. "Ira was the guy who did it all. Felix didn't do shit."[26]

After the 1992 election of Bill Clinton as the first Democratic president in 12 years, Rohatyn expected a high-profile position in the White House, even a cabinet position after years of faithful service to the party. But he was ignored by Clinton for a cabinet post. Some in the New York media thought Rohatyn's days as a star banker were almost over. It was time for a new generation of deal makers. The press hailed Steven Rattner, an up-and-coming Lazard banker, as one of Wall Street's brightest lights.[27]

Rattner was the subject of a glowing profile in the pages of *Vanity Fair* in January 1994. Rattner was close to the Clintons, a noted Democratic party fund-raiser who also knew how to court the press. He was a former *New York Times* reporter and friend of the newspaper's publisher, Arthur Sulzberger Jr. In short, as *New York* magazine writer Suzanna Andrews said, "a younger, yuppie version of Rohatyn."[28]

Rohatyn exploded with jealousy. In an interview with Andrews, he called Rattner "monomaniacal" and accused him of "social climbing." Andrews's interview with Rohatyn, which was originally intended to gather views on public relations man Gershon Kekst, instead became an expose on the Rohatyn-Rattner rift. "Felix Loses It," screamed the March 1996 cover of *New York* magazine. Andrews noted Rohatyn's unhappiness at Lazard and the general discontent many partners had with David-Weill's leadership.[29]

A year later, Rohatyn retired from Lazard after nearly 40 years at the firm. He accepted Clinton's offer to be U.S. ambassador to France. Over the intervening years, the firm would lose its most senior bankers. Harris left in 1998. Gerald Rosenfeld, Kendrick Wilson, Bob Lovejoy, Rattner, and Luis Rinaldini also departed.[30] David-Weill's divide-and-rule management style had exerted a toll on the firm.

"The worst thing in the world is when you believe in your own baloney," Harris said years later reflecting on his Lazard days. "The truth was Lazard was never any different than anyone else. We all put our pants on one leg at a time. Michel didn't understand the panache, the perception of Lazard, was that we were different was the key thing. We weren't really that different. When you start to believe this you have trouble. Unfortunately he had some people around him telling him how great he was."[31]

■   ■   ■

First Boston had a renaissance on Wall Street in the 1980s under George Shinn. Shinn decided to go and get a PhD at Columbia University and turned the firm over to Peter Buchanan. He didn't have the vision of Shinn, and he didn't like Bruce Wasserstein.[32]

Bill Lambert, Jim Maher, and Wasserstein had discussions in 1987 with Michel David-Weill and Felix Rohatyn about joining Lazard. In the end, they pulled back. The three thought it was one person's firm, David-Weill's, rather than a true partnership.[33] Buchanan got wind of the discussion and called Joe Perella up. He said he was 90 percent sure Wasserstein was going to leave First Boston.[34]

"I went and saw Bruce," recalled Perella. "I said, 'Bruce, what the fuck is going on?' He said, 'Well, you and I are generating over 50 percent of the profits of the firm and we don't have a seat at the table. We're on the management committee, but basically they don't ask us anything. They pat us on the head and say, "Keep making money." In the meantime, they periodically take these $25 million, $50 million hits on the trading floor for lack of discipline. It's very frustrating.'"[35]

Wasserstein wanted to run a Wall Street firm. Perella didn't have that aspiration. He was never the threat to First Boston's management that Wasserstein was. Wasserstein wanted a path that would lead to running

First Boston one day. Buchanan decided he wasn't going to give what Wasserstein wanted. He began to plot Wasserstein's dismissal.[36]

"I went in and saw them and said, 'I know what you guys are up to, and if you fire any bullets at Bruce, they go through me,'" recalled Perella. "'If you shoot him, I'm quitting. I hired Bruce, I discovered him, I decided to marry him, and I'll decide if we're going to get a divorce, not you.' 'Why are you doing this?' Buchanan said. 'I thought you were one of us.' I said, 'We built this business together. What you are talking about is very destabilizing. People always looked at us as a team. I'm not about to have Bruce go off and go into competition with us at another firm. If you shoot him, the bullet goes through me.'"[37]

There was a rapprochement of sorts between Buchanan and Wasserstein and Perella negotiated by Jim Maher. Buchanan promised to study all of First Boston's businesses. The reports the merger department got back was that the best parts were being left on the cutting room floor.[38]

In January 1988, Perella was in Japan. Buchanan sent out a First Boston "broadcast" or memorandum on yellow paper, so it would stick out amongst all the intracompany mail. It said to all employees: "We're pleased to report that the strategic review of all First Boston's businesses are complete. The conclusion reached is that no changes are necessary." Perella and Wasserstein resigned February 2, 1988.[39] Within 18 months, First Boston imploded. The firm wiped out its capital in a bad bridge loan and was taken over by Credit Suisse. Perella and Wasserstein made their first fortunes by tendering their shares to Credit Suisse. Each had millions of dollars' worth of First Boston stock.[40]

Wasserstein and Perella started their eponymous firm on the day they resigned by asking Marty Lipton for help. They went to Wachtell's offices and an exodus followed them from First Boston. Perella and Wasserstein had a conference room and after a week had 25 people there. Wachtell's phone system was crashing every day because the merger bankers were busy dialing their clients and overloading the law firm's switchboard. Wachtell asked the former First Boston bankers to find office space.[41]

That year, American Express had bought E. F. Hutton and had fired a lot of people. One of Wasserstein's and Perella's bankers got wind that an entire investment banking floor of a building on West 52nd Street was empty. He went over to discover that all the telephones worked and the Quotrons were on. Only the art work had been removed. Perella called Shearson Lehman Hutton chairman Peter Cohen and rented the space.[42]

Wasserstein Perella earned fees its first month courtesy of Henry Kravis, who gave the firm the Tropicana sale. Perella sold 20 percent of the firm to Nomura in the first six months for $100 million and set up a merger joint venture. Some high-yield bond sales and traders from Salomon Brothers joined the firm. The firm also set up a mezzanine fund to finance its buyout fund. At the end of 1988, tiny Wasserstein Perella was ranked number two in global mergers after advising Kohlberg Kravis Roberts on its acquisition of RJR Nabisco. It was, as Perella recalled, "a jet-propelled start."[43]

■   ■   ■

Eric Gleacher and Steve Waters also advised KKR on the RJR buyout. Both men were again working together at Morgan Stanley. For Waters, being on the winning side on RJR was sweet revenge. He had been ousted as co-head of mergers at Shearson Lehman Hutton by his partners Tom Hill and Peter Cohen, who advised Ross Johnson's management group, which lost the RJR deal to KKR.[44]

In the RJR battle, Waters was asked by Henry Kravis to tell Shearson, the adviser to the management buyout proposal, that KKR was prepared to split the deal with Ross Johnson's team at $90 a share. "The word came back from Peter Cohen and Tom Hill, 'This is our deal.' Tell Henry to go fuck himself," recalled Waters. "So I called Jim Robinson of American Express, per Henry's request, and said, 'I'm not sure you want me to repeat that. I was told that's up to you, but that's the message.'"[45]

Waters and Hill ran Shearson's merger department from 1985 to 1988 and guided the firm to the top of the league table in mergers. Strangely, Cohen and Hill weren't happy. Cohen wasn't comfortable with ex–Lehman Brothers bankers such as Waters. Hill wanted to run the department by himself. He disparaged Waters at management meetings. When Waters questioned Cohen's bonus decisions, he found his position had become untenable and resigned.[46]

Waters got 10 job offers, including 2 from Morgan Stanley. Joe Fogg ran one merger effort at the firm. Eric Gleacher ran the official merger department. Waters asked Bob Greenhill, the head of investment banking, what he should do. Greenhill told him to work for Gleacher.[47]

In January 1990, Gleacher quit to found his own firm. His parting with Morgan Stanley was not amicable. Waters, who was appointed co-head of the merger department at Morgan Stanley with Bruce Fiedorek, battled with Gleacher who wanted to poach some Morgan Stanley bankers to work at his firm. Gleacher and Waters have had little contact since.[48]

■ ■ ■

Throughout the 1980s, Greenhill continued to pursue deals. Morgan Stanley had an aerospace analyst who went and saw Jeff Williams, who was running the transaction business development group. He told Williams there was a company out on the West Coast called Hughes Aircraft, which didn't make aircrafts. It made satellites, rockets, and weapons. The company was owned by the Howard Hughes Medical Trust after the death of its eccentric billionaire founder. The aerospace analyst believed Hughes Aircraft was going to be brought up for sale.[49]

Together with a banker, the aerospace analyst found Howard Hughes Medical Institute financials after discovering that as a tax-exempt charter charity in Delaware, it had to file appraisals. Irv Shapiro, who was in the process of retiring as chairman of DuPont, was going to be on the board of Howard Hughes Medical Institute. Shapiro was a very good friend of Morgan Stanley. He was a very close friend of Frank Petito, Greenhill's mentor, and Joe Flom, who was Shaprio's Harvard Law School classmate and would hire him as a Skadden partner.[50]

Greenhill and Jeff Williams took the train to Willmington, Delaware to see Shapiro. They sat down with Shapiro in his new Skadden office. Greenhill gave Shapiro the Morgan Stanley book on the Howard Hughes Medical Trust. A few weeks later, the institute asked various investment banks to present their plans to sell the trust. In the presentation by various investment banks, Greenhill, with his customary flair, made the presentation to the medical trustees by himself. Morgan Stanley was hired and sold Hughes Aircraft to General Motors.[51]

In the 1980s, Greenhill began flying lessons. He purchased a plane and outfitted the interior in "Morgan Stanley blue." One partner remembers Greenhill flying his plane into Chicago's Meigs Field on the waterfront of downtown Chicago. As he approached the field, Greenhill whipped around Sears Tower.

"We were so close, one could see the color of the ties of guys in the windows," one former Morgan Stanley managing director recalled.[52] Once flying his plane with a couple of colleagues to see Data General's chief executive, Greenhill asked the Data General CEO to send along a helicopter to pick him up. During the helicopter ride to the company's headquarters, Greenhill asked the helicopter pilot how to fly the machine. After the business meeting Greenhill asked the helicopter pilot if he could fly the helicopter. Taken to a deserted field, Greenhill seized the controls and maneuvered the helicopter off the ground. Then the tail of the machine began to dip close to the ground and the helicopter nose pointed skyward.[53]

"I thought we were going to die," said Carter McClelland, a Morgan Stanley banker trapped in the back with Jeff Williams.[54] Greenhill righted the helicopter with assistance from the pilot and flew it up and down the field.

His vacations were equally adventuresome. Greenhill took his family on monthlong canoe trips in isolated parts of Canada. Once dropped by a biplane on a river north of the Arctic Circle with no guide, the Greenhills spent weeks paddling to the Arctic Ocean. Greenhill's son, Robert Jr., recalled: "It was raining, when you put your tent up it was raining, when you took it down it was raining, you ate in the rain. It was freezing."[55] The conditions elicited little sympathy from his father. "Well, you can sit out here in the rain, or you can paddle and get to camp," Bob Greenhill told his children.[56]

In Morgan Stanley politics, Greenhill was less successful in bending the firm to his will. After Parker Gilbert retired as Morgan Stanley chairman, Richard Fisher became chairman and demoted Greenhill from president and appointed his protégé John Mack in his place.[57] It was a huge blow to Greenhill personally. He had desperately wanted to run Morgan Stanley after Parker Gilbert retired and hoped when Fisher left the firm he would get his chance. If Greenhill was disappointed, few knew. He showed close friends no emotion over the decision. He had a defense mechanism. When things didn't go his way, Greenhill just focused on what was next, not what happened yesterday.[58]

Years later, Greenhill said: "I'd like to have run Morgan Stanley. Was it a smart thing to do? Not necessarily. I'm not the greatest person focusing on details, budgets, and that sort of thing."[59]

More humiliation for Greenhill was to follow. Fisher and other members of the management committee met while Greenhill was away on a business trip. Fisher decided that Greenhill should be axed from the management committee. It was, as one former managing director at the firm said, a "palace coup."[60]

"Greenhill was not a manager. No patience," Fisher said years later.[61] Greenhill wasn't going to stand for being ousted in such a manner. He talked with friends, including Sandy Weill about starting a boutique merger advisory firm. Weill instead coaxed him to join Smith Barney Shearson as its chairman.[62]

Greenhill timed his departure from Morgan Stanley so that it created the most impact within the firm and in the press. He waited until June 1993, when John Mack was traveling in Asia and Richard Fisher was in Switzerland. Fisher's hotel switchboard shut down in the evening, and Mack was in the air when Greenhill resigned. He had the movers come in and take out his beloved rolltop desk as well as all of his corporate files and Rolodex.[63] Greenhill then marched across town and held a news conference, with Sandy Weill by his side. In his trademark bright yellow suspenders, he vowed to make Smith Barney the "firm of tomorrow."[64] He began recruiting 21 of his former Morgan Stanley colleagues.

"He was the largest, or one of the largest individual shareholders of Morgan Stanley, a huge rainmaker in terms of the business, and came to personify the firm in terms of its image on Wall Street and the corporate community," recalled Bruce Fiedorek, who was then co-head of mergers at the firm with Steve Waters. "When he left, it was shocking."[65]

Greenhill and Joe Flom remained close. They sometimes holidayed together. Claire Flom recalled a trip made to a West Texas ranch owned by a friend of the Greenhills.

"I always travel with a Scrabble set. We had time one morning, so I pulled it out," recalled Claire. "I played a game with Joe. Greenhill was hovering over the table. I won. That offended Greenhill. He tries, but he doesn't really think that women are in the same league as men. I played him and I won. Our host was standing there bug-eyed, and I said, 'Why don't I play the two of you?' and I beat them both. That was very good for them. It's a sobering thing. You may be king of the hill, but it doesn't always make you the winner."[66]

Chapter 17

New Horizons

In 1990, John Weinberg retired as Goldman Sachs's senior partner. Since 1976, he had run the firm first with John Whitehead and then by himself. An ex-Marine, he was a touchstone for many at Goldman Sachs. At the end of every business year, Weinberg would say to his troops: "You guys that are feeling good, don't feel so good. You guys that are feeling bad, don't feel so bad."[1] He kept people centered from an emotional and philosophical point of view and made it feel like a family firm, said one former Goldman Sachs banker, while his former partner Whitehead made it feel like a professionally managed firm.[2]

Steve Friedman and Bob Rubin became co–senior partners after Weinberg's retirement. Like Whitehead and Weinberg's partnership, they felt they were "kindred sprits" in their vision of the firm.[3]

Morgan Stanley had been a publicly traded investment bank for several years. Before he retired, John Weinberg had asked Friedman and Rubin to examine whether Goldman Sachs should go public, the first time the firm's partnership had formally entertained such a suggestion. Friedman and Rubin argued in favor of the firm's selling stock. It was expanding its trading operations, and senior partners such as Weinberg were about to leave, pulling a lot of capital from the firm. Others among the 50-member partnership weren't so sure and voiced their opposition to going public.[4] "At that point, it may have been inevitable, but many of us didn't feel that psychologically the firm was ready for it," recalled Geoff Boisi.[5]

Friedman and Rubin, who were in favor of Goldman Sachs selling stock to the public to shore up the firm's capital base, were disappointed. Boisi's and Friedman's once-close relationship soured. Once thought a candidate to become senior partner at the firm, Boisi shocked his fellow partners by deciding to retire at the end of 1991 at the ripe old age of 42. After 22 years of 18-hour days, he felt he needed a break from Wall Street. The demands of work had taken a toll on Boisi's family life.[6]

In 1993, Boisi reentered Wall Street by forming a boutique merger advisory firm, the Beacon Group, with former Goldman Sachs partners. Beacon would advise on the merger of Chase Manhattan Bank and J. P. Morgan, and Schroders' sale of its investment bank to Citigroup. Boisi would sell Beacon to J. P. Morgan for more than $500 million and make more money from the sale, about a fifth of the proceeds, than he did during his 20-year career at Goldman Sachs. Like his father, Boisi was appointed a J. P. Morgan vice chairman and served on the company's management committee.[7]

It was not a happy two and a half years, however, for Boisi at J. P. Morgan. Charged with creating a Goldman Sachs–like investment bank at J. P. Morgan bore the brunt of animosity of firings in the wake of the collapse in markets and an economic recession that followed the September 11, 2001, terrorist attacks. J. P. Morgan and its investment bank were also caught up in the scandals of Enron and WorldCom, where the bank had lent money to the bankrupt companies before Boisi's arrival. Bill Harrison, J. P. Morgan's chairman, retreated from his earlier collegiality and support. Boisi departed and formed another boutique firm, Roundtable.[8]

In 1992, Robert Rubin left Goldman Sachs to join Bill Clinton's administration. Some of Steve Friedman's partners advised him to appoint one or two others to help manage the firm. Friedman, the banker, would handle client relations, and others would handle the trading side.[9]

"Friedman had tremendous confidence in his own abilities, maybe to a fault," recalled a former Goldman Sachs partner. "I had a conversation with him when he took over the firm after Rubin left when I warned him of the dangers of trying to do it all himself. It wasn't my own insights but a message from a variety of people at the firm who thought the job of running the entity was getting to be too much for one. I suggested to him that he appoint several vice chairmen to help take some of the load off his shoulders as well as avoid a political battle in terms of succession."[10]

Friedman ignored the suggestion. Doctors diagnosed the Goldman Sachs senior partner as having an irregular heartbeat. His health had suffered after 28 years at Goldman Sachs.[11]

"What you don't want to do is fly internationally, get jet lag, and stimulate yourself with caffeine, all of which I was doing," said Friedman. "You were always very tired, always jet lagged, and overdosing with coffee. It was pretty common for people to say, 'What's wrong with you? You look green.'"[12]

Friedman decided to retire. "I set the retirement in motion in 1994, which was a lousy year," recalled Friedman. "The last quarter, after I told the management committee to work out the succession, was really the bad quarter, with the Russian default and bond market slump. The last three months of that year I spent getting diagnosed, sorting out the right medication."[13]

Friedman's children, like many on Wall Street, had paid a price for their father's singular focus on his career. At one wedding anniversary, Friedman's children performed skits for their parents. One was entitled "Great Parenting Moments from Mom," which roasted Barbara Friedman. Then there was a skit on "Great Parenting Moments from Dad." It consisted of a long silence.[14]

Friedman was appointed George Bush's chief economic adviser in 2002. He resigned after two years and later rejoin Goldman Sachs as a member of its board.[15]

■ ■ ■

At Wasserstein Perella in the early 1990s, there was also a raft of resignations and internal turmoil. Bruce Wasserstein had become more independent of Joe Perella and wanted to make more decisions on his own. The two founders talked less and made decisions independently, as opposed to together.[16]

Seeking a chief financial officer, Perella interviewed a candidate. "After seeing Joe, I'm convinced this is a great job and the management team has signed off on this. I walk into Bruce's office after seeing Perella, and he says, 'I don't care what he said, we really do need you,'" the job candidate recalled.[17]

Wasserstein Perella had invested in British retailer Isosceles, which went bankrupt and put a taint on the firm's name. An economic recession at the beginning of the 1990s had caused the merger cycle to collapse, along with some of Wasserstein's reputation.[18] In 1989, *Forbes* put Wasserstein on its cover with a nickname: "Bid-'em-up Bruce."

In 1988, Wasserstein had engineered the highly leveraged takeover of Federated Department Stores and Allied Stores by Robert Campeau. The retailer couldn't cope with the debt on its balance sheet and filed for bankruptcy. Pete Peterson was a Federated board member. He was also chairman of Blackstone, which had bid to buy Federated. Blackstone dropped to $58 a share.[19]

"In came Bruce, Drexel, and high rollers wanting to do a deal," recalled Peterson. "They were talking about paying a huge premium at $74.50. A sizeable portion of it was this paper. I said, 'If we're backing out of this thing at $58 and this bid is $74.50, this paper they are now promoting as being tremendously valuable just intuitively doesn't make much sense.' We said, 'If that paper is such a great buy, why don't you sell it to someone who appreciates it? I'll be goddamned—they did it and paid in cash. They were bankrupt within months.'"[20]

In July 1993, Perella shook hands with Wasserstein and said he would leave. They settled on a September 1 departure date.[21]

"I said to myself, 'I've been with Bruce 16 years. I think it's time for me to be on my own,'" recalled Perella. "I didn't want to fight with him over control of the firm. Neither one of us had enough shares to control the situation. Some marriages last forever. Some end in divorce. We had a civilized divorce. We didn't raise our voices. We didn't fight."[22]

Reflecting on their relationship years later, Perella said of Wasserstein and himself: "One was a lawyer, the other was an accountant. One was tall and thin, and the other was shorter and plumper. One was Italian and the other was Jewish. One went to Michigan, one went to Lehigh, both went to Harvard Business School. Bruce was a Baker Scholar, Joe wasn't. Bruce had a higher IQ, Joe had better people skills. At a moment in time, they formed a partnership that gave the world what they needed and wanted in that business. It was very effective. The odd couple that made it work for 16 years. They were complementary. We agreed on a lot of things, most importantly who had talent and who didn't. The thing that we differed the most in was our personalities. Joe was more an outgoing guy and Bruce was shy. Joe was more of an emoter. Bruce was more reserved."[23]

Bruce Fiedorek was in a car with Morgan Stanley chairman Richard Fisher when he got a call from Skadden partner Peter Atkins. Atkins called to say Perella was going to announce he was leaving Wasserstein Perella.[24]

"I wasn't 100 percent sure it was the best personality fit, but I thought there was a decent chance it was," recalled Fiedorek. "I told Fisher about the call from Atkins, and I thought it was really important that Morgan Stanley at least thought about hiring Joe. Joe then went through the lengthy mating dance with most of Wall Street over two months, which I'm sure he really enjoyed. He had offers from a lot of people but came to Morgan Stanley."[25]

Richard Fisher and John Mack would appoint Perella head of corporate finance. Morgan Stanley's investment bankers had suffered from a lack of charismatic leadership following Bob Greenhill's resignation. Perella sought to make the firm's bankers sell their skills and look for new business. He traveled the world developing the firm's relationships. He also sought to improve Morgan Stanley's internal communication. "I thought internal communications sucked there," recalled Perella. "They had a very protective mentality. It was 'my client information.' You've got to reach a level of communication at a firm in order to exploit the power of the brain bank."[26]

At Wasserstein Perella there was an exodus of bankers who had reached prominence under the two founders. Gary Parr and Ray McGuire departed and would end up together with Perella at Morgan Stanley. Chuck Ward went back to his old firm that was now CS First Boston. There was a feeling that Wasserstein Perella was sinking, according to one who worked there.[27] Wasserstein hired Fred Seegal, the former co-head of corporate finance of Salomon Brothers, to help right the ship as president. Seegal's hiring bolstered the firm's internal optimism as he enjoyed a reputation as a deal maker.[28]

But Seegal and Wasserstein clashed. Seegal was never part of Wasserstein's inner circle, which consisted of Robert Pruzman and Michael Biondi. When the firm had trouble meeting payroll, Wasserstein tried to change Seegal's contract. It was watertight, and Seegal would make a lot of money when the firm was sold.[29]

By 1995, the firm was giving equity out to employees in lieu of salaries because the firm was in a precarious state. Bill Lambert, who sometimes came to work in torn jeans and a sweater two or three days a week, helped keep the firm afloat with deals from a cadre of loyal chief executives. Robert Pruzan, considered by many at Wasserstein Perella as one of its brightest employees, would sometimes turn up at the office at 2 AM unannounced to check that analysts and associates were working.[30]

Wasserstein seemed out of touch speaking with chief executives, telling them in meetings they had to sign confidentiality agreements when discussing potential acquisitions. He still courted the press, lavishing time on reporters he trusted, ensuring he got newsprint while the firm struggled during a downturn.[31]

In the 1970s and 1980s, bankers brimming with chutzpah, such as Wasserstein, forced their way into boardrooms and chief executive suites and steamrolled them into doing deals. Wasserstein and his competitors were the stars, sucking all the oxygen in the room toward them. By the 1990s, chief executives knew how to do deals and wanted a banker who could function more as a quiet therapist, not a commando out front leading the way. Wasserstein didn't fit the new mold.

"Bruce wasn't really running the firm [Wasserstein Perella]," said a former Wasserstein Perella banker. "He is a chess player, Machiavellian with people, motivated by glory and money. He wants to be the star in the room, but times changed in the 1990s and CEOs became the stars. Bruce could not handle that."[32]

■   ■   ■

Bob Greenhill had run into troubles at Smith Barney. Sandy Weill "swallowed hard and went along" with Greenhill's insistence of a seven-year

deal plus a share of the firm's profits as well as a $20 million sign-
ing bonus in stock. Greenhill's bankers that he recruited from Morgan
Stanley were similarly well compensated, causing friction within Smith
Barney. At first, Greenhill had some notable successes, including advising Viacom on its acquisition of Paramount. But he was also frustrating
others at Smith Barney, as he did at Morgan Stanley. Greenhill was on the
road or in the air flying his plane, pursuing deals rather than managing
the 10,500 brokers at Smith Barney.[33]

Weill made Jamie Dimon Smith Barney's chief operating officer under Greenhill to manage the investment bank, given Greenhill's frequent
business trips. Dimon criticized Greenhill at management meetings and
complained about the banker to Weill. Greenhill and his wife in turn,
in private dinners with Weill and his wife, let vent their bitterness at
Dimon's insults. At one, Gayle Greenhill broke down in a "cathartic
outburst."[34]

Greenhill resigned in January 1996, after it was clear Weill would
not fire Dimon. His watertight contract enabled him to claim $200
million.[35] Before the end of the month, he had set up his own firm,
Greenhill & Company, on Park Avenue, with a driver and a secretary.[36]

Like Steve Schwarzman and Pete Peterson at Blackstone, and Bruce
Wasserstein and Joe Perella at Wasserstein Perella, Greenhill had been
inspired to establish his own firm by the success of James Wolfensohn's
Wolfensohn & Company, which concentrated on just giving merger
advice.

Wolfensohn's firm never had more than 100 employees, yet attracted
such heavyweights as Greenhill's mentor at Morgan Stanley, Frank Petito,
who as chairman was succeeded by former Federal Reserve chairman
Paul Volcker. The firm's clients included DuPont, Chase Manhattan
Bank, Daimler Benz, and BHP, all of whom paid an annual fee of
$250,000 retainer. Wolfensohn charged a success fee based on transac-
tions. It advised Hong Kong and Shanghai Bank's acquisition of Midland
Bank and the *New York Times* purchase of the *Boston Globe*. In the last year
of its decade-and-a-half existence, Wolfensohn advised on $60 billion of
takeovers.[37]

"We would recommend against more things than we would recommend for," recalled Wolfensohn. "Not as a matter of principal, but
because we were independent. Seventy percent of our business was

reviewing stuff that came in from others. Five out of six times we would say no."[38]

Greenhill began recruiting former Morgan Stanley bankers such as Tim George and Scott Bok to his firm, as well as established British bankers such as Simon Borrows and James Lupton. Borrows first met Greenhill in 1997 when Greenhill had advised ING on its purchase of U.S. brokerage Furman Selz from Robertson Stephens.[39]

At the celebration dinner, ING chairman Aad Jacobs said that ING would like to buy a stake in Greenhill & Company for an outpost in New York. "Bob said the firm was not for sale but 'we would like Simon to open our London office,'" recalled Borrows.[40]

On Easter 1998, Borrows resigned from ING after reading in the *Financial Times* that the firm would now concentrate on advising small and medium-size companies instead of advising on large takeovers, which had been Borrows's business. He went to see Aad Jacobs. "It was good of you to advise me through the FT about our change in strategy. I quit," recalled Borrows.[41]

"I went to my house in the country," said Borrows. "Bob phoned and said, 'I want to fly over and meet you to discuss what you do next. See you at Claridge's Easter Monday at 8 PM.'"[42]

Greenhill thrived at his boutique because it seemed that working in a small place without the bureaucratic infighting and the administrative responsibilities of managing thousands of employees suited him. He could get on and do what he most liked—doing deals. He had successfully maintained a vast array of relationships through the years. Greenhill, like Jim Wolfensohn, perfected the art of mixing business and pleasure. Tennis camps and golf outings were augmented by a personal concern in the welfare of the CEO's children. Sometimes Greenhill dispatched his lieutenants to MBA programs to argue for the admission of a child of a chief executive.[43]

Greenhill was a consistent presence.

"People had ups and downs, and during the downs one of the first calls you will have is from Bob Greenhill," said his friend Bruce Schnitzer.[44]

■ ■ ■

Michel David-Weill turned to Bruce Wasserstein to revive Lazard. In 2000, Wasserstein had convinced Dresdner Bank to pay $1.6 billion for Wasserstein Perella. Wasserstein made $600 million on the sale. The price paid by Dresdner was considered outrageous by Wasserstein Perella's staff. At the time of the sale, Wasserstein was again having trouble meeting payroll at his firm.[45] "That's what you call a great deal, having an amazing sense of timing, a sense of leverage, feeling the need in the other party and just pushing it to advantage," said one Wasserstein admirer.[46]

In the Credit Lyonnais building on 6th Avenue, Wasserstein Perella had spent millions on its offices, lining them in wood and marble. Every desk was oak. One in the boardroom was 20 feet long, made of a single piece of wood. Such luxury may have helped convince Dresdner the firm was more valuable than it really was.[47]

Wasserstein's tenure at Dresdner Kleinwort Wasserstein lasted less than a year. He fled to Lazard where Wasserstein extracted an agreement from David-Weill, with whom he had been in talks for months, that he alone would run Lazard. "The key to that whole negotiation was they couldn't fire him for five years," said a Lazard banker. "He had five years to get something done, and Michel couldn't chop his knees off."[48]

Wasserstein set about gathering a loyal coterie of bankers who had worked for him in the past. They included Gary Parr, Chuck Ward, Michael Biondi, and Jeff Rosen. Then he set about dismantling David-Weill's hold over the firm. Lazard's nonworking partners, including David-Weill's family, owned 36 percent of the firm. The non-working partners, even if they didn't own a majority stake in Lazard, effectively controlled it and exercised their power through David-Weill. Wasserstein sought to take control of the firm by buying out David-Weill and the non-working partners.[49]

In the summer of 2004, Wasserstein gathered together a group at his East Hampton home and outlined his plan to wrest Lazard from David-Weill's control. He would take the firm public and use the proceeds to buy out David-Weill and other shareholders. "We all looked and said, 'You're fuckin' crazy, Bruce; you're never going to take this public," recalled one.[50] The next year, Lazard did go public. Wasserstein had to push the leverage of the firm as high as it would go in order to buy out David-Weill, pay off the non-working partners, and secure the most valuable pieces of the firm, the merger and asset management business, as the basis of the new Lazard.[51] After a hiccup in the stock price of Lazard within the first few weeks of trading when the shares fell below their IPO price, Lazard's stock climbed, helped by the frenzied merger activity of 2005, 2006, and 2007, which swelled the firm's coffers. As with the sale of Wasserstein Perella to Dresdner, Wasserstein's timing was impeccable. The Lazard IPO helped him reclaim some of his lost mystique. Wachtell partner Adam Chinn who helped plan the Lazard IPO coined a phrase, "don't bet against Bruce."

"Bruce has an uncanny ability to demand more out of people than they can possibly provide, and get it," said Chinn. "He's a great motivator of people. You have to rely on other people because you can't get everything done yourself. Bruce is better at that than anyone I've ever met."[52]

■   ■   ■

Wasserstein may not have been able to take Lazard public if it weren't for Bob Greenhill. A year earlier than Lazard, Greenhill & Company had sold stock, the first U.S. investment bank since Goldman Sachs to go public. It would inspire not only Lazard to go public but Roger Altman's Evercore Partners, Thom Weisel's Thomas Weisel Partners, and Steve Schwarzman's Blackstone.

Before filing its prospectus with its name, "Greenhill & Company," in green, lawyers had unsuccessfully lobbied for a clause among the "risk factors" section. The lawyers wanted a paragraph on what effect an unexpected death of the firm's founder would have on business. Greenhill himself managed to dissuade the lawyers from inserting such a paragraph.[53]

Greenhill & Company had won renown in 1999 for being picked by the Clinton administration to serve as its investment banking adviser on Microsoft. The government wanted Greenhill to draw up a plan of what should be done if Microsoft were broken up as a result of antitrust action. Bob Greenhill initially had refused. Clinton's antitrust czar, Joel Klein, called Greenhill to tell him he couldn't refuse the assignment. "Bob, you don't understand—I don't accept no," said Klein. Greenhill, in his audacious style, extracted a guarantee. If the government did something that went against the firm's advice, Greenhill could resign and state publicly why it did so. Klein agreed. "Consider yourself a client," said Greenhill.[54]

It was not the last time that Greenhill, a lifelong Republican, would get the Clinton White House to agree to his terms. Flying to do business one day, Greenhill got a call on his plane's satellite phone from Fred Green, president of Nantucket Golf Club. Greenhill had helped form, fund-raise, and plan the building of the course and clubhouse. Green told Greenhill the White House had called. President Clinton wanted to play 18 holes with a member, Senator John Kerry.[55]

Greenhill told Green if the president wanted to play golf at Nantucket Golf Club, the White House and Kerry had to agree to a number of conditions. No other vehicles were to be let past the front gates of the club except those of the president and his guests. Two tees were to be closed while Clinton was playing with Kerry, the one behind him and the one in front of him. Green was also to ask Kerry for a resignation letter. If anything untoward happened during the visit by Clinton, Kerry would agree to resign from the club.[56]

It was perhaps not surprising that when a group of eight former Morgan Stanley executives after Richard Fisher's memorial service in December 2004 sought to oust Philip Purcell, they turned to Greenhill. Joe Perella resigned from Morgan Stanley, disgusted with Purcell's management and his firing of anyone he saw as a threat to his position as chief executive.[57] No other Wall Street firm would act as an adviser to dissidents seeking to ouster a chief executive of an investment bank. The Morgan Stanley dissidents turned to Greenhill and his firm.

"They needed a practitioner who was going to advise them, but they didn't want to go outside the family," said Perella. "They went to a boutique who understood the Morgan Stanley culture who was one of them."[58] Greenhill's counsel that maintaining steady pressure on Purcell would lead to an erosion of his standing and authority at Morgan Stanley proved the right advice. Purcell resigned after just a few months, much to Greenhill's surprise, and was replaced by the man who helped oust Greenhill from the firm, John Mack.[59]

Perella followed in the wake of Greenhill and found his own boutique investment bank, Perella Weinberg Partners, with Goldman Sachs's former senior partner John Weinberg's nephew, Peter Weinberg, and his closest colleague at Morgan Stanley, Terry Meguid. At his offices in the

GM Building on Fifth Avenue and Central Park South, Perella seemed one day more concerned about the scratches his young associates were making to the firm's conference room tables with their aluminum take-out food containers than the demands of a start-up investment bank.[60]

Muttering that people have to respect their environment and the property of the firm, he rubbed and cursed at the scratches on the table. Perella said he didn't miss the use of the Morgan Stanley corporate jet for business. Still, flying the red-eye back from the West Coast on Jet Blue, Perella said, was trying to his lanky frame, now in its 60s.[61]

In Perella Weinberg's reception area hung a massive Jean-Michel Basquiat painting that clearly showed the artist's origins in graffiti. Perella paused before it, asked his guest if he liked it, and then excused himself to take a client call. He continued to work until midnight, heading back to his office after dinner to try and ensure that his firm could mirror the success of other boutiques such as Greenhill's.[62]

In October 2007, Bob Greenhill, then 71, relinquished the title of chief executive at his firm to his younger partners, the New York–based Scott Bok and the London-based Simon Borrows. Greenhill remained chairman. He showed few signs of slowing down. Greenhill's father, now in his 90s, plays golf with his son on Sea Island, Georgia, where Bob Greenhill has a home. Raymond Greenhill does 50 push-ups daily. Bob Greenhill arrives at work at 7 AM, and after checking his e-mails and phone messages, heads off for an hour of exercise with a personal trainer.[63]

On the walls of Greenhill & Company on Park Avenue, Gayle Greenhill has enlarged photographs of Captain Robert Scott and his four companions, who froze to death in March 1912 after reaching the South Pole. The negatives of the photographs that hang on Greenhill & Company's walls were found next to their frozen bodies. The photographs of Scott and his men betray not only their exhaustion but their sheer disappointment to find that Roald Amundsen's Norwegian expedition had beaten them by a month to become the first men to stand at the South Pole.[64]

"That's what I like about expeditions," said Greenhill, betraying no sympathy looking at the photographs of Scott's men. "They're uncertain." He turned and walked back into his office and sat down at his Wendell Castle desk. Behind Greenhill's desk is a large grainy black-and-white photograph of a lone man walking down a road.[65]

Notes

Introduction

1. Martin Lipton, "Merger Waves in the 19th, 20th and 21st Centuries," from "The Davies Lecture," Osgoode Hall Law School, York University, Canada, September 14, 2006.

Chapter 1

1. Much of the material of this chapter came from the author's taped interviews with leading characters in the book as well as others who were partners at Wall Street law firms or investment banks in the 1960s, 1970s, and 1980s.
2. The establishment of Morgan Stanley of offices at 2 Wall Street is from the firm's web site.
3. John Whitehead, *A Life in Leadership: From D-Day to Ground Zero* (New York: Basic Books, 2005), 75–77.
4. John Gutfreund, former Salomon Brothers Chairman, in a taped interview with the author in 2006.
5. Whitehead, *A Life in Leadership,* 72–73.
6. Ace Greenberg, former Bear Stearns chairman, in a taped interview with the author in 2007.
7. "House Divided," *Time,* September 16, 1935.

8. John Adams Morgan, Morgan Joseph chairman, in a taped interview with the author in 2005.

9. Former Morgan Stanley partners and managing directors told the author in taped interviews in 2007 about the protocol on securities offerings and fees.

10. Former Morgan Stanley partners and managing directors, 2007.

11. Richard Fisher, former Morgan Stanley chairman, in an interview with the author in 2004.

12. Former Morgan Stanley partners and managing directors, 2007.

13. Bob Baldwin, former Morgan Stanley chairman, in a telephone interview with the author in 2004.

14. John Adams Morgan, 2005.

15. Former Morgan Stanley partners, in taped interviews with the author in 2007.

16. Joel Cohen, Davis Polk former partner, in a taped interview with the author in 2007.

17. Harvey Miller, Weil Gotshal & Manges partner, in a taped interview with the author in 2007. Martin Ginsburg, Ruth Bader Ginsburg's husband, confirmed the accuracy of Miller's account in an e-mail to the author.

18. Unnamed partner at a law firm in a taped interview with the author in 2007.

19. Joel Cohen, former Davis Polk partner, in a taped interview with the author in 2007.

20. Bankers and lawyers active on Wall Street during the conglomerate era, in taped interviews with the author in 2007.

21. Bankers and lawyers active on Wall Street during the conglomerate era, 2007.

22. Warren Hellman, former Lehman Brothers partner, in a taped interview with the author in 2007.

23. Hellman, 2007.

24. Hellman, 2007.

25. Skadden partners in taped interviews with the author in 2007.

26. Arthur Fleischer, Fried, Frank, Harris, Shriver & Jacobson senior partner, in a taped interview with the author in 2007.

Chapter 2

1. Joe Flom, Skadden, Arps, Slate, Meagher & Flom partner; Claire Flom, wife of Joe Flom; and Marty Lipton, Wachtell, Lipton, Rosen & Katz partner, provided the bulk of the material including quotes, unless otherwise stated, in a series of taped interviews with the author in 2007.

2. Fin Fogg, of counsel at Skadden, in a taped interview with the author in 2007.

3. Morris Kramer, Skadden partner, in a taped interview with the author in 2007.

4. Arthur Fleischer, Fried, Frank senior partner, in a taped interview with the author in 2007.

5. Harvey Miller, Weil Gotshal partner, in a taped interview with the author in 2007.

6. Miller, 2007.

7. Miller, 2007.

8. Miller, 2007.

9. Miller, 2007.

Chapter 3

1. Ira Harris, former Salomon Brothers partner, in taped interviews with the author in 2007.

2. Billy Salomon, former Salomon Brothers managing partner, in a telephone interview with the author in 2007.

3. "The Success of Salomon," *Time,* August 3, 1970.

4. James Wolfensohn, former Salomon Brothers partner, in a taped interview with the author in 2007.

5. Salomon, 2007.

6. Ned Jannotta, William Blair chairman, in a taped interview with the author in 2007.

7. Jannotta, 2007.

8. Bob Lovejoy, former Lazard partner, in a taped interview with the author in 2007.

9. Sandy Robertson, founder of Robertson Stephens, in a taped interview with the author in 2007.

10. "A Discussion about the Life of Felix Rohatyn," *Charlie Rose* television show, December 21, 2000; Cary Reich, *Financier: The Biography of Andre Meyer* (New York: William Morrow), 218.

11. Bob Herbert, "Acts of Quiet Courage," *New York Times,* April 11, 2005.

12. Reich, *Financier,* pp. 218, 219.

13. Ibid., 219.

14. From Lazard's Web site (www.lazard.com).

15. Former Lazard partner who worked with Pierre David-Weill and Andre Meyer, in a taped interview with the author in 2007.

16. Former Lazard partner who worked with Pierre David-Weill and Andre Meyer, 2007.

17. Reich, *Financier,* pp. 89–91, 245–270.

18. Former Lazard partner who worked with Andre Meyer, in a taped interview with the author in 2007.

19. New York lawyer, in a taped interview with the author in 2007.

20. Former Lazard partner who worked with Meyer and Rohatyn, in a taped interview with author in 2007.

21. "A Discussion about the Life of Felix Rohatyn," 2000.

22. Arthur Fleischer, Fried, Frank senior partner, in a taped interview with the author in 2007.

23. Former Lazard partner, in a taped interview with the author in 2007.

24. Former Lazard partner, 2007.

25. "A Discussion about the Life of Felix Rohatyn," 2000.

26. J. Tomilson Hill, former First Boston merger banker, in a telephone interview with the author in 2006.

Chapter 4

1. Former Goldman Sachs partners Steve Friedman, John Whitehead, Geoff Boisi, and Robert Rubin provided the biographical and other material including quotes in a series of taped interviews with the author in 2007. Whitehead's autobiography, *A Life in Leadership: From D-Day to Ground Zero* (New York: Basic Books, 2005), pp. 75–135, was also very helpful. Rubin's autobiography, *In an Uncertain World* (New York: Random House, 2003) pp. 66–103 was likewise helpful.

Chapter 5

1. Richard Fisher, former Morgan Stanley chairman, in an interview with the author in 2004.

2. Bob Baldwin, former Morgan Stanley chairman, in a telephone interview with the author in 2004.

3. Former Morgan Stanley partner in an interview with author in 2007.

4. Fred Whittemore, former Morgan Stanley partner, in a taped interview with the author in 2007.

5. Bob Greenhill, former Morgan Stanley partner; Gayle Greenhill, Bob Greenhill's wife; Raymond Greenhill, Bob Greenhill's father; and Robert Greenhill Jr., Bob Greenhill's son, provided the biographical material on Bob Greenhill, unless indicated otherwise, in interviews with the author in 2004.

6. Jack McAtee, former Davis Polk partner, in a taped interview with the author in 2007.

7. McAtee, 2007.

8. Fisher, 2004.

9. Fisher, 2004; and Bob Greenhill, 2004.

10. Fisher, 2004.

11. Bob Greenhill, 2004.

12. Bill Hambrecht, Hambrecht & Quist founder, in a taped interview with the author in 2007.

13. Jerry Pearlman, former Harvard Business School classmate of Richard Fisher's and Bob Greenhill's, in a taped interview in 2007.

14. Fisher, 2004.

15. Harvard College Web site (www.hbs.edu/news/releases/AAA/fisher.html). Alumni Achievement Award, Richard Fisher, 2001.

16. Harvard College Web site (www.hbs.edu/news/releases/AAA/fisher.html), 2001.

17. McAtee, 2007.

18. Steve Waters, former Morgan Stanley managing director, in a taped interview with the author in 2007.

19. Barton Biggs, former Morgan Stanley strategist, in a telephone interview with the author in 2004.

20. Morris Kramer, Skadden partner, in a taped interview with the author in 2007.

21. Skadden partners, in taped interviews with the author in 2007.

22. Peter Atkins, Skadden partner, in a taped interview with the author in 2007.

23. Former Morgan Stanley managing directors in interviews with the author in 2007.

24. Claire Flom, wife of Joe Flom, in a taped interview with the author in 2007.

25. Joe Flom, Skadden partner, in a taped interview with the author in 2007.

26. Former Morgan Stanley partners and managing directors and Skadden partners, in taped interviews with the author in 2007.

27. Dow Jones Indexes Web site (www.djindexes.com/mdsidx/index.cfm?event=showAvgStats#no7).

28. Former Morgan Stanley partners and managing directors, in taped interviews with the author in 2007.

29. Chip Baird, Charles Baird's son, in telephone and e-mail interviews with the author in 2007.

30. Kramer, 2007.

31. Kramer, 2007.

32. Steve Friedman, former Goldman Sachs chairman, in a taped interview with the author in 2007.

33. Kramer, 2007.

34. Kramer, 2007.

35. Friedman, 2007.

36. Kramer, 2007.

Chapter 6

1. Statement by Charles Schwab Corporation on deregulation of brokerage commissions. PRNewswire, San Francisco, April 28, 2005.

2. John Whitehead, former Goldman Sachs co-chairman, in a taped interview with the author in 2007.

3. Whitehead, 2007.

4. Whitehead, 2007.

5. Whitehead, 2007.

6. Geoff Boisi, former Goldman Sachs partner, in a taped interview with the author in 2007.

7. Steve Freidman, former Goldman Sachs Chairman, in a taped interview with the author in 2007.

8. Freidman, 2007.

9. Freidman, 2007.

10. Freidman, 2007.

11. Boisi, 2007.

12. Boisi, 2007.

13. Freidman, 2007.

14. Boisi, 2007.

15. Marty Lipton, in a taped interview with the author in 2007.

16. Lipton, 2007.

17. Lipton, 2007.

18. Lipton, 2007.

19. Lipton, 2007.

20. Lipton, 2007.

21. Boisi, 2007.

22. Boisi, 2007.

23. Boisi, 2007.

24. Boisi, 2007.

25. Jim Freund, Skadden partner, in a taped interview with the author in 2007.

26. Joe Flom, Skadden partner, in a taped interview with the author in 2007.

27. Flom, 2007.

28. Fin Fogg, Skadden partner, in a taped interview with the author.

29. "Joseph Flom," *The American Lawyer,* March 1989.

30. Victor Lewkow, Cleary, Gottlieb, Steen & Hamilton partner, in a taped interview with the author in 2006.

31. Morris Kramer, Skadden partner, in a taped interview with the author in 2007.

32. Kramer, 2007.

33. Lipton, 2007.

34. Lipton, 2007.

35. Lipton, 2007.

36. Lipton, 2007.

37. Lipton, 2007.

38. Lipton, 2007.

39. Lipton, 2007.

40. Lipton, 2007.

41. Kramer, 2007.

42. Kramer, 2007.

43. Jim Freund, "Dinner Tribute to Joe Flom," *University of Miami Law Review* 54(4) (July 2000): 855.

44. Freund, "Dinner Tribute to Joe Flom," p. 856.

45. Adam Chinn, former Wachtell partner, in a taped interview with the author in 2007.

46. Chinn, 2007.

47. Former Lazard partner in a taped interview with the author in 2007.

48. Former Lazard partner, 2007.

49. Former Lazard partner, 2007.

50. Scott Newquist, former Morgan Stanley managing director, in a taped interview with the author in 2007.

51. Bruce Fiedorek, former Morgan Stanley managing director, in a taped interview with the author in 2007.

52. Newquist, 2007.

53. Fiedorek; and Peter Atkins, Skadden partner, in taped interviews with the author in 2007.

54. Newquist, 2007.

55. Newquist, 2007.

56. Newquist, 2007.

57. Bob Greenhill, former Morgan Stanley partner, in an interview with the author in 2004.

58. Newquist, 2007.

59. Newquist, 2007.

60. Former Morgan Stanley partners and managing directors, in taped interviews with the author in 2007.

61. Newquist, 2007.

62. Jeff Williams, former Morgan Stanley managing director, in a taped interview with the author in 2007.

63. Bruce Schnitzer, former Marsh & McLennan chief executive, in an interview with the author in 2004.

Chapter 7

1. Joe Flom, Skadden partner, in a taped interview with the author in 2007.

2. Joe Perella, former First Boston managing director, supplied his biographical information and quotes, which, unless otherwise stated, are from taped interviews with the author in 2007.

3. Chip Baird, former First Boston merger banker, in an e-mail to the author in 2007.

4. "Mellon into First Boston," *Time,* July 8, 1946 and Perella, 2007.

5. Steve Schwarzman, former Lehman Brothers partner, in a taped interview with the author in 2007.

6. Warren Hellman, former Lehman Brothers partner, in taped interview with the author in 2007.

7. Hellman, 2007.

8. Hellman, 2007.

9. Hellman, 2007.

10. Hellman, 2007.

11. Pete Peterson, former Lehman Brothers chairman, in a taped interview with the author in 2007.

12. Peterson; and Eric Gleacher, former Lehman Brothers partner, in taped interviews with the author in 2007.

13. Eric Gleacher, former Lehman Brothers partner, in a taped interview with the author in 2007.

14. Gleacher, 2007.

15. Steve Waters, former Lehman Brothers partner, in a taped interview with the author in 2007.

16. Waters, 2007.

17. Waters, 2007.

18. Eric Gleacher, former Lehman Brothers partner, supplied his biographical information and quotes, which, unless otherwise stated, are from a taped interview with the author in 2007.

19. Gleacher, 2007.

20. Gleacher, 2007.

21. Stephen Schwarzman, "Lehman's Merger Maker," *New York Times,* January 13, 1980.

22. Schwarzman, 2007.

23. Schwarzman, 2007.

24. Waters, 2007.

25. Gleacher, 2007.

26. Gleacher, 2007.

27. Joe Perella, former First Boston managing director, in a taped interview with the author in 2007.

28. Perella, 2007.

29. Perella, 2007.

30. Baird, 2007.

31. Baird, 2007.

32. Brian Young, former First Boston merger banker, in a taped interview with the author in 2007.

33. Baird, 2007.

34. Perella, 2007.

35. Baird, 2007.

36. Perella, 2007.

37. Jim Maher, former First Boston managing director, in a taped interview with the author in 2007.

38. Perella, 2007.

39. William Cohan, *The Last Tycoons* (New York: Doubleday, 2007), 540.

40. "Dressing Up Lazard," *Bloomberg Markets* (February 2003): 29.

41. Ibid.

42. Sam Butler, Cravath special counsel, in a taped interview with the author in 2006.

43. Butler, 2006.

44. Butler, 2006.

45. Perella, 2007.

46. Butler, 2006.

47. Perella, 2007.

48. Perella, 2007.

49. Butler, 2006.

50. Perella, 2007.

51. Former First Boston bankers and competitors remember Wasserstein in taped interviews conducted by author in 2007.

52. Maher, 2007.

53. Perella, 2007.

54. Perella, 2007.

55. Perella, 2007.

56. Perella, 2007.

57. Perella, 2007.

58. Young, 2007.

59. First Boston merger bankers' specialties from a copy of a marketing document issued by the firm and given to the author and from taped interviews with former First Boston bankers.

60. Maher, 2007.

Chapter 8

1. Bruce Fiedorek, former Morgan Stanley managing director, in a taped interview with the author in 2007.

2. Fiedorek, in 2007.

3. Fiedorek, in 2007.

4. Scott Newquist, former Morgan Stanley managing director, in a taped interview with the author in 2007.

5. Former Morgan Stanley managing director, in a taped interview with the author in 2007.

6. Former Morgan Stanley managing director, 2007.

7. Former Morgan Stanley managing director, 2007.

8. Fiedorek, 2007.

9. Newquist, 2007.

10. Former Morgan Stanley merger bankers, in an interview with the author in 2007.

11. Bob Lessin, former Morgan Stanley managing director, in a taped interview with the author in 2007.

12. Robert Niehaus, former Morgan Stanley managing director, in a taped interview with the author in 2007.

13. Fiedorek, 2007.

14. Lessin, 2007.

15. Jeffrey Williams, former Morgan Stanley managing director, in a taped interview with the author in 2007.

16. Former Morgan Stanley managing director, 2007.

17. Former Morgan Stanley managing director, 2007.

18. Former Morgan Stanley managing director, 2007.

19. Former Morgan Stanley managing director, 2007.

20. Newquist, 2007.

21. Bill Hambrecht, H&Q founder, in a taped interview with the author in 2007.

22. Hambrecht, 2007.

23. Hambrecht, 2007.

24. Sandy Robertson, Robertson Stephens founder, in a taped interview with the author in 2007.

25. Robertson, 2007.

26. Hambrecht, 2007.

27. Hambrecht, 2007.

28. Hambrecht, 2007.

29. Hambrecht, 2007.

30. Robertson, 2007.

31. Hambrecht, 2007.

32. Hambrecht, 2007.

33. Hambrecht, 2007.

Chapter 9

1. Steve Friedman, former Goldman Sachs chairman, in a taped interview with the author in 2007.

2. Friedman, 2007.

3. Friedman, 2007.

4. Friedman, 2007.

5. Friedman, 2007.

6. Friedman, 2007.

7. Former Goldman Sachs partner, in a taped interview with the author in 2007.

8. Friedman, 2007.

9. Friedman, 2007.

10. Friedman, 2007.

11. Geoff Boisi, former Goldman Sachs partner, in a taped interview with the author in 2007.

12. Chris Flowers, former Goldman Sachs partner, in a taped interview with the author in 2007.

13. Flowers, 2007.

14. Friedman, 2007.

15. Boisi, 2007.

16. Boisi, 2007.

17. Boisi, 2007.

18. Boisi, 2007.

19. Boisi, 2007.

20. Boisi, 2007.

21. Boisi, 2007.

22. Boisi, 2007.

23. Boisi, 2007.

24. Fritz Hobbs, former head of mergers at Dillon Read, in a taped interview with the author in 2007.

25. Boisi, 2007.

26. Boisi, 2007.

27. Boisi, 2007.

28. Friedman, 2007.

29. Friedman, 2007.

30. Flowers, 2007.

31. Friedman, 2007; and Boisi, 2007.
32. Friedman, 2007; and Boisi, 2007.
33. Boisi, 2007.
34. Former Goldman Sachs merger banker, in a taped interview with the author in 2007.
35. Former Goldman Sachs merger banker, 2007.
36. Former Goldman Sachs merger banker, 2007.
37. Former Goldman Sachs merger banker, 2007.
38. Former Goldman Sachs merger banker, 2007.
39. Flowers, 2007.
40. Flowers, 2007.
41. Former Goldman Sachs merger banker, 2007.
42. Former Goldman Sachs merger banker, 2007.

Chapter 10

1. Jeffrey Rosen, former White Weld banker, in a taped interview with the author in 2007.
2. Rosen, 2007.
3. Former Lazard partner, in a taped interview with the author in 2007.
4. Former Lazard partner, 2007.
5. Former Lazard partner, 2007.
6. Gerald Rosenfeld, former Salomon Brothers banker, in a taped interview with the author in 2007.
7. Jim Freund, Skadden partner, in a taped interview with the author in 2007.
8. Joe Flom, Skadden partner, in a taped interview with the author in 2007.
9. Diane Cardwell, "Coffee and Eggs, Movers and Shakers," *New York Times,* June 5, 2005.
10. Marty Lipton, Wachtell partner, in a taped interview with the author in 2007.
11. "A Discussion about the Life of Felix Rohatyn," *Charlie Rose,* December 21, 2000.
12. Morris Kramer, Skadden partner, in a taped interview with the author in 2007.
13. Luis Rinaldini, former Lazard partner, in a taped interview with the author in 2007.
14. Former Lazard partner, 2007.

15. Rosenfeld, 2007.

16. Former Lazard partner, 2007.

17. Former Lazard partner, 2007.

18. Jeffrey Williams, former Morgan Stanley managing director, in a taped interview with the author in 2007.

19. Williams, 2007.

20. Louis Perlmutter, former Lazard partner, in a taped interview with the author in 2007.

21. Rinaldini, 2007.

22. Ken Miller, former head of Merrill Lynch mergers department, in a taped interview with the author in 2007.

23. Former Lazard partner, 2007.

24. Former Lazard partner, 2007.

25. Former Salomon Brothers executive, in a taped interview with the author in 2007.

26. Former Salomon Brothers executive, 2007.

27. James Wolfensohn, former Salomon Brothers partner, in a taped interview with the author in 2007.

28. Lipton, 2007.

29. Sandy Robertson, Robertson Stephens founder, in a taped interview with the author in 2007.

30. Ira Harris, former Salomon Brothers partner, in a taped interview with the author in 2007.

31. Harris, 2007.

32. Harris, 2007.

33. Harris, 2007.

34. Perlmutter, 2007.

35. Dick Griffin, "Salomon's Man in Chicago," *New York Times,* February 13, 1977.

Chapter 11

1. Marty Lipton, Wachtell partner, in a taped interview with the author in 2007.

2. Federal Reserve Web site (www.federalreserve.gov/boarddocs/speeches/ 2004/20040716/default.htm and www.bookrags.com/biography/paul-volcker/); James Wolfensohn, Wolfensohn & Company founder, in a taped interview with the author in 2007.

3. Thomson Financial data.

4. Boone Pickens, former Mesa Petroleum chief executive, in a taped interview with the author in 2007; and interviews with investment bankers by the author in 2007.

5. Joe Perella, former First Boston managing director, in a taped interview with the author in 2007.

6. Perella, 2007.

7. Perella, 2007.

8. Bob Lovejoy, former Lazard partner, in a taped interview with the author in 2007.

9. Perella, 2007.

10. Perella, 2007.

11. Perella, 2007.

12. Perella, 2007.

13. Chuck Ward, former First Boston merger banker, in a taped interview with the author in 2007.

14. Perella, 2007.

15. Fritz Hobbs, former Dillon Read head of mergers, in a taped interview with the author in 2007.

16. Lawyer who worked closely with Wasserstein in mergers in the 1980s, in a taped interview with the author in 2007.

17. Lawyer who worked closely with Wasserstein in mergers in the 1980s, 2007.

18. Lawyer who worked closely with Wasserstein in mergers in the 1980s, 2007.

19. Pickens, 2007; Lovejoy, 2007; and Pete Peterson, Blackstone Group founder, in a taped interview with the author in 2007.

20. Peterson, 2007.

21. Peterson, 2007.

22. Former First Boston merger bankers, in taped interviews with the author in 2007.

23. Former Anderson Clayton executive, in a taped interview with the author in 2007.

24. Former Anderson Clayton executive, 2007.

25. Former Anderson Clayton executive, 2007.

26. Former Anderson Clayton executive, 2007.

27. Former Anderson Clayton executive, 2007.

28. Former Anderson Clayton executive, 2007.

29. Former Anderson Clayton executive, 2007.

30. Former Anderson Clayton executive, 2007.

31. Steve Schwarzman, former Lehman Brothers partner, in a taped interview with the author in 2007.

32. Schwarzman, 2007.

Chapter 12

1. Joe Perella, former First Boston managing director, in a taped interview with the author in 2007.

2. Former Morgan Stanley partners and managing directors, in taped interviews with the author in 2007.

3. Tim Metz, former *Wall Street Journal* reporter, in a taped interview with the author in 2006. Metz wrote the Olinkraft story for the newspaper.

4. Metz, 2006.

5. Metz, 2006.

6. Metz, 2006.

7. Metz, 2006.

8. Scott Newquist, former Morgan Stanley managing director, in a taped interview with the author in 2007.

9. Boone Pickens, former Mesa Petroleum CEO, in a taped interview with the author in 2007.

10. Former Morgan Stanley managing director, in a taped interview with the author in 2007.

11. Former Morgan Stanley managing director, 2007.

12. Steve Waters, former Lehman Brothers partner, in a taped interview with the author in 2007.

13. Pete Peterson, former Lehman Brothers chairman, in a taped interview with the author in 2007.

14. Eric Gleacher, former Lehman Brothers partner, in a taped interview with the author in 2007.

15. Gleacher, 2007.

16. Gleacher, 2007.

17. Former Morgan Stanley partners and managing directors, 2007.

18. Former Morgan Stanley managing director, 2007.

19. Gleacher, 2007.

20. Gleacher, 2007.

21. Gleacher, 2007.

22. Gleacher, 2007.

23. Gleacher, 2007.

24. Former Morgan Stanley managing directors in interviews with the author in 2007.

25. Former Morgan Stanley managing directors, 2007.

26. Former Morgan Stanley managing directors, 2007.

27. Former Morgan Stanley managing directors, 2007.

28. Warburg Pincus partner in taped interview with the author, 2007.

29. Warburg Pincus partner, 2007.

30. Former Morgan Stanley managing directors, 2007.

31. Former Morgan Stanley partner, 2007.

32. Former Morgan Stanley managing directors, 2007.

33. Former Morgan Stanley managing director, 2007.

34. Former Morgan Stanley managing director, 2007.

35. Former Morgan Stanley managing directors, 2007.

36. Ken Auletta, *Power, Greed and Glory on Wall Street: The Fall of Lehman Brothers,* (New York: Warner Books, 1986). Extracts from the book printed in the *New York Times,* February 17, 1985, and February 24, 1985, and used as resource and reference material by the author.

37. Waters, 2007.

38. Steve Schwarzman, former Lehman Brothers partner, in a taped interview with the author in 2007.

39. Former Lehman Brothers managing director, 2007.

40. Peter Solomon, former head of mergers at Lehman Brothers, in a taped interview with the author in 2007.

Chapter 13

1. Fred Joseph, former Drexel CEO, in a taped interview with the author in 2007.

2. Joseph, 2007.

3. Joseph, 2007.

4. Joseph, 2007.

5. Joseph, 2007.

6. Joseph, 2007.

7. Former Drexel executives, in taped interviews with the author in 2007; and James Stewart, *Den of Thieves* (New York: Simon & Schuster, 1992), 51–53.

8. Former Drexel managing director, in a taped interview with the author in 2007.

9. James Sterngold, Legendary Wall Street Outsider at Center of U.S. Inquiry, (*New York Times*, December 22, 1988).

10. Former Drexel managing director, 2007.

11. Former Drexel managing director, 2007.

12. Boone Pickens, former Mesa Petroleum CEO, in a taped interview with the author in 2007.

13. Joseph, 2007.

14. Joseph, 2007.

15. Joseph, 2007.

16. Former Drexel managing director, 2007.

17. John Whitehead, former Goldman Sachs co-chairman, in a taped interview with the author in 2007.

18. Joseph, 2007.

19. Former Drexel managing directors, 2007.

20. Former Drexel managing directors, 2007; and Bryan Burrough and John Helyar, *Barbarians at the Gate* (New York: HarperCollins, 1990), 234.

21. Former Drexel managing directors, 2007.

22. Former Drexel managing directors, 2007.

23. Joseph, 2007.

24. Steve Waters, former Lehman Brothers partner, in a taped interview with the author in 2007.

25. Former head of mergers at an investment bank, in a taped interview with the author in 2007.

26. Pickens, 2007.

27. Pickens, 2007.

28. Tony James, former Donaldson Lufkin & Jenrette head of mergers, in a taped interview with the author in 2007.

29. Pickens, 2007.

30. John Sorte, former Drexel managing director, in a taped interview with the author in 2007.

31. Sorte, 2007.

32. Bob Lovejoy, former Davis Polk partner, in a taped interview with the author in 2007.

33. Lovejoy, 2007.

34. Sorte, 2007.

35. Waters 2007.

36. Stewart, *Den of Thieves*, 72–81.

37. Sorte, 2007.

38. Sorte, 2007.

39. Sorte, 2007.

40. Ace Greenberg, former Bear Stearns chairman, in a taped interview with the author in 2007.

41. Stewart, *Den of Thieves*, 161.

42. Greenberg, 2007.

43. Sorte, 2007.

44. Sorte, 2007.

Chapter 14

1. Harvey Pitt, former Fried Frank partner, in a taped interview with the author in 2007.

2. Pitt, 2007.

3. James Stewart, *Den of Thieves* (New York: Simon & Schuster, 1992), 113–114.

4. Marty Lipton, Wachtell partner, in a taped interview with the author in 2007.

5. Lipton, 2007.

6. Lipton, 2007.

7. Former head of mergers at an investment bank, in a taped interview with the author in 2007.

8. Jack McAtee, former Davis Polk partner, in a taped interview with the author in 2007.

9. Charles Cox, U.S. Securities and Exchange Commission Commissioner, "The Law of Insider Trading—How They Get Caught." Remarks to Piedmont Economic Club, Greenville, South Carolina, November 20, 1986, p. 8. A copy of the speech is on the SEC Web site (www.sec.gov/news/speech/1986/112086cox.pdf).

10. Pitt, 2007.

11. Steve Waters, former Lehman Brothers partner, in a taped interview with the author in 2007.

12. Former Goldman Sachs partner, in a taped interview with the author in 2007.

13. Sarah Bartlett, "A Top Trader at Goldman, Sachs Pleads Guilty to Insider Trading," *New York Times,* August 18, 1989.

14. Ibid.

15. Richard B. Stolley, "The End of an Ordeal," *Fortune,* October 4, 1993.

16. James Sterngold, "Insider Figure Is Sentenced to 30 Days in Jail," *New York Times,* January 13, 1987.

17. The author's telephone interview with former Goldman Sachs partner Robert Freeman in 2008. Freeman sent the author an October, 18, 1991, 29-page letter from his lawyers at Kaye, Scholar, Fierman, Hays & Handler to publishers Simon & Schuster which took issue with what Freeman and his attorneys allege are factual errors made by James Stewart in his book, *Den of Thieves.* Freeman also sent the author a 143-page document further outlining the inaccuracies in Stewart's book, the mistakes made by prosecutors at the U.S. Attorney's office, and the lies of Marty Siegel.

18. Steve Friedman, former Goldman Sachs chairman, in a taped interview with the author in 2007.

19. Former Goldman Sachs bankers and partners, in taped interviews with the author in 2007.

20. Former Goldman Sachs partner, 2007.

21. John Whitehead, former Goldman Sachs co-chairman, in a taped interview with the author in 2007.

22. Friedman, 2007.

23. Friedman, 2007.

24. Aloysius Ehrbar, "Have Takeovers Gone Too Far?" *Fortune,* May 27, 1985.

25. Eric Gleacher, former head of mergers at Morgan Stanley, in a taped interview with the author in 2007.

26. Bob Lovejoy, former Davis Polk partner, in a taped interview with the author in 2007.

27. John Sorte, former Drexel managing director, in a taped interview with the author in 2007.

28. Sorte, 2007.

29. Sorte, 2007.

30. Fred Joseph, former Drexel CEO, in a taped interview with the author in 2007.

31. Sorte, 2007.

32. Sorte, 2007.

33. Ken Miller, former head of mergers at Merrill Lynch, in a taped interview with the author in 2007.

34. Joseph, 2007.

35. Sorte, 2007.

36. Sorte, 2007.

37. Fritz Hobbs, former Dillon Read head of mergers, and Steve Friedman, former Goldman Sachs chairman, in taped interviews with the author in 2007.

38. Martin Lipton and Paul Rowe, "Pills, Polls and Professors: A Reply to Professor Gilson," Delaware court decision on Unocal. *Delaware Journal of Corporate Law* 27(1) (2002). Opinion on Boone Pickens's career ending as a raider by John Sorte, former Drexel managing director, in a taped interview with the author in 2007.

39. Nicholas Kristof, "Unocal May Refinance Its $4.1 Billion in Debt," *New York Times,* August 24, 1985.

40. Hobbs, 2007.

41. Pauline Yoshihashi, "Goldman, Kidder, Cited in Unocal Insider Suit," *New York Times,* April, 15 1987.

42. Stephen Labaton, "Drexel as Expected, Pleads Guilty to 6 Counts of Fraud," *New York Times,* September 12, 1989; Kurt Eichenwald, "Milken Defends 'Junk Bonds' as He Enters His Guilty Plea," *New York Times,* April 25, 1990.

43. Sorte, 2007.

44. "Study in Milken's Name; Overpaid Executives? Takes One to Know," *New York Times,* July 29, 1993.

45. Boone Pickens, former Mesa Petroleum CEO, in a taped interview with the author in 2007.

46. Kurt Eichenwald, "Wages Even Wall Street Can't Stomach," *New York Times,* April 3, 1989.

47. Partner at a New York law firm, in a taped interview with the author in 2007.

48. Joseph, 2007; and Sorte, 2007.

49. Sorte, 2007.

50. Joseph, 2007.

51. Lipton, 2007.

Chapter 15

1. Martin Lipton and Paul Rowe, "Pills, Polls, and Professors: A Reply to Professor Gilson," *Delaware Journal of Corporate Law* 27(1) (2002): 5.

2. Fin Fogg, of counsel at Skadden, in a taped interview with the author in 2007.

3. Martin Lipton, "Pills, Polls and Professors Redux," *University of Chicago Law Review* 69(3) (Summer 2002): 1041.

4. John Whitehead, former co-chairman of Goldman Sachs, in a taped interview with the author in 2007. Goldman Sachs was a private partnership until 1999 and didn't disclose its annual income from mergers.

5. Former head of mergers at Smith Barney, in a taped interview with the author in 2007.

6. Former head of mergers at Smith Barney, 2007.

7. Harvey Miller, Weil Gotshal partner, in a taped interview with the author in 2007.

8. Lipton and Rowe, "Pills, Polls, and Professors: A Reply to Professor Gilson," p. 3.

9. Martin Lipton, "Takeover Bids in the Target's Boardroom," *The Business Lawyer* 35 (November 1979).

10. Ibid., p. 106.

11. Martin Lipton, "Twenty-Five Years after Takeover Bids in the Target's Boardroom: Old Battles, New Attacks and the Continuing War," *The Business Lawyer* 60 (Spring 2005): 1373.

12. Lipton, "Takeover Bids in the Target's Boardroom."

13. Boone Pickens, former Mesa Petroleum CEO, in a taped interview with the author in 2007.

14. U.S. House of Representatives. Subcommittee on Telecommunications, Consumer Protection, and Finance of the Committee on Energy and Commerce, Testimony of Martin Lipton, March 28, 1984.

15. Martin Lipton, "Discussion Memorandum: Warrant Dividend Plan," September 15, 1982.

16. Marty Lipton, Wachtell partner, in a taped interview with the author in 2007.

17. Lipton, 2007.

18. Lipton, "Pills, Polls and Professors Redux," p. 1044.

19. Lipton, 2007.

20. Former Goldman Sachs merger banker and partner, in a taped interview with the author in 2007.

21. Lipton, 2007.

22. Lipton, 2007.

23. Morris Kramer, Skadden partner, in a taped interview with the author in 2007.

24. James Freund, former Skadden partner, in a taped interview with the author in 2007.

25. Lipton, "Pills, Polls and Professors Redux," pp. 1045–1046; and Lipton, 2007.

26. Kramer, 2007.

27. Lester Crown, Henry Crown & Company president, in a taped interview with the author in 2007.

28. Ronald Grover, "Why Carl Icahn Wants to Spoil American's Deal," BusinessWeek, January 22, 2001.

29. Lawrence Zuckerman and Maureen Milford, "TWA Judge Dismisses Icahn Group Bid," *New York Times,* March 12, 2001.

30. Crown, 2007.

31. Lipton, 2007.

32. Relational Investors' Web site (www.rillc.com/team_principals.htm).

33. Ann Zimmerman and Joann S. Lublin, "Home Depot Bows to Whitworth Again," *Wall Street Journal,* February 13, 2007.

34. Andrew Ross Sorkin, "Questioning an Adviser's Advice," *New York Times,* January 8, 2008.

35. Adam Chinn, former Wachtell partner, in a taped interview with the author in 2007.

Chapter 16

1. Gerald Rosenfeld, former Lazard partner, in a taped interview with the author in 2007.

2. Bob Lovejoy, former Lazard partner, in a taped interview with the author in 2007.

3. Former Lazard partner, 2007.

4. Former Lazard partner, 2007.

5. Former Lazard partner, 2007.

6. Former Lazard partners, 2007.

7. Former Lazard partners, 2007.

8. Lovejoy, 2007.

9. Lovejoy, 2007.

10. Lovejoy, 2007.

11. Former Lazard partners, 2007.

12. Former Lazard partner, 2007.

13. Former Lazard partner, 2007.

14. Ira Harris, former Salomon Brothers partner, in a taped interview with the author in 2007.

15. John Gutfreund, former Salomon Brothers chairman, in a taped interview with the author in 2006.

16. Gutfreund, 2006.

17. Harris, 2007.

18. Peter Solomon, former Lehman Brothers partner, in a taped interview with the author in 2007.

19. Harris, 2007.

20. Former Lazard partner, 2007.

21. Former Lazard partner, 2007.

22. Harris, 2007.

23. Harris, 2007.

24. William Cohan, *The Last Tycoons* (Doubleday, 2007), 354.

25. Fritz Hobbs, former Dillon Read head of mergers, in a taped interview with the author 2007.

26. Hobbs, 2007.

27. Suzanna Andrews, "Felix Loses It," *New York* magazine, March 11, 1996.

28. Ibid.

29. Ibid.

30. Former Lazard partners, 2007.

31. Harris, 2007.

32. Joe Perella, former First Boston managing director, in a taped interview with the author in 2007.

33. Jim Maher, former First Boston managing director, in a taped interview with the author in 2007.

34. Perella, 2007.

35. Perella, 2007.

36. Perella, 2007.

37. Perella, 2007.

38. Perella, 2007.

39. Perella, 2007.

40. Perella, 2007.

41. Perella, 2007.

42. Perella, 2007.

43. Perella, 2007.

44. Bryan Burrough and John Helyar, *Barbarians at the Gate* (New York: HarperCollins, 1990).

45. Steve Waters, former Lehman Brothers co-head of mergers, in a taped interview with the author in 2007.

46. Former Shearson Lehman Hutton managing director, in a taped interview with the author in 2007.

47. Waters, 2007.

48. Waters, 2007.

49. Jeff Williams, former Morgan Stanley managing director, in a taped interview with the author in 2007.

50. Williams, 2007.

51. Bob Greenhill, former Morgan Stanley partner, in an interview with the author in 2004.

52. Former Morgan Stanley managing director, 2007.

53. Carter McClelland, former Morgan Stanley managing director, in an interview with the author in 2004.

54. McClelland, 2004.

55. Robert Greenhill Jr., son of Bob Greenhill, in a telephone interview with the author in 2004.

56. Bob Greenhill, 2004.

57. Former Morgan Stanley partners and Bob Greenhill's friends, in taped interviews with the author in 2007.

58. Former Morgan Stanley partners and Bob Greenhill's friends, 2007.

59. Bob Greenhill, 2004.

60. Former Morgan Stanley managing director, 2007.

61. Richard Fisher, former Morgan Stanley chairman, in an interview with the author in 2004.

62. Sandy Weill and Judah Kraushaar, *The Real Deal: My Life in Business and Philanthropy* (New York: Warner Business Books, 2006), 252.

63. Former Morgan Stanley managing director, 2007.

64. Weill and Kraushaar, *The Real Deal,* p. 253.

65. Bruce Fiedorek, former Morgan Stanley co-head of mergers, in a taped interview with the author in 2007.

66. Claire Flom, in a taped interview with the author in 2007.

Chapter 17

1. Former Goldman Sachs merger banker, in a taped interview with the author in 2007.

2. Former Goldman Sachs merger banker, 2007.

3. Steve Friedman, former Goldman Sachs chairman, in a taped interview with the author in 2007.

4. Geoff Boisi, former Goldman Sachs partner, in a taped interview with the author in 2007.

5. Boisi, 2007.

6. Boisi, 2007.

7. Boisi, 2007.

8. Boisi, 2007.

9. Former Goldman Sachs partner, 2007.

10. Former Goldman Sachs partner, 2007.

11. Friedman, 2007.

12. Friedman, 2007.

13. Friedman, 2007.

14. Friedman, 2007.

15. Friedman, 2007.

16. Former Wasserstein Perella bankers, in taped interviews with the author in 2007.

17. Former Wasserstein Perella job candidate, in a taped interview with the author in 2007.

18. Former Wasserstein Perella bankers and competitors, in taped interviews with the author in 2007.

19. Pete Peterson, Blackstone Group founder, in a taped interview with the author in 2007.

20. Peterson, 2007.

21. Perella, 2007.

22. Perella, 2007.

23. Perella, 2007.

24. Bruce Fiedorek, former Morgan Stanley co-head of mergers, in a taped interview with the author in 2007.

25. Fiedorek, 2007.

26. Perella, 2007.

27. Former Wasserstein Perella banker, 2007.

28. Former Wasserstein Perella banker, 2007.

29. Former Wasserstein Perella banker, 2007.

30. Former Wasserstein Perella banker, 2007.

31. Former Wasserstein Perella banker, 2007.

32. Former Wasserstein Perella banker, 2007.

33. Sandy Weill and Judah Kraushaar, *The Real Deal: My Life in Business and Philanthropy* (New York: Warner Business Books, 2006), 253–258.

34. Weill and Kraushaar, *The Real Deal,* p. 259.

35. Jack McAtee, friend of Bob Greenhill's, in a taped interview with the author in 2007.

36. Bob Greenhill, former Smith Barney chairman, in an interview with the author in 2004.

37. James Wolfensohn, founder of Wolfensohn & Company, in a taped interview with the author in 2007.

38. Wolfensohn, 2007.

39. Simon Borrows, Greenhill & Company co-president; Tim George, Greenhill & Company managing director; and Scott Bok, Greenhill & Company co-president, in interviews with the author in 2004.

40. Borrows, George, and Bok, 2004.

41. Borrows, George, and Bok, 2004.

42. Borrows, George, and Bok, 2004.

43. Former Morgan Stanley managing directors in interviews with author, 2007.

44. Bruce Schnitzer, friend of Bob Greenhill's, in an interview with the author in 2004.

45. Former Wasserstein Perella banker, 2007.

46. Former Wasserstein adviser, in a taped interview with the author in 2007.

47. Former Wasserstein Perella banker, 2007.

48. Lazard banker, in an interview with the author in 2007.

49. Former Lazard partners, in taped interviews with the author in 2007.

50. Former Wasserstein adviser, 2007.

51. Wall Street securities firm analyst, in a taped interview with the author in 2007.

52. Former Wachtell partner, in a taped interview with the author in 2007.

53. Greenhill & Company managing directors, in interviews with the author in 2004.

54. Bob Greenhill, Greenhill & Company founder, in an interview with the author in 2004.

55. Former Bob Greenhill confidant, in an interview with the author in 2008.

56. Former Bob Greenhill confidant, 2008.

57. Perella, 2007.

58. Perella, 2007.

59. Perella, 2007.
60. Perella, 2007.
61. Perella, 2007.
62. Perella, 2007.
63. Greenhill, 2004.
64. Greenhill, 2004.
65. Greenhill, 2004.

References

The foundations of this book were gathered from about 200 hours of taped interviews with more than 80 Wall Street people in New York; Greenwich, Connecticut; Washington D.C.; Chicago; Los Angeles; San Francisco; and London. Some of those interviewed agreed to speak on the record, some only on the condition their name not be used. Nearly everyone who was interviewed was given the chance to comment.

Felix Rohatyn, Bruce Wasserstein, and Michael Milken were the three main characters in the book who refused to be interviewed. I relied on interviews and recollections of their former and current colleagues, as well as the work of journalists, to paint a portrait of the men.

Books

Books that provided a great source of information and portraits of Wall Street people include:

- Bruck, Connie (1988). *The Predator's Ball* (New York: Simon & Schuster).

- Burrough, Bryan, and John Helyar (1990). *Barbarians at the Gate* (New York: HarperCollins).
- Reich, Cary (1983). *Financier: The Biography of Andre Meyer* (New York: John Wiley & Sons).
- Stewart, James (1992). *Den of Thieves* (New York: Simon & Schuster).

Other books which were read during the course of research were:

- Cohan, William (2007). *The Last Tycoons: The Secret History of Lazard Freres & Co.* (New York: Doubleday). I am grateful to William Cohan for speaking with me about his experiences and observations of Lazard.
- Johnston, Moira (1986). *Takeover* (New York: William Morrow).
- Levine, Dennis, and William Hoffer (1991). *Inside Out: an Insider's Account of Wall Street* (New York: G. P. Putnam's Sons).
- Pickens, Boone (2000). *The Luckiest Guy in the World* (Frederick, MD: Beard Books).
- Rubin, Robert and Jacob Weisberg (2003). *In An Uncertain World: Tough Choices from Wall Street to Washington* (New York: Random House).
- Stone, Dan (1990). *April Fools: An Insider's Account of the Rise and Collapse of Drexel Burnham* (New York: Donald I. Fine Inc.).
- Wasserstein, Bruce (2000). *Big Deal: Mergers and Acquisitions in the Digital Age* (New York: Warner Books).
- Weill, Sandy, and Judah Kraushaar (2006). *The Real Deal: My Life in Business and Philanthropy* (New York: Warner Business Books).
- Whitehead, John (2005). *A Life in Leadership: From D-Day to Ground Zero* (New York: Basic Books).

Articles

James Fox in Skadden's library helpfully provided copies of articles on Joe Flom. They included one article written by Joe Flom himself in the 1989/1990 issue of *Career Insights* and Joe Flom's "Mergers & Acquisitions: The Decade in Review," *University of Miami Law Review* 54(4), July 2000.

Other articles on Joe Flom and Skadden include one in the Fall 1998 issue of *Directors & Boards* entitled "The Lion in Winter." In December

1999, *The American Lawyer* named Flom one of its "Lawyers of the Century" and wrote a short profile on him. In 1989, Steven Brill wrote a profile on Flom and Skadden in the March 1989 issue of *The American Lawyer.*

Fin Fogg was kind enough to give me a copy of his "Skadden, Arps—A Brief History," February 2006. I am also grateful to Jim Freund, who kindly lent me his "Dinner Tribute to Joe Flom," printed in the *University of Miami Law Review* 54(4), July 2000.

Marty Lipton's office at Wachtell was most helpful supplying me with many of his articles. They included:

- Martin Lipton and William Savitt, "The Many Myths of Lucian Beb-chuk," by" a copy of which was given to me before its publication in the May 2007 issue of the *University of Virginia Law Review.*
- Martin Lipton, "Twenty-Five Years after Takeover Bids in the Target's Boardroom: Old Battles, New Attacks and the Continuing War," *The Business Lawyer* 60, August 2005.
- Martin Lipton and Paul Rowe, "Pills, Polls and Professors: A Reply to Professor Gilson," *Delaware Journal of Corporate Law* 27(1), 2002.
- Martin Lipton, "Pills, Polls and Professors Redux," *University of Chicago Law Review* 69(3), Summer 2002.
- Martin Lipton, "Discussion Memorandum: Warrant Dividend Plan," Wachtell, Lipton, Rosen & Katz. September 15, 1982.
- U.S. House of Representatives, Subcommittee on Telecommunications, Consumer protection and Finance of the Committee on Energy and Commerce. Testimony of Martin Lipton, March 28, 1984, revised.
- Martin Lipton, "Takeover Bids in the Target's Boardroom" *The Business Lawyer* 36, November 1979.
- Martin Lipton and Jay Lorsch, "A Modest Proposal for Improved Corporate Governance," *The Business Lawyer* 48, November 1992.
- Martin Lipton, "Some Thoughts for Boards of Directors," Aspen Publishers, March 1, 2004, Section 2.
- Jay Lorsch and Martin Lipton, "The Fight for Good Governance," *Harvard Business Review,* January–February 1993.
- Martin Lipton, "Merger Waves in the 19th, 20th and 21st Centuries," The Davies lecture, Osgoode Hall Law School, York University, September 14, 2006.

- Martin Lipton, "Bubbles and Their Aftermath." Address to the Commercial Club of Chicago, Illinois, November 2002.
- Martin Lipton," An End to Hostile Takeovers and Short-Termism," *Financial Times,* Wednesday, June 27, 1990.

Numerous articles by reporters at the *New York Times, Wall Street Journal, BusinessWeek, Fortune, Forbes,* and *Time* from 1935 to 2008 were read. Where direct reference was made of the articles, it is indicated in the endnotes.

About the Author

Brett Cole is the Korean correspondent for *The Economist*. From 2003 to 2007, he covered Wall Street for Bloomberg News in New York, reporting on the investment banks and private equity firms. Prior to New York, he worked for the news agency in Tokyo, Taipei and Sydney where he profiled investment bankers, their deals and their firms. He can be contacted at cole.r.brett@gmail.com.

Index